$\boxed{\textbf{F}}$

Albert Morehead's Classic Work

ON

the Principles of Bidding Judgment

BIDDING

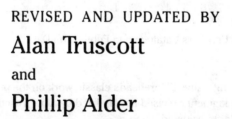

REVISED AND UPDATED BY
Alan Truscott
and
Phillip Alder

A FIRESIDE BOOK

PUBLISHED BY
Simon & Schuster Inc.

NEW YORK LONDON TORONTO SYDNEY TOKYO SINGAPORE

Fireside
Simon & Schuster Building
Rockefeller Center
1230 Avenue of the Americas
New York, New York 10020

Copyright © 1964 by Albert H. Morehead
Revised edition copyright © 1974 by Andrew T. Morehead
and Philip D. Morehead
Revised edition copyright © 1990 by Alan Truscott

First Fireside Edition 1990

FIRESIDE and colophon are registered trademarks
of Simon & Schuster Inc.

Designed by Stanley S. Drate/Folio Graphics Co. Inc.

Manufactured in the United States of America

10 9 8 7 6 5 4 3 2 1

Library of Congress Cataloging in Publication Data

Truscott, Alan F.
    On bidding : Albert Morehead's classic work on the principles of
    bidding judgment / revised and updated by Alan Truscott and Phillip
    Alder.—1st Fireside ed.
        p.   cm.
    Rev. ed. of: Morehead on bidding, 1974.
    "A Fireside book."
    1. Contract bridge—Bidding.   I. Alder, Phillip.   II. Morehead,
Albert H. (Albert Hodges), date.   Morehead on bidding.   III. Title.
GV1282.4.T76 1990
795.41'52—dc20   89-21966
ISBN 0-671-66463-8   CIP

Contents

P A R T   II

BIDDING CONVENTIONS

P A R T   III

THE PROCESS OF CARD VALUATION

P A R T IV

THE THEORY AND STRATEGY OF BIDDING

PART I

Standard American Bidding, Expert Style

1 Point-Count Valuation

Bidding begins with hand valuation. Perhaps the most surprising development in bridge in the 1950s and 1960s was that expert players in all countries, after more than twenty-five years of disagreement on methods of valuation, almost unanimously adopted the "4-3-2-1 point-count."

This means (not that anyone really needs to be told) that each ace in one's hand is counted as 4 points, each king 3, each queen 2, and each jack 1.

The following would be called a 10-point hand:

♠ 10 6 2   ♡ J 7 3   ◇ Q 8 4   ♣ A K 9 5

This is also the classic "average hand," the hand that every player at the table would hold, varying only by suits, if one dealt out a new deck of cards without shuffling it.

Since the 4-3-2-1 point-count has achieved almost universal acceptance, it will be used in this book to describe the relative strength of each hand cited.

However, the 4-3-2-1 point-count as it is presented in bridge books differs in one essential from how it is used by experts. To explain the difference, it is necessary to delve briefly into the history of bridge science.

ORIGIN AND USE OF POINT-COUNT BIDDING

In their efforts to educate the average bridge player by substituting rule for reason, bridge authorities have used many different kinds of formulas for estimating the strength of a hand.

There have been tables of quick tricks, honor tricks, high-card tricks, primary and secondary tricks. There have been point-counts in which the numerical values assigned to the honors from ace down have been 7-5-3-2-1 (the Robertson point-count), 6-4-3-2-1 (the Reith or New England count), 1½-1-½ (the Winslow count), 3-2-1-½ (the Four Aces count), and the presently popular 4-3-2-1 count supposedly developed by Bryant McCampbell (and probably by others independently) and publicized first by Milton Work and then by Charles Goren.

Since no method is entirely accurate, theoretically it matters little which one is used. The true process of hand valuation is not simple; it will be the subject of an entire section of this book in later pages. From the standpoint of the bridge teacher and writer, the important thing is that the average player be able to understand and willing to use a particular method.

The 4-3-2-1 count that is now dominant dates back to 1915 or before, and was espoused by some of the most respectable authorities during the 1920s and thereafter, but it never achieved mass acceptance until Goren adopted it in 1949.

The 4-3-2-1 count and other point-count schedules missed out in their earliest years because they were devised only to count the high-card content of a hand. Experts know that every bridge hand's value depends on its distribution as much as on its high cards. If only the original 4-3-2-1 count of high cards were applied, the following hands might seem equivalent:

	1.		2.	
	♠	K Q J	♠	K Q J 10 7 6
	♡	K Q J	♡	K Q J 10 7 6
	◇	7 6 5 3	◇	5
	♣	7 6 5	♣	—

Each hand is worth 12 points in high cards, but number one can hardly be expected to win more than four or five tricks, while number two is almost sure to win ten tricks with either spades or hearts as trumps. Such a difference is too great to be tolerated in any method of valuation.

Two major efforts to modify the basic point-count to allow for distributional values were made in the late 1940s. A third was developed more recently.

1. Short Suits

In 1948, a Toronto actuary named William Anderson, who happened to be a bridge enthusiast, worked out the following simple table:

Doubleton	one point
Singleton	two points
Void	three points

He suggested adding these to the basic point-count to represent the true potential of a hand. This plan was offered to Ely Culbertson, the authority of the thirties. Culbertson had retired from bridge and was intent on a political quest to give enforcement powers to the embryonic United Nations. His bridge organization was still wedded to the unsatisfactory honor-trick method, and rejected the Anderson plan.

Anderson then offered his idea to Goren, who welcomed it with open arms and used it in a series of books that achieved public acceptance and pushed Culbertson into the background.

Some minor modifications were introduced, to reflect the presence or absence of aces, and to allow for inadequately guarded honors.

For the purpose of initial valuation, this has some obvious flaws. Hands with 5-3-3-2 and 4-4-3-2 shapes each contain one distributional point, but there is a clear advantage in having a five-card suit. Also, in this method 7-3-3-0, a powerful distribution, is equivalent to 7-2-2-2, which is noticeably weaker.

2. Long Suits

While Goren was making use of Anderson's short-suit plan, the late Fred Karpin, a leading player-teacher living near Washington, D.C., was advocating a long-suit approach:

Five-card suit	one point
Six-card suit	two points
Seven-card suit	three points, etc.

This method does better than the short-suit count in that it separates 5-3-3-2 from 4-4-3-2. But it is equally unsatisfactory in distinguishing 7-3-3-0 from 7-2-2-2, and it treats 4-3-3-3 as the equivalent of 4-4-4-1.

This method has been relied upon by William Root, a top-ranked player-writer-teacher who contributed much to the first edition of this book. Most teachers, however, have accepted the short-suit count.

3. Assets

A third method that capitalizes on the strengths of the first two is the asset method, developed in the seventies and featured in several books by Dorothy and Alan Truscott.

Singleton	one asset
Void	two assets
Five-card or longer suit	one asset

For initial valuation, assets are counted in the same way as distributional points in the other methods. This gives a result much closer to expert practice than the other approaches, and the purpose of such additions has always been to give the inexperienced player rules that will allow him to match the accumulated wisdom of the experts.

The weakness of the asset method is that it gives equal value to balanced one-suited hands with 5-3-3-2, 6-3-2-2, and 7-2-2-2 distributions. This is unimportant for the purposes of minimum opening bids, however, because 6-3-2-2 and 7-2-2-2 hands usually shade into the area of the weak two-bid and the preemptive three-bid.

FINE TUNING

Experts throughout the world have adopted the 4-3-2-1 count for high cards, but they do not use any distributional count, preferring to trust experience and intuition in measuring the value of long suits and shortages.

If an expert says, "I had a fourteen-count," he is referring only to high-card points. He is likely to add his actual distribution: "With 6-4-2-1 shape." If he wishes to be specific, he will say, "With 4-6-1-2."

But if an inexperienced player claims to have had 14 points, he may or may not have them all in high cards. He may be counting distributional points as he has learned them from a teacher or a book. As he increases in skill, he will abandon this useful crutch.

Once the basic valuation has been done, counting distribution consciously or unconsciously, there are many more subtle factors to consider. Among them are:

1. Aces
The 4-3-2-1 count undervalues the ace. Some have suggested counting it as 4½. Goren suggests adding a point for owning all four aces, and subtracting a point for an aceless hand.

This has some merit, but leaves a one-ace hand equal to one with three aces. Note that the old, abandoned Four Aces count (3-2-1-½) gave the ace 50 percent more value than a king, rather than 33 percent more. All experts take into account the presence or absence of aces in their hand.

2. Tens

Tens are not considered in the 4-3-2-1 count, but should be. They have an important role to play, especially in combination with one or two higher honors. It is quite reasonable for anyone, expert or beginner, to count half a point for each ten held.

A sensible alternative is to look at aces and tens in combination. Add a point if the hand has a bunch of aces and tens, six or more out of the possible eight. Deduct a point if the hand has two or fewer.

3. Intermediates

Even nines and eights have their uses, and an expert will sometimes be influenced in borderline situations by their presence or absence. The nine is particularly potent in combinations such as K-10-9 and Q-10-9.

4. Unguarded Honors

Singleton kings, queens, and jacks have limited value, and all the distributional counts devalue them by a point. Goren also deducts one point for a doubleton queen or jack when a suit bid is contemplated. The expert makes such allowances instinctively, knowing such cards are likely to be more effective in defense than in attack. A defender is much more likely than a declarer to score a singleton king, for example.

5. Honors in Long Suits

Conversely, it is a distinct advantage to have honor cards in long suits. Consider these three hands:

1. ♠ A Q J 3 2	2. ♠ A 5 4 3 2	3. ♠ 6 5 4 3 2
♡ A 4 3 2	♡ J 4 3 2	♡ A 4 3 2
◇ 4 3 2	◇ Q 3 2	◇ A J 2
♣ 2	♣ A	♣ Q

All three hands have the same 11 points, with two aces and no tens, and the distributions are identical. However, hand one is an automatic opening because of the strength in the long suit (note that the long-suit count fails here), while hand two is a borderline opening, and number three is a decidedly undesirable opening with its weak suit and singleton queen.

6. Rebid Problem

The only hands that present serious rebid problems are those with a five-card suit (usually a major) and a shortage in the suit immediately below. Examples are 5-2-4-2, 4-5-1-3, 5-1-3-4, 5-2-3-3, and 1-3-4-5. Goren takes this problem very seriously, allowing a pass when the total count is 13. This factor must be taken into account, although it does not affect the playing potential of the hand. But remember that more often than not, the dreaded response in the short-suit-below will not happen.

Modern experts are, however, less restrained in this area. This is partly because one Goren limitation has been abandoned: a sequence such as 1♠–2◇–2NT no longer shows extra values but can be a minimum.

Rather than assigning a specific weight to all of the above, the expert may simply announce that he had a "good" 15 or a "bad" 13. This means that he has the given point-count, but that all the other factors—aces, tens, intermediates, unguarded honors, long-suit honors, and so on—suggest optimism or pessimism.

REVALUATION

All three of the methods of distributional valuation provide changes as circumstances dictate.

1. Short Suits

In raising partner's suit, Goren revises the point-count adjustment. The doubleton remains worth one point, but the others improve:

Doubleton	one point
Singleton	three points
Void	five points

One point is deducted if the support is only three cards in length rather than four, or if the distribution is 4-3-3-3.

This has obvious weaknesses: it does not consider five-card support, or the rebid by the opener.

2. Long Suits

The revaluation here augments rather than replaces the previous count. Once a good fit is found, the supporter—whether opener or responder—adds points for short suits, employing the same scale used by Goren for the original evaluation:

Doubleton	one point
Singleton	two points
Void	three points

Again, one point is deducted if the support is three cards rather than four.

3. Assets

Revaluation in this method is quite different, and depends on the degree of fit that has been uncovered:

Known Fit	Prospects	Assets
None	Poor	Worthless
Eight cards	Normal	Unchanged
Nine cards	Good	Double
Ten cards	Excellent	Triple, etc.

This operates for any player at any stage of the auction. For example, suppose your partner deals and bids one spade. The opponents are silent and you have:

♠ 2　♡ A 8 7 3 2　◇ K 6 5 4 2　♣ 9 2

You started with 3 assets, but they became worthless when your partner bid spades. So far there is a misfit.

You respond one notrump, and your partner rebids two hearts, a revelation. You know there is at least a nine-card fit and your assets not only come back to life but also double from 3 to 6. You count 13 points, for a total of 26, and bid four hearts.

A second example:

♠ A 9 8 7 5 4 3　♡ A Q 5　◇ A 3 2　♣ —

You open one spade, and partner bids three spades, a limit bid promising the equivalent of about 11 points and four trumps. With an eleven-card fit, your 3 assets have quadrupled to 12, making your total count 26. The combined count is more than enough to reach the 33 needed for a small slam. There is no danger of two quick losers, and six spades rates to be the best contract, so bidding it immediately is reasonable. (However, there is a chance of seven, and the best way to investigate is by jumping to five clubs, showing the void and asking partner to ignore any honors he holds in the suit.)

In the long-suit count, this hand begins at 17 points and revalues to 20: not enough for a slam. The short-suit count does not provide for opener's rebids.

♠
♡
2 **The Opening**
♢ **Bid**
♣

Since contract bridge was first played in 1925, nearly every bid has changed in meaning, but there has been least change in the standards for opening bids.

There have been noticeable trends among the leading players. Around 1930, very light opening bids were fashionable. Then, as increasing numbers of players learned to make trap passes early and come in later with penalty doubles, the trend was to greater conservatism in opening bids. This caused doubling to become less frequent, whereupon bids became lighter again.

In the 1980s, the majority of players arrived at the middle of the road. They now open most hands in which they have only 13 or 14 points and a few hands in which they have only 12 points but have a strong major suit. They are flanked by two groups of extremists. One of these groups is called the "open on anything" school. To this group the following hand is an obligatory opening bid (usually one club).

♠ 10 7 6 3   ♡ A 7   ◇ Q J 3   ♣ K J 7 6

At the other extreme we have the followers of the Roth-Stone system, whose watchword is that an opening bid must be "sound" (which means "strong"). Not only would this group pass the hand shown above, it would pass the following hand:

♠ A Q 6 4 2   ♡ A 6 5   ◇ Q 7 4   ♣ 7 4

The middle-of-the-roaders would pass the first of the two hands shown above, primarily because it has only 11 points in high cards; they would bid one spade on the other hand, because it has 12 points, the primary suit (spades), and a respectable five-card major that they would not mind partner leading. Also, to pass and then overcall one spade on the next round is more dangerous: one spade doubled is more likely to be an expensive final contract following an overcall than after an opening bid.

To the majority of experts, aces and kings are more important than queens and jacks. Experience has shown that declarer's side is usually at a disadvantage if it does not have at least two of the four aces. Therefore, an aceless hand is not bid unless it is a sound opening bid. Consider the two following hands, one of which was previously cited:

1. ♠ A Q 6 4 2	2. ♠ J 7 6 5 4
♡ A 6 5	♡ Q J 10
◇ Q 7 4	◇ K Q
♣ 7 4	♣ Q J 2

As mentioned above, most experts will bid one spade on the first hand. Most experts will start with a pass on hand two. By standard valuation methods, the two hands are equivalent, each having 12 points in high cards and 13 points net, no matter which of the three methods of adding points for distribution is used. But possession of at least one ace in a borderline hand is essential, and possession of two aces in

such a hand is usually sufficient to sway the decision from a
pass to an opening bid.

The trick-taking power of a hand is nonetheless important, and between two hands of equivalent high-card content
the line is often drawn on the basis of intermediates:

1.	♠ J 2	2.	♠ J 10
	♡ Q 4 3 2		♡ Q 10 9 8
	◇ A J 2		◇ A J 10
	♣ K J 3 2		♣ K J 10 9

The extreme light bidders would not dream of passing either
hand, and the Roth-Stone "sound" bidders would not dream
of bidding either hand. However, the middle-of-the-road bidders will pass number one because of its poor intermediates,
whereas those useful tens and nines will persuade them to
open number two.

THE FIVE-CARD MAJOR

Even more than between the light bidders and the sound
bidders, there used to be a split between those who would
open the bidding in the first or second seat in a four-card
major and those who would not open in a major suit unless it
had at least five cards. Nowadays, though, in most of the
bridge-playing world and especially in North America, the
five-card-majorites far outnumber the four-card supporters.

The doctrine of the five-card major suit goes far back in
bridge history. Geoffrey Mott-Smith was the first to advance
it, and he made a virtual religion of it. In a 1927 book he
proposed bidding first in a five-card major ahead of any
longer minor suit—presumably even an eight-card minor
suit—and he championed the principle that an opening bid
in a major suit should always guarantee at least a five-card
suit, while any opening bid in a minor suit would deny a five-
card major.

Mott-Smith was born too early. During the formative
years of contract bridge, most experts were happy to open in

a four-card major suit. They argued that if you could not open in a four-card major, you would often have to open in a weak minor suit, making it easier for the opponents to overcall, since your left-hand opponent might be strong enough to overcall at the one-level but not at the two-level. The bidding could be so high when it came around to you again that you would never get a chance to show your four-card major. And, as mentioned above, there was a risk that partner might make a fatal lead in your weak minor suit.

In the 1950s and 1960s, though, the five-card-major principle gained ground, as part of the Roth-Stone and Kaplan-Sheinwold systems.

There are advantages, for both opener and responder. Packing this extra information into the opening bid may give opener a chance to make a more informative rebid when otherwise he would have to repeat his suit to show five cards; the responding player can safely raise with three trumps at his first turn, and occasionally can do so with a king doubleton or queen doubleton (or even jack doubleton in competition) without waiting for a rebid of the suit.

Originally, most experts stayed with the four-card-major style, but as the efficacy of the five-card style was demonstrated, particularly in conjunction with the forcing one-notrump response (see Part II, Chapter 2), the pendulum started to swing in favor of the five-card-major approach; and now, in the 1980s, the ball is deep in the five-card-major court.

However, there are still some contentious hands, in particular those with five spades and five clubs:

♠ A J 10 6 3   ♡ 7 2   ◇ 8   ♣ A K 7 5 2

Many players would open one club on this hand to keep the bidding low as long as possible. Partner's response will likely be one diamond or one heart; the opening bidder can then bid one spade, showing both of his suits at the lowest possible level.

However, a player would also have bid one club and rebid one spade on the following hand:

♠ A J 10 6   ♡ 7 2   ◇ 8 3   ♣ A K 7 5 2

How is partner to know when he has a five-card major suit on this auction? The opener has to bid the major suit a second time, which might prove to be awkward. And the matter is likely to become worse if the opponents enter the auction. So most experts open the 5-5 hand with one spade, preferring to tell partner about the five-card major immediately, and hoping to be able to bid the club suit later on. If it proves that the suit is lost and the correct contract was in clubs, unlucky. No system bids all hands perfectly, and emphasis must be placed on the major suits.

REQUIREMENTS FOR OPENING BIDS

Every expert has joined in the statement that with 14 points one must open the bidding; almost all authorities recommend opening the bidding with 13 points; with 12 points there are occasional hands that because of their long suits and solidity are acceptable opening bids.

Here again, however, experts and average players (or the teachers of average players) are likely to be talking two different languages.

♠ K Q 10 6 3   ♡ A Q 7 5 4   ◇ 8 2   ♣ 5

The expert calls this an 11-point hand with good distribution and a major two-suiter, and he opens one spade although it contains "only" 11 points. The instruction books that add points for short suits call it a 14-point hand, since they count 2 points for the singleton and 1 for the doubleton, and as a 14-point hand it is a compulsory opening bid. The long-suit advocates add 2 points, 1 for the fifth card in the spade suit and 1 for the fifth heart card, and arrive at a total of 13 points. With the good suits, this is an automatic opening bid. Finally, those who count assets reach 14 points, adding 1 point for each of the five-card suits and 1 for the singleton. Once more, an opening bid. Two of the three methods arrive at the same figure; and all four advocate opening one spade.

	1.	♠ A 6 5	2.	♠ K 6 5
		♡ K 7 5 3		♡ A Q 10 7
		◇ K 8 4		◇ K 4 3
		♣ A 9 2		♣ J 7 2

Hand one contains 14 high-card points, and so conforms to the opening-bid requirements of virtually all authorities. They would recommend opening one club.

The vast majority of experts would also open hand two, which has 13 points, although Roth-Stoners would never dream of opening on such a hand. The five-card majorites open this hand one club, despite the poor suit (though take away the jack of clubs and they would pass), while the few remaining four-card-major supporters might bid one heart.

All these opening bids are flawed, and patently the best bid to show the strength and nature of the hand in one fell swoop is the weak notrump opening bid. The weak notrump enjoyed a resurgence of popularity hand in hand first with the Kaplan-Sheinwold system and then with Precision Club, but today it has retreated into the background, with even some Precision Club pairs using a strong notrump. However, it is the best bid to show a balanced hand with just enough strength to open the bidding.

Hands that count only to 12 points including distributional values are seldom opened unless the hand in question contains a six-card major. Unless an expert is wedded to a fairly rigid system and heavy weak two-bids, he will usually open one spade on the following hand:

> ♠ A Q J 10 7 6   ♡ 6 3   ◇ K 6 5   ♣ 7 2

He will pass with:

> ♠ 10 8 6 5 3 2   ♡ 5 3   ◇ A Q J   ♣ K 7

The other important factor with a borderline hand is the quality of the suit in which the bidding will be opened. If the suit is poor, it is more likely that the expert will pass; but with a strong suit, he will open the bidding. The critical difference is not on offense but on defense; with a weak suit, he must worry about his partner making a fatal lead in the suit should his side be outbid. This factor applies in the two hands considered above. In the second hand, the expert is reluctant to bid on a suit without the top cards when he has a hand of only moderate strength. The opponents may well play the hand, so he hesitates to bid a suit he does not want his partner to lead.

WHO'S GOT THE SPADES?

We will have more to say—much more—in a later section on the function of the spade suit in hand evaluation, but here it will suffice to mention briefly the part that the spade suit plays in determining a player's choice between a bid and a pass.

In the first or second position, the decision to bid is seldom controlled by the suits that one holds. There are two opposing factors and they balance each other. When a player has strength in the major suits, he has an advantage over his opponents and this gives him an incentive to open the bidding. When a player's strength is chiefly in the minor suits, he may be at a disadvantage, but it is important to him to get his bid in lest he be shut out later—perhaps by reason of the opponents' higher-ranking suits.

The following minor-suit hand is opened by many of the experts, as dealer or second hand:

♠ 6 2   ♡ J 6 3   ◇ K Q 9   ♣ A J 10 5 4

The hand is substandard in high cards, but the holder of it would be embarrassed if one opponent opened one spade and the other raised to two spades. Partner could hold:

♠ 7 3   ♡ A Q 9 7 4 2   ◊ 10 8 5 3   ♣ 6

He could not safely overcall a bid of one spade with two hearts, and a weak jump overcall of three hearts is very risky opposite a passed partner. But the opponents can probably make two or three spades, while four hearts might succeed. And if the opponents venture as far as four spades, that contract might be defeated.

Transpose the spade and diamond holdings, and more experts would pass than would bid. They would not be so afraid of being shut out by an opposing spade suit.

When third hand, a player may often open the bidding on a substandard hand. He does this on the assumption that fourth hand is bound to have enough to bid anyway, and he may as well get in the first blow, both to interfere with the opponents' bidding and to inform his partner of a good suit to lead. This latter being essential, a player should not make a weak third-hand opening bid unless his suit is a strong one, such as K-Q-10-x-x or A-J-10-x-x (or even K-Q-J-x), something he wants his partner to lead.

There is always some danger in opening a relatively weak hand, since partner will assume full opening-bid values and may take the bidding too high. The late Doug Drury devised the convention bearing his name to handle this exact predicament. The details of Drury may be found on page 174.

A player should not open the bidding in third seat on only 10 or 11 points unless his strength is largely in the major suits. Fourth hand, after three passes, does not open without sound values unless he has some strength in spades. In borderline cases, it is normal to apply the Rule of Fifteen. This rule states that fourth hand should open the bidding if the number of high-card points plus the number of spades totals 15 or more.

1. ♠ K 6 3   2. ♠ 7 2
    ♡ 9 5   ♡ 9 5
    ◇ A 7 4   ◇ A 8 7 4
    ♣ K Q 10 8 2   ♣ A Q J 6 5

In the fourth seat, the same expert bid one club on hand one, but passed on number two. The first was accepted because it could support spades. The second was rejected because even if partner had spades or hearts there would be no support for him, and if the opponents had those suits there would be little defense against them.

A player should fear to open the following hand in fourth position:

♠ 8 2   ♡ 5   ◇ K Q 10 6 3   ♣ A Q 7 5 4

To bid could unleash whatever major-suit forces the opponents might have, and if partner has the major suits, the hand will be a misfit.

There was a time when this hand would have been opened in first or second position, to avoid being shut out of the bidding. General adoption of the Unusual Notrump (see page 231) has converted the hand to a pass in most experts' book because its holder can show its nature better by passing originally and making a notrump overcall later, promising a minor two-suiter. The hand is still an acceptable third-hand one-diamond bid, but some good players make it a practice to pass it in any position and await developments.

On the following deal from the final of the 1986 Rosenblum Cup, the winning American team benefited from a light opening bid on board sixteen.

Dlr: West   ♠ Q 7 4
Vul: E-W   ♡ 4
                   ◇ Q 8 5 4
                   ♣ A Q 10 8 4

♠ 6 5 3 2   ♠ K 9
♡ 8 6   ♡ A J 10 7 5 2
◇ 10 7 2   ◇ A J 6
♣ K 9 7 6   ♣ J 2

                   ♠ A J 10 8
                   ♡ K Q 9 3
                   ◇ K 9 3
                   ♣ 5 3

Open Room:

West	North	East	South
Nishat	*Silverman*	*Nisar*	*Lipsitz*
Pass	1♣	1♡	Dble (a)
Pass	2♣	2♡	Dble (b)
Pass	Pass	Pass	

(a) Negative   (b) Penalty

Closed Room:

West	North	East	South
Woolsey	*Fazli*	*Manfield*	*Zia*
Pass	Pass	1♡	1♠
Pass	3♡ (c)	Pass	4♠
Pass	Pass	Pass	

(c) High-card raise to three spades

First, Neil Silverman chose to open a 10-count that most
would pass with nine minor-suit cards, and then Nisar
Ahmed was seduced by his sixth heart into bidding twice,
with fatal consequences. (Though North-South would have
reached three notrump after the opening bid and made that
contract.)

Bobby Lipsitz led the five of clubs, Silverman won with the queen and switched to his trump, declarer finessing the jack. South was sort of endplayed, and chose to continue with the ace and another spade. Nisar won with the king and continued with the ten of hearts. Lipsitz won and played a third round of spades, declarer ruffing. Nisar cashed the ace of hearts but was forced to lead diamonds from hand. Therefore, he lost two tricks in that suit, eight in all and conceded an 800-point penalty.

In the other room, Zia Mahmood would have reduced the loss if he had bid three notrump over three hearts. However, he jumped to four spades. Kit Woolsey led a trump to the four, nine, and jack. A successful finesse of the queen of clubs was followed by a heart from the dummy, East rising with the ace. Afraid that declarer had five spades and would be able to utilize dummy's club suit, Eddie Manfield switched to a low diamond, which ran to dummy's queen.

Declarer had several ways to make the hand from this point, the easiest being to lead a diamond from the dummy. East rated to hold the king of spades because West probably would have bid one notrump or two hearts with two black kings. Also, as East-West were using Flannery (see page 161), East was unlikely to hold four spades. In fact, though, declarer led a spade to the king and ace, and tried to cash the king and queen of hearts. West ruffed the latter of these, and dummy overruffed. East rose with the ace on the diamond lead from the dummy and cashed the ten of hearts, on which Woolsey discarded his last diamond. A diamond ruff gave the defenders their fourth trick. The swing of thirteen IMPs helped the United States on their way to victory in the World Championship.

♠
♡
3 Responses and
Their Effects on
◇ Other Bids
♣

The bidding practices that were current some thirty-five to forty-five years ago, and are still espoused in many bridge instruction books, have changed radically in at least three departments of the game: the choice of suit for an opening bid; the strength required for certain responses; and the strength required for certain rebids.

This is no accident; nearly any change in one aspect of bridge bidding can necessitate changes in several others.

Within three or four years of the birth of contract bridge—meaning by 1930—bridge experts had unanimously adopted the principle of "keeping the bidding open light." The principle has not changed but its application has. The bidding is still kept open "light"—the responding hand passes his partner's opening bid fewer than one time in twenty. But the different types of response have become more rigidly defined.

There was a time, in the earliest years of contract bridge, when a player might pass his partner's opening one-spade bid on the following hand:

♠ 6 3   ♡ Q 8 2   ◇ J 7 5 4   ♣ K 7 6 3

Once the principle of keeping the bidding open was established, such a hand became an obligatory one-notrump response.

The reason for this is that an opening bid at the one-level can contain up to 20 (and on rare occasions even 21 or 22) points, and with a combined total of 26 points it is desirable to play in a game contract. Also, game is often available with less high-card power, and in the days when the responding hand was passing with 6 points, many game contracts and their game bonuses were being missed.

Once the idea of responding with only 6 high-card points was accepted, it became common for the responding hand to keep the bidding open with only 5 points, particularly if the opening bid were in a minor and responder was short in that suit. Sometimes, for tactical purposes—as when the responding hand is non-vulnerable and does not wish to reveal his weakness to his vulnerable opponents, lest they enter the bidding and reach a game—a player might respond on even fewer than 5 high-card points.

Another change from the early days of contract bridge can be seen on the following hand, in which a player responding to his partner's one-spade opening would have bid two hearts, rather than suppress his major:

♠ 6   ♡ K Q J 5 4   ◇ J 7 5 4   ♣ 7 6 3

Similarly, on the following hand the response would have been two diamonds, it having been thought at the time that one must not distort the picture of one's distribution for the mere purpose of showing weakness:

♠ 6 3   ♡ Q 8 5 2   ◇ K J 10 7 5 2   ♣ 6

Today the response on each of the hands shown above would be one notrump (which most experts play as forcing—see page 122). At the time, the only voice crying in the wilderness was S. Garton Churchill, a Brooklyn expert who went on to win several national championships. He advocated a one-notrump response, saying that more points were needed for a two-level response in a new suit, but the best players rejected and even scoffed at the idea that they were to embrace so enthusiastically twenty years later.

The principle that the experts ultimately adopted in responding, as previously they had done in rebidding, is this: *The primary objective is to try to find an eight-card or better major-suit fit; but, within that framework, it is more important to show the general strength of the hand than to show the location of the strength or the distribution of the hand.* When one bid may be made to serve two or all three of these purposes, it is of course the preferred bid. When there is a choice, it should be made in favor of the bid that best shows how strong the hand is.

The validity of this approach will be discussed at greater length in later sections of this book. For the time being, it suffices to note that it exists and is generally accepted.

THE REVERSE AND TWO-NOTRUMP REBIDS

Among several outstanding cases in which the new guidelines have affected bidding practices, there are two bids—the reverse and the two-notrump rebid after a two-over-one response—that once were considered invariably strong and no longer are; and at least one action—the preference bid after a two-over-one response—that once was considered invariably weak and no longer is.

It is just as well that the reverse bid has been redefined in many cases, because it has always mystified the bridge student. The neophyte considers it one of the conventions of bridge, such as the convention that makes an opening two-club bid strength-showing and usually game-forcing. Reverse bids actually never were that; it's just that the experts' logical interpretation of some bidding sequences caused these bids to be, and to be read as, strong. For example,

West	North	East	South
			1 ◇
Pass	1 ♠	Pass	2 ♡

South's two-heart rebid is a reverse—it reverses the order of the suits since it is natural with two suits to bid the higher-ranking first. Also, it forces the responder to go up to the three-level to return to the opening bidder's first suit: here, three diamonds. When South bids two hearts, he risks finding North with a hand like this:

♠ Q 9 8 6 4   ♡ 7 3   ◇ A 7 2   ♣ 7 6 3

North's spades are too weak to rebid, North does not have enough club protection to bid two notrump safely, certainly North cannot pass two hearts when he has a low doubleton and South probably does not have more than a four-card suit, and so North shows preference by returning to three diamonds. (That was the old-fashioned way of doing it, one that still enjoys support in a large section of the bridge-playing world. However, present-day experts adopt a more scientific approach. The most common is to bid the fourth suit or two notrump, whichever is cheaper, as a warning. The responder is telling the opener that he has a weak hand; opener rebids in the lowest contract he is willing to play, and responder corrects if necessary. Any other bid by the responder is natural and game-forcing.) South had to anticipate the fact that North might have such a problem, so by bidding two hearts South announced sufficient strength to play in a contract of three diamonds with very little support from North. A hand that can undertake a contract for nine tricks with so little support must be a strong hand. *Ergo,* the reverse bid of two hearts shows a strong hand.

Such is the case when the response is a one-over-one or one notrump. But in this bidding sequence, there is not necessarily any such implication:

West	North	East	South
			1 ◇
Pass	2 ♣	Pass	2 ♡

North's two-club bid has shown substantial strength, so North-South are unquestionably safe in undertaking a contract at the three-level. Therefore, many partnerships have agreed that South's rebid of two hearts does not necessarily show great strength, it just describes his distribution: four or more hearts and five or more diamonds. He may have only a fair hand and be bidding on the basis of the support he can rely upon receiving from his partner. Others play that the two-heart rebid shows only 4-4 in the red suits, rebidding two diamonds with at least five and waiting for responder to bid a four-card major if he holds one.

A rebid of two notrump by the opening hand after a two-level response was once used invariably to show considerable strength. Consider the following hand:

♠ Q J 9 7 6   ♡ 5 4   ◇ A J 8   ♣ K Q 3

After opening one spade and receiving a two-heart response, players had to rebid two spades, as a two-notrump bid would be taken as showing a stronger hand. Today, as the response at the two-level promises extra values, the opener is allowed to rebid two notrump without promising anything more than a minimum opening bid.

The following deal was bid according to today's style. It developed into one of those situations in play that *bridgeurs* like to talk about.

Dlr: South
Vul: Both

```
                    ♠ A 9
                    ♡ 8 6 2
                    ◇ K 6 2
                    ♣ A Q 10 6 4
    ♠ Q J 6 4                       ♠ 10 8 5
    ♡ K J 7 4 3                     ♡ Q 10 9
    ◇ 9 4 3                         ◇ Q J 7
    ♣ 5                             ♣ J 9 8 7
                    ♠ K 7 3 2
                    ♡ A 5
                    ◇ A 10 8 5
                    ♣ K 3 2
```

West	North	East	South
			1 ◇
Pass	2 ♣	Pass	2NT
Pass	3NT	Pass	Pass
Pass			

By the standards that controlled bidding from the late thirties into the early fifties, South would not have been strong enough for a rebid of two notrump. Probably he would have opened the bidding with one club so as not to let himself be in an embarrassing position if his partner responded two clubs to one diamond.

No embarrassment is felt now. Because South knew his partner was strong, and because South had a notrump type of hand, he simply bid two notrump. Over an old-style two-notrump rebid, which would have shown considerable strength, North might then have probed for a slam. By modern bidding, North could content himself with a simple raise to three notrump because he had already shown his strength with his two-club response.

West opened the four of hearts and East played the queen. South let East hold this trick, and took his ace of hearts when East led back the ten.

South cashed his king of clubs and then led a low club to dummy's queen. This revealed the fact that East had a club stopper. South could run only eight tricks—two spades, the heart already won, two diamonds, and three clubs—without letting East into the lead. By letting East take his jack of clubs, South could establish dummy's last club as his ninth trick; but unfortunately (for South), as soon as East got in with a club the defenders could run three more heart tricks to defeat the contract.

South found the solution in a time-honored play that all can profit from knowing. He led the eight of hearts from dummy to permit the defenders to run their three established hearts first.

On the eight of hearts East played the nine, South discarded a spade and West won with the jack. West cashed the king of hearts, dummy discarded a diamond, East a spade, and South a diamond.

If West led his last heart, he would squeeze his partner. And if he led anything but his last heart, he would never get in again to take the last heart. South could give up a club trick to East, establishing dummy's other club as his ninth trick, and the defenders would get only four tricks.

West did not happen to note the possible consequences of his lead of the last heart, or the fact that he was helpless; he did lead the last heart. A club was thrown from the dummy, East parted with another spade and South also discarded a spade.

West led the queen of spades, and South took the ace and king. On the second of these, East had to discard either a club or a diamond. A club discard would make dummy's fourth club good, and a diamond discard would make South's ten of diamonds good. East chose to throw the diamond, and South ran off the remaining tricks with the king, ace, and ten of diamonds and the ace of clubs.

The preference bid, which used to be a denial of strength, in some cases has become a strength-showing bid. The following bidding sequence is typical:

West	North	East	South
			1♠
Pass	2♣	Pass	2♦
Pass	2♠		

At one time, North's return to two spades would have been noncommittal at best, and South in all probability would now pass. In the 1960s, since North's hand had to be so strong for the two-club response, South would very likely have bid again—unless he had a minimum. North's bidding showed that he was too strong for a simple raise to two spades on the first round. He would often have the kind of hand that is jocularly called a "two-and-a-half spade bid," not quite strong enough for a jump to three spades, which would have been forcing to game, but too good for a single raise. Such a hand might be the following:

♠ K 7 5 3   ♡ 9 5   ◇ J 6 3   ♣ A K 6 2

Today, with the wise adoption of the limit raise by North American experts, this hand would bid three spades immediately, inviting but not forcing game. And after the sequence given above, not only must South bid again following North's preference bid of two spades, but the auction is game-forcing. And there is another inference available to South: North probably only holds three-card spade support. With four-card support, he would usually make an immediate forcing spade raise, bidding either three notrump or two notrump (see Part II, Chapter 8).

AN OLD STORY IN NEW FORM

The following deal typifies a situation that is quite old and has nothing to do with the modern relaxation of reverse-bid standards, but the new definitions of those standards may save many players from going wrong on such hands.

Dlr: South
Vul: None

	♠ K 8 5 3	
	♡ A J 10 9 7	
	◇ A J 8	
	♣ 3	

♠ 10		♠ J 9 7 6
♡ K 8 2		♡ Q 6 4
◇ 9 4 3		◇ 10 6 2
♣ A K J 9 5 2		♣ 10 6 4

	♠ A Q 4 2	
	♡ 5 3	
	◇ K Q 7 5	
	♣ Q 8 7	

West	North	East	South
			1 ◇
2 ♣	2 ♡	Pass	2 ♠
Pass	4NT	Pass	5 ◇
Pass	6 ♠	Pass	Pass
Pass			

Against six spades, West opened the king of clubs, then shifted to a diamond.

Because the spades did not break, South had to lose a trick in that suit to East, as well as a heart trick to East's queen. The slam was down two, but even if the spades had broken 3-2 as expected, it would have been a hopeless contract, losing at least one heart and one club.

North, supporting his Blackwood bid of four notrump and his later insistence on a slam, argued, "But you reversed; I thought you had a strong hand."

North's hand had to be strong when he bid two hearts. South had no choice but to rebid, because North's response was forcing, and it would be highly artificial if a system prevented South from showing his spade suit at this point, where he could show it so cheaply.

What the North player should remember before making a bid like two hearts is that South has bid one diamond prepared to rebid safely over any response by North: over one heart, South could bid one spade and keep the bidding low; but when North bid two hearts, he created a situation that South could not have anticipated. Therefore, North's hand has to be a strong one. North did have this strength and he went wrong only in misinterpreting the strength shown by South's rebid. He should have expressed his slam interest in spades by making a splinter bid of four clubs (see page 169) and leaving the next move to his partner. Here, South would sign off in four spades, but if a slam were available, he would move toward the six-level himself.

THE WEAK ONE-OVER-ONE RESPONSE

Since a one-over-one response is forcing, it may range from a weak hand hoping to survive up to something that has its holder already contemplating a slam.

Paradoxically, when a player makes one of those weak, tactical one-over-one responses, he worries more that partner will be very strong rather than that partner will be weak. If his partner is weak, the opponents will probably enter the bidding and the opening side will be out of trouble.

The following deal resulted in a contract calculated to produce shivers of fear in almost any bridge player, but because the declarer recognized one of the elementary aspects of bridge technique the ending was a happy one.

```
Dlr: South          ♠ Q 7 6
Vul: Both           ♡ 9 4 2
                    ◇ Q 8 7 5 3
                    ♣ 9 3
     ♠ J 4                          ♠ A 10 9 5 2
     ♡ J 10 8 5                     ♡ K 6 3
     ◇ J 10 9                       ◇ K 4 2
     ♣ K 6 4 2                      ♣ J 7
                    ♠ K 8 3
                    ♡ A Q 7
                    ◇ A 6
                    ♣ A Q 10 8 5
```

West	North	East	South
			1♣
Pass	1◇	Pass	2NT
Pass	Pass	Pass	

North shuddered as he passed two notrump, probably wishing he had passed over one club. He could take only cold comfort from the fact that any rescuing bid would make matters worse.

West opened the jack of hearts, East played the six, and South won with the queen.

There was little point to trying for the finesse in clubs with no sure entry to the dummy, so South next led the ace of clubs.

Then South led the queen of clubs, hoping to drop the doubleton jack. This was the only correct play; the queen should always be led in such cases. It could not have helped him to play for, and find, the doubleton king of clubs, for he would still have to lose a trick to the guarded jack.

South was fortunate: the jack of clubs fell under the queen, West winning with the king. South won a heart continuation, cashed three club tricks, and later got a spade and a diamond, making his contract.

4 The Opening Two-Bid

Most systems employ some special opening bid to show an unusually powerful hand, one that will produce game by itself or with the most meager support—including unbiddable support—from partner, and a hand that gives high hopes of a slam if partner has anything better than that.

The earliest such bid to be introduced was the two-bid in a suit, which is called the forcing two or the strong two, and was once called the two-demand or the two-command. By this system, any opening bid of two in a suit shows a hand of the greatest power, forces partner to respond, and forces both players then to keep on bidding until game has been reached. This two-bid still enjoys a reasonable popularity among rubber-bridge players and the older generation of average players, but among tournament players it is virtually extinct.

Most experts use an opening one-club bid (see page 157) or two-club bid as an artificial strength-showing bid.

Most of those who follow the two-club system use other two-bids as weak, preemptive bids. Outside America there are advocates of two-bids that are strong but not game-forcing; some demand ace-showing responses after a two-club opening bid, often employing a two-diamond opening bid for the other strong hands not quite worth a game-force.

Among those who do use two clubs as their most powerful opening bid, there is no uniformity as to the best responses. As mentioned above, some like aces to be shown, some prefer showing aces and kings (control-showing, as it is called), some like natural responses, some use two diamonds as either a weak response or a waiting bid with no good suit to show, and some even use two diamonds as the only positive response, all higher bids being weaker.

For the purpose of this discussion it makes no difference which of these systems is used. The forcing two-bid as used by some players and the forcing artificial two-club bid as used by others are almost always equivalent. That is, a hand on which a member of the former school would open two spades is a hand on which the latter school would open two clubs and show the spade suit later. However, we will assume that the two-club style is being employed.

Whichever kind of original forcing bid he uses, the expert employs it sparingly. Particularly if using the two-club system, that opening bid is overworked and so should be avoided if possible.

Either of the following hands would be an opening two-club bid for the average player, the opening bidder planning to rebid two spades. But there are some experts (believe it or not) who would bid only one spade on hand number one, and many experts would content themselves with a bid of one spade on hand two:

1. ♠ A K Q 8 4	2. ♠ A Q 10 9 6 3
♡ A K 10 6 5	♡ K Q 10 5
◇ A 7	◇ A K
♣ 3	♣ 4

The advantage of the one-bid is that partner's response means something. When partner makes an unforced response to a one-bid, he shows definite values. When he makes a forced response (except a positive response, of course) to a two-club bid, he shows nothing that the two-bidder can count on.

The advantage—not the only one—of the strong two-bid is that game may still be reached when partner is too weak to respond to a one-bid and the opponents are too weak to overcall.

The strong two-bid does not make it more difficult to reach a slam; nor, admittedly, does it facilitate reaching a slam except in the rare cases when a one-bid would be passed out and not even game would be reached.

The purpose of the forcing two-bid should not be to facilitate reaching a slam, but to guard against missing a game. The probable strength of the other three hands, not the strength of the two-bidder's hand, determines the advisability of opening with a two-bid. The following hand promises a sure game, but it is merely a one-spade bid:

♠ K Q J 10 6 5   ♡ A K Q J 8   ◊ 5 3   ♣ —

Over a one-spade bid, someone—partner or an opponent—will surely be strong enough to bid, so the chance to reach game will not be lost.

When an opening hand is "missing" six of the top cards (aces, kings, and queens), it is likely that the bidding will be kept open. If partner has two such cards, he will probably be able to make some response; if partner is weaker than that, one of the opponents will probably be able to reopen the bidding. But when the opening hand has all but four or five of the aces, kings, and queens, he is in danger of being dropped in a one-bid. The following hand, with all but four of the top cards, would certainly be opened with a two-club bid:

♠ A K Q 7 5   ♡ A Q J 6   ◊ A Q 5   ♣ K

The king of clubs, being singleton, is unlikely to contribute to the trick-taking power of the hand, but its presence affects the ability of the other players to keep the bidding open.

There is a distinct change from the days when experts felt some loss of face in opening with a two-bid. They seemed, they thought, to be insulting their partners' boldness in keeping the bidding open. The late P. Hal Sims, who had the largest expert following of the early 1930s and who was captain of the team called the Four Horsemen, which for about two years won all the principal team championships, rather famously bid only one heart on the following hand:

♠ A K 8 3   ♡ A K Q 5 4   ◇ A K Q 10   ♣ —

The Sims system included a game-forcing opening two-bid on a hand that had "a sure game"; perhaps Sims did not feel that this hand would surely take ten tricks with hearts as trumps. The hand might conceivably have lost one diamond, two hearts, and two spades.

Sims came out reasonably well on the hand because, over the one-heart bid, his left-hand opponent made a preemptive club bid, which kept the bidding open for him. Eventually he got to six hearts and made it, and that was the normal contract on the hand. Nevertheless, his refusal to make a two-bid on such a hand was a reminder of an incident reported by Colonel Frank Cook, who wrote a humorous column in a bridge magazine of the 1920s.

According to Colonel Cook, a reader sent in this question:

"I held the ace of spades five times, the ace of hearts four times and the ace of diamonds four times, with no club in my hand. What should I have bid?"

Colonel Cook closed his eyes and visualized the correspondent's hand:

♠ A A A A A   ♡ A A A A   ◇ A A A A   ♣ —

"I would pass," the Colonel replied. "Against the players I know, I wouldn't dare bid," he continued somberly, "unless I had a club in my hand."

USE OF A STRONG TWO-BID TO AVOID LATER OVERBIDDING

There is a recognized advantage to making a forcing bid on a hand that is powerful in top tricks but doubtful in playing strength: by starting with a slight overbid one may avoid more dangerous overbidding later. For example:

Dlr: South
Vul: N-S

	♠ Q 10 6 5	
	♡ 8	
	◇ J 10 6 3	
	♣ K J 7 2	
♠ 8 4 3		♠ J
♡ 10 4 3 2		♡ K J 9 7 5
◇ Q 8 4 2		◇ 7 5
♣ A 8		♣ Q 10 9 5 4
	♠ A K 9 7 2	
	♡ A Q 6	
	◇ A K 9	
	♣ 6 3	

Some experts would not consider South's hand strong enough for more than a one-bid. South did make a one-bid on it, and the record shows what happened:

West	North	East	South
			1 ♠
Pass	2 ♠	Pass	3 ◇
Pass	4 ♠	Pass	4NT
Pass	5 ♣	Pass	5 ♠
Pass	Pass	Pass	

Unfortunately, five spades went down. West opened a heart, but the free finesse did South no good. After drawing trumps, he went after the diamonds and West was in with the queen.

He led his low club and South guessed wrong, putting in the jack. The defenders got two club tricks.

South could well have bid a simple four spades when one spade was raised. And clearly he should not have used Blackwood with two club losers when he had no guarantee that his partner held a control in the suit; but the real problem was the opening bid. Today, most experts would open two notrump, showing some 20–22 points and a balanced hand. This is not ideal with a low doubleton and a five-card major, but experience has shown that it is the best opening bid, immediately showing both the strength and balanced nature of the hand. After bidding two notrump, the opener may sit back and leave further moves to his partner. Here, North would use Stayman to uncover the fit in that suit, and four spades would be the final contract. He would have no thoughts of a slam.

STRONG BALANCED HANDS

It used to be said, truly, that two notrump was the expert's favorite strength-showing bid. It shows a strong hand and will rarely be passed if partner has a smattering of strength. But it is a reasonably safe bid because partner is not required to carry on to game if he is weak, it facilitates slam bidding because partner can expect a fit with any suit he has when his hand is unbalanced, and it guarantees enough high-card strength so that partner can carry on to a slam on his own if he has a fairly good hand with a respectable suit.

The strength shown by a two-notrump opening has come down in the last ten or twenty years. It used to show 22–24 points, but opening with a one-bid when holding 21 points is dangerous; partner might pass with four or five points when game is available. As mentioned above, most experts today use a range in the region of 20–22 points. When holding 23 or 24 points, the opening bid is an artificial two clubs, with a two-notrump rebid defining the hand.

Similarly, a three-notrump opening bid used to show some 25–27 points, and is still so listed in many bridge books. However, the trend has been away from the three-notrump opening bid on such hands. The bid is expressive and accurate, and in the deal given below did no harm, but psychologically the opening three-notrump bid on such a strong hand has proved difficult for the responder to control. Today, experts usually open two clubs and rebid three notrump to show this type of hand. Obviously, this could still prove awkward for the responder, but does have the advantage that the three-notrump opening is released for an alternative meaning and, more important, if the responder happens to give a positive response to the two-club opening, valuable bidding space will have been conserved in the quest for the best slam contract.

In this deal, though, the problem was just the opposite: North had so much less than should be expected that South made his contract only by resorting to a brilliant maneuver.

Dlr: South
Vul: N-S

```
                    ♠ 3 2
                    ♡ 10 7
                    ◇ 8 6 5 3
                    ♣ Q 10 9 4 3
    ♠ Q 10 7                          ♠ J 8 6 5
    ♡ 8 5 4 2                         ♡ Q J 9
    ◇ J 9 7 4                         ◇ K 10 2
    ♣ 7 6                            ♣ K 8 2
                    ♠ A K 9 4
                    ♡ A K 6 3
                    ◇ A Q
                    ♣ A J 5
```

West	North	East	South
			2 ♣
Pass	2 ◇	Pass	3NT
Pass	Pass	Pass	

West led the two of hearts, dummy's ten was played on the bare but unavailing chance that West might have underled the queen-jack, and East's jack forced South's ace.

To inexperienced players, it might seem that South's only chance to make his contract would be to find a singleton or doubleton king of clubs in the hand of either opponent. However, South used a different method of play and made his contract despite his failure to find the king of clubs singleton or doubleton. After winning with the ace of hearts, South led the jack of clubs and overtook with the queen in the dummy.

If East won this trick with the king, South would have had at least nine sure tricks in two spades, two hearts, one diamond, and four clubs, so East played low.

The nine of clubs was next led from the dummy and East had no choice but to play low again, so South finessed by playing his five of clubs, and the nine won.

This left the lead still in the dummy, and South took the opportunity to finesse his queen of diamonds, which won. Now declarer had nine tricks: two spades, two hearts, two diamonds, and three clubs.

South was lucky, but the play of the club suit is still worth studying as an example of how to win three tricks in such a suit even when you cannot reach dummy for a finesse.

No doubt some readers are asking whether declarer would have played the same way if West had held the doubleton king of clubs and had ducked on the first round. Maybe, maybe not. Here, though, East took time to consider his play at trick two, making it clear he held the king. It would take an expert defender to play low smoothly, and then he would have deserved to defeat the contract.

♠
♡
5 Forcing
◇ Responses and
♣ Rebids

In 1929, when the game of contract bridge was very new, a woman in Cleveland, Ohio, attended a lecture by Ely Culbertson, one of the most reputable authorities. She was a serious student and she was equipped with an open notebook and a sharp pencil for recording the lecturer's pearls of bridge wisdom.

The whole idea of forcing bids was new then, too, and the lecturer devoted his time to explaining such bids: opening two-bids, jump bids, one-over-one bids, cue-bids, and so on. While he talked, the serious woman in his audience busily plied pencil on notebook.

On his way out of the hall, the lecturer curiously glanced at the woman's notebook. The page was covered with doodling except for two words, her sole notes on the lecture. The two words were "Never pass."

Yet the bids that the lecturer wished to have treated as forcing then would not have represented ten percent of the bids that are treated as forcing today.

Waggishly, S. Garton Churchill said in 1931 that his next book would be on the subject of non-forcing bids and would have 500 pages. "All the pages," he added thoughtfully, "will be blank."

By the ultrarefined bidding system used by the leading American players today, it is almost as hard to pass as that woman thought it was in 1929. Forcing bids no longer need be two-bids or jump bids—in fact, jump bids are considered somewhat unsporting, perhaps because they make matters easier for partner. Almost any suit-bid is likely to be forcing, and some simple bids turn out unexpectedly to be forcing to game.

FORCING BIDS THAT ARE NOT JUMPS

Forcing bids were an American invention, and perhaps for that reason American players have always used many forcing bids, while Europeans, using fewer, have, until recently, won the World Championship from American teams year after year.

As early as 1927 Culbertson proposed that opening two-bids and jump shifts be forcing, and it was twenty years before anyone disputed this theory; even today, the two-club opening and jump shifts are almost universally treated as forcing.

It was also Culbertson who (in 1929) proposed the first forcing bid that was not a jump—the bid that came to be called the one-over-one. For example:

West	North	East	South
			1 ◇
Pass	1 ♡	Pass	

The one-heart bid is a one-over-one and is forcing: South must bid again. The bid is still so interpreted by nearly every player in the world, good or bad.

In less than a year—some time before the end of 1930—Culbertson had abandoned this theory, concluding that it was unsound. But his original argument had been too convincing; American experts had taken up the one-over-one principle and nothing that has happened or that has been said since has persuaded them to abandon it. Even Culbertson was forced to backtrack five years later and call the one-heart response forcing because all the good players were treating it as such.

The extension of the one-over-one principle—the idea that a new-suit bid at the one-level even by the opener should be forcing—lasted only a few years and then was generally abandoned.

For example:

West	North	East	South
			1♣
Pass	1♡	Pass	1♠
Pass			

At one time, the idea was that South's one-spade rebid was forcing and North must bid again; but this gave way to the principle that if North were allowed to pass the one-club bid, he might now pass the one-spade rebid. Suppose the opener holds this hand:

♠ A J 5 3   ♡ 9 5   ◊ A 7 4   ♣ K 10 5 4

It is customary to open one club on this hand and rebid one spade over partner's expected response of one diamond or one heart. However, if the one-spade rebid were forcing, it would be dangerous to open the bidding in the first place.

SUIT OVER SUIT

Nevertheless the suit-over-suit principle, proposed as early as 1932 and rejected by most experts at that time, soon came to be a tenet of the American bridge religion and is generally followed today. By 1935 it was firmly established in American practice that any new-suit response to an opening was forcing for one round, whether the response was at the one-level or the two-level. In the following sequence:

West	North	East	South
			1 ◇
Pass	2 ♣	Pass	?

South had to bid again, and if he could not conveniently bid over two clubs the conclusion was that he should not have opened the bidding in the first place.

After that it did not take long to arrive at a system whereby the suit-over-suit principle, rejected in 1932, became an effective part of every popular system—as it still is.

The new-suit bid is not forcing when partner's previous bid was one notrump, unless responder has reversed.

West	North	East	South
			1 ◇
Pass	1 ♡	Pass	1NT
Pass	2 ♣	Pass	

North's two-club bid, though a rebid in a new suit, is not played as forcing (unless it is being used as the modern Checkback convention—see page 63). North may have a weak hand, but has bid two clubs because he has unbalanced distribution that would make it dangerous to play in notrump. For example:

♠ 7   ♡ K 8 7 5 3   ◇ 8 4   ♣ K J 6 4 2

But if North had rebid two spades over one notrump, this would be a reverse and would be forcing.

By the usual definition as published in most popular bridge books, a new-suit non-jump rebid is forcing only when made by the responding hand. In the following sequence:

West	North	East	South
			1 ♡
Pass	1 ♠	Pass	2 ♣
Pass	2 ◇		

South's rebid of two clubs is not forcing because South is the opening hand, but North's rebid of two diamonds is forcing because North is the responding hand. Also because almost every expert today plays "fourth suit forcing."

The opener may make a forcing suit-over-suit bid if his partner has responded at the two-level. For example:

West	North	East	South
			1 ♠
Pass	2 ♣	Pass	2 ◇

In the modern game in North America, North's initial bid is usually treated as forcing to game unless followed by a three-club rebid, so South's two-diamond rebid must logically be forcing. In fact, even before the game-forcing two-over-one became popular, as the responder still promised at least a good ten points for his two-level response, many experts played that a new suit by opener would be forcing for one round.

This approach, as already mentioned in Chapter 2, has affected the opener's reverse. For example:

West	North	East	South
			1 ◇
Pass	2 ♣	Pass	2 ♡

In days of yore, this bid showed extra values. Today, though, many experts, especially those who live on the East Coast, treat this bid only as shape-showing, indicating at least five diamonds and four hearts, and not promising any extra high-card values. It is a playable method, but can cause problems when neither the opener nor the responder knows whether his partner is minimum or not.

Another bid that used to be treated as non-forcing but is played as forcing by most experts today is the opener's reverse after a one-over-one response. For example:

West	North	East	South
			1 ◇
Pass	1 ♠	Pass	2 ♡

With an unsuitable minimum that preferred hearts to diamonds and did not have long spades, the responder used to be able to pass. Now, the situation is forcing; and most pairs use some scientific sequences to distinguish between strong and weak responding hands (see page 35).

THE NEW FORCING BIDS

To summarize, the following have all become forcing bids in American practice, either because they are defined as forcing or because they may be so strong that it is not safe to pass them:

• Any bid in a new suit by the responder, except over one notrump.
• Any rebid by the opener if the response was at the two-level.
• Any reverse by the opener.

This hand exhibits the advantage of taking things slowly.

Dlr: North
Vul: None

```
                    ♠ A K 6 5
                    ♡ 4
                    ◇ J 8 5 3
                    ♣ A Q 8 7
    ♠ J 9 8 2                      ♠ Q 10 4 3
    ♡ Q 8                          ♡ K J 9 7 2
    ◇ Q 10 9 2                     ◇ 6
    ♣ 6 5 2                        ♣ J 9 4
                    ♠ 7
                    ♡ A 10 6 5 3
                    ◇ A K 7 4
                    ♣ K 10 3
```

West	North	East	South
	1♣	Pass	1♡
Pass	1♠	Pass	2◇
Pass	3◇	Pass	4♣
Pass	4◇	Pass	6◇
Pass	Pass	Pass	

Normally, North would open one diamond with 4-4 in the minors, but here the clubs were much stronger and he did not anticipate rebid problems holding a four-card spade suit.

South, with a hand potentially playable in three suits, took it gently, bidding a simple one heart, and then asking for further information with a "fourth suit forcing" two diamonds. He learned that partner had a three-suited hand short in hearts, which was good news. He showed his club support, learned that partner was definitely happy to play in diamonds opposite length, and jumped to the slam.

West, in an effort to find a safe lead, opened the six of clubs. Dummy played low, East put up the jack, and South won with the king. Declarer then led the king and ace of diamonds, for if the outstanding diamonds were 3-2 he could establish the dummy's hand. But the diamonds did not break.

South could now get twelve tricks only if he found West with at least three clubs and one heart and guessed his distribution correctly. South cashed the ten of clubs and played a club to the queen. Then he cashed the ace and king of spades and ruffed a spade in hand. Next, he cashed the ace of hearts, ruffed a heart in the dummy, and ruffed the last spade in hand. Finally, he led a heart. West could do nothing to prevent dummy's jack of diamonds from winning the twelfth trick for South.

NOTRUMP BIDS

Any simple suit bid that is forcing but does nothing to define more closely the strength of the hand suffers from an inherent weakness: partner still does not know the power of the hand opposite, and cannot make a judgment about how high to aim. But whenever a player bids in notrump, his partner feels at home. The bid will be limited, and it is easy to assess the combined power of the hands. At least, that used to be the situation. Now, notrump bids seem no longer to be limited, non-forcing, and descriptive. There is the forcing one-notrump (see page 122); the Jacoby two-notrump (see page 165), or the three-notrump forcing raise response to an opening bid of one spade or one heart; Lebensohl (see page 226); and so on. However, in these cases, the partner of the notrump bidder will normally define his hand more closely, and it is up to the ambiguous notrump bidder either to select the final contract or to make his intentions apparent to his partner. Examples will be given in the descriptions of these conventional notrump bids.

PREFERENCE BIDS

As already mentioned in Chapter 3, another erstwhile sign-off bid that has changed character, with far-reaching ramifications, is the preference bid.

In the following sequence, North's two-spade bid used to be limited and South was expected to pass unless he had noticeable extra values, but it is now game-forcing:

West	North	East	South
			1♠
Pass	2♣	Pass	2♢
Pass	2♠	Pass	?

No bid by North (except the limited three clubs, which shows a good six-card suit and some ten high-card points) can sound weak when his earlier two-club response said that his hand is strong.

When the first response has promised no great strength, a preference bid is still weak; it can be and often is passed:

West	North	East	South
			1♡
Pass	1♠	Pass	2♢
Pass	2♡	Pass	?

The logical meaning of North's two-heart bid is this: North probably lacked either the heart support or the general strength to raise to two hearts in the first place; therefore North's return to hearts promises no more than the original one-spade response, which could have been made on a weak hand. The only additional information given by the preference bid of two hearts is that North likes hearts better than diamonds. North may have such a hand as:

♠ 10 8 7 6 3   ♡ J 5   ♢ 6   ♣ A 7 6 4 3

He cannot reasonably pass two diamonds and he is too weak and unsuitable for any other action. He must bid two hearts.

South must appreciate this fact and will pass two hearts unless his hand is exceptionally strong and two diamonds was something of an underbid.

But if the two-heart preference bid is to be used as a warning and pass-inviting bid, it is similarly reasonable to expect a jump by North to three hearts to promise only a good, not an overwhelming, hand. Holding this:

♠ A K J 5   ♡ Q 7 3   ♢ 6 3   ♣ 7 6 4 2

North could hardly respond anything but one spade to one heart. (Even if employing Flannery—see page 161—bidding a forcing one-notrump and then three hearts is a reasonable description of the hand, but is not as accurate as starting with one spade, the suit in which most of this hand's values lie. And a limit raise of three hearts with only three-card support is unattractive whenever there is a sensible alternative: that ninth trump is usually worth an extra trick.) The one-spade bid shows the location of his strength and does not given an exaggerated picture of his heart support. But when South has rebid two diamonds, how can North merely bid two hearts on this hand and let his partner think it may be as weak as the previous one?

The solution, once considered old-fashioned but now having regained acceptance among good players, is for North to bid three hearts over two diamonds. Logically, the jump to three hearts shows more than a hopeless hand but less than enough to force to game—if North wished to guarantee game he could jump to *four* hearts. South should be permitted to pass a jump to three hearts with a hand like this:

♠ 7 3   ♡ A 9 8 4 2   ◇ A K 8 4   ♣ J 9

These combined North-South hands will probably make three hearts but are unlikely to make game.

TOURNAMENT STYLE

The gap between the social and the tournament player widened in the 1970s and 1980s, in terms of style and conventions. The best evidence for this is the polls taken by *The Bridge World* magazine in 1968 and 1984, with responses from about 120 experts and some 1,400 readers, almost all of whom were knowledgeable tournament players. The following summarizes the changes during the sixteen-year period.

1. The four-card-major opening bid was abandoned, just as the strong two-bid had been earlier. In addition, the idea that one notrump should be a forcing response to a one-heart or one-spade opening became standard, with the corollary that two-level responses are strong (usually twelve points or more) and promise further bidding.

2. Some bids that used to be forcing became non-forcing, and *vice versa:*

       a. All second-round jumps (except a jump shift) by a responder who bid at the one-level became invitational, not forcing. For example:

Opener	Responder
1♣	1♡
1♠	2NT/3♣/3♡/3♠

All these rebids by responder are now treated as invitational and non-forcing.

       b. A minor-suit raise (1♣–2♣ or 1♢–2♢) became strong and forcing, promising at least ten high-card points. The jump raise of the minor (1♣–3♣ or 1♢–3♢) became weak.

       c. A jump in a minor suit in response to a one-notrump opening (1NT–3♣ or 1NT–3♢) became a weak sign-off, requiring a pass by the opener.

       d. After an opposing take-out double, a new suit at the one-level (e.g., 1♣–[Dble]–1♡) became forcing.

       e. After a one-level overcall of partner's opening bid, jump shifts (e.g., 1♣–[1♡]–2♠) became weak.

       f. Unless by a passed hand, fourth-suit bids that were either reverses (e.g., 1♢–1♡–2♣–2♠) or at the three-level (e.g., 1♡–1♠–2♢–3♣) became game-forcing.

3. Some bids that used to be natural became artificial:

       a. After an opening bid of one or two notrump, a red-suit response became a transfer, showing at least five cards in the major suit immediately above the bid suit. This transfer concept was endorsed by most experts and an astonishing 97 percent of readers. As a corollary, minimum spade responses now indicate minor-suit hands.

b. After a third- or fourth-seat major-suit opening bid, a two-club response (e.g., Pass–1♠–2♣) is strong and promises a fit. This is the Drury convention (see page 174). The corollary is that a one-notrump response by a passed hand may have as many as twelve points, so the opener should bid again unless he is minimum or subminimum.

c. After a one-notrump rebid, two of a minor is an artificial probe announcing at least game interest.

Many pairs use New Minor Forcing, in which two of the unbid minor (e.g., 1♣–1♠–1NT–2◇ or 1◇–1♡–1NT–2♣) is the artificial inquiry. (When both minors have been bid, the auction having begun 1♣–1◇–1NT, two clubs is used as NMF.)

Some pairs always bid two clubs regardless of the auction. This is often called Checkback.

A few pairs employ both two clubs and two diamonds, the former starting invitational sequences and the latter being an immediate game-force.

d. After a major-suit opening, a two-notrump response (e.g., 1♡–2NT) became an artificial bid promising a strong hand with slam interest and a good fit for the opener. This Jacoby two-notrump bid asks the opener to show a singleton or void if he has one. The opener's weakest action is a jump to game in his suit.

e. If a one-notrump opening is overcalled, a response of two notrump (e.g., 1NT–[2♡]–2NT) became artificial. This bid, called Lebensohl (or Lebensold—see page 226), asks the opener to rebid three clubs. Responder may have a weak hand with a long suit, or a game-going hand with a stopper in the opponent's suit, in which case he will continue with a Stayman-type cue-bid or a rebid of three notrump.

Another use of the same idea occurs after a take-out

double of an opposing weak two-bid. A two-notrump bid again forces three clubs.

    f. After a strong and artificial two-club opening, the responder shows abject weakness by responding first two diamonds and then three clubs if the opener rebids in a major (e.g., 2♣–2◇–2♠–3♣). If the opener rebids three clubs, three diamonds serves the same purpose.

4. Two sophisticated slam conventions have become standard:

    a. Roman Key Card Blackwood, which treats the king of the agreed trump suit as an ace, has replaced traditional Blackwood as the preferred ace-asking method (see page 191).

    b. The splinter bid, an unusual jump, shows a fit with partner, slam interest, and at most one card in the suit bid. Examples are: 1♡–4♣; 1♣–1♠–4◇; 1♠–2♡–4♣; 2♣–2◇–2♡–4♣.

Treating the jump rebid in the opener's minor as non-forcing would have side-stepped the problems encountered in the next deal.

```
Dlr: North          ♠ Q 10 8 5
Vul: E-W            ♡ Q
                    ◇ A 7
                    ♣ A 8 6 4 3 2
     ♠ K 9 4 3                      ♠ A J
     ♡ A 9 8 2                      ♡ J 7 6 4
     ◇ 9 8 5 4                      ◇ K 10 6 3 2
     ♣ J                           ♣ 10 5
                    ♠ 7 6 2
                    ♡ K 10 5 3
                    ◇ Q J
                    ♣ K Q 9 7
```

West	North	East	South
	1♣	Pass	1♡
Pass	1♠	Pass	1NT
Pass	Pass	Pass	

In a rubber-bridge game, North would have rebid two clubs over one notrump. But as this deal occurred in a match-pointed pair event, in which it is better to make a notrump contract than the same number of tricks in a suit contract, North passed one notrump to take advantage of the higher trick score in notrump.

South, playing in one notrump, did not even make seven tricks. West led the four of diamonds, dummy's seven was played, and East won with the king. East returned a low diamond to dummy's ace. South could have run his six clubs, but instead he tried to sneak an extra trick by leading the queen of hearts. However, West won with the ace, East took three more diamond tricks, and then East cashed the ace of spades and led a spade to West's king for the setting trick.

South played badly. He should have cashed his clubs to assure himself of seven tricks and his contract. Here, he had reason to hope that any pair playing in clubs would be held to eight tricks. Two clubs scores 90, the same as one notrump. And a contract of three clubs would be too high.

The fact remains that North probably could have made game in notrump. East's normal opening lead would have been the three of diamonds, giving North two diamond tricks. North would have led a heart, and could not have been prevented from winning one heart, two diamonds, and six clubs, the nine he needed for his three-notrump contract.

The problem was the limitation placed on South by the forcing nature of jump bids. South did not want to bid two clubs over North's one spade, because two clubs is a weak bid that might be passed, leaving North-South in a low-scoring club contract. South was afraid to jump to three clubs because that would have been a forcing bid and South was not strong enough to force North to bid again.

In the actual circumstances, an invitational three-club bid would have told North that he could probably win six club tricks in notrump—not that he would bid that on this particular hand. He would pass three clubs and probably make the contract after a diamond lead from East. Unfortunately, South did not know that his partner held a six-card club suit; North might have held only four clubs, or even three. North did not know his six clubs were all trick-winners; South might have held only one or two valueless clubs.

Logically, South should have been able to bid three clubs merely to show that his hand had more strength than he would need to bid two clubs. He could have risked a jump to three clubs if North had been free to pass when holding a weak or ill-fitting hand. But when a jump bid is forcing, one can hardly expect partner to pass, however weak or ill-fitting his hand.

FOURTH SUIT FORCING

Many years ago, most European experts embraced a principle called Fourth Suit Forcing. When a partnership has previously bid three of the suits, a bid in the fourth suit forces a response (as it has always done in American bidding, too), but does not necessarily show strength in the fourth suit (as it traditionally has in American bidding). It is used whenever the responder has no clear-cut bid available, and asks the opener to describe his hand further, placing emphasis on bidding notrump with a stopper in the fourth suit.

In an early book, *Blueprint for Bidding* by Terence Reese and Albert Dormer, the following example is given. South holds

♠ A K 8 7 5   ♡ 10 7   ◇ 9 5 3   ♣ A Q 2

and the bidding begins:

West	North	East	South
	1♡	Pass	1♠
Pass	2♣	Pass	?

South cannot bid notrump without a diamond stopper, but does not wish to have the bidding stop short of game. The fourth-suit bid in diamonds keeps the bidding low, promises better-than-minimum responding values, and assures South of another chance.

In traditional American bidding, South would promise a control in diamonds and so would be faced with a most unappetizing problem. Because of this, most American experts have adopted Fourth Suit Forcing.

What strength is shown by the fourth-suit bidder? Many use the simple approach, that the bid is forcing to game. However, the more discerning bidder only has this arrangement when the bid is made at the three-level. One level lower, it is better to play that the bid is forcing for one round, promising some eleven points or more.

To make things more difficult, though, there are certain fourth-suit bids that are most definitely *not* forcing.

West	North	East	South
	1◇	Pass	1♠
Pass	2♣	Pass	2◇
Pass	2NT	Pass	3♡

South was too weak to bid two hearts over two clubs. Instead South bid two diamonds, a simple preference bid that invited a pass by North. How can South, who revealed such weakness, now make a forcing bid that would inevitably result in a game contract? He cannot. South should hold something like:

♠ Q 8 7 5 3   ♡ K J 8 7 4   ◇ 9 4   ♣ 7

Having discovered from North's two-notrump bid that his partner has some strength in hearts, and a generally strong hand, South fixes the contract in what is likely to be the best combined trump suit.

A similar principle applies in other auctions.

West	North	East	South
	1 ♡	Pass	2 ♡
Pass	2NT	Pass	3 ♣

South holds

♠ 7   ♡ Q 7 5   ◇ 10 4 3   ♣ A 10 8 7 5 4

The obvious first response is a raise to two hearts. The rebid in clubs shows at least a six-card suit, and the opener is being invited to pass.

♠
♡
6 An Approach to the Jump Shift
♢
♣

In the formative years of contract bridge bidding systems there were "jumpers" and there were "minimum bidders." In responding to an opening bid such as one heart, the jumpers would jump to two spades or three clubs on merely a strong, game-going hand; the minimum bidders would respond only one spade or two clubs on such a hand, reserving the jump response for possible slam hands.

The argument revolved around such cases as the following:

♠ 9 4	♠ A J 10 6 5
♡ A J 10 6 5	♡ K 2
♢ A K 3	♢ 7 4
♣ 10 5 2	♣ A K J 3

West deals and opens one heart. North passes. What should East respond?

"One spade!" cried the minimum bidders. "Two spades!" shouted the jump bidders.

The minimum bidders maintained that the one-over-one saved a round of bidding. Their argument was plausible. Look, they said:

West	East	or	West	East
1 ♡	1 ♠		1 ♡	2 ♠

Doesn't the former save a round of bidding against the latter?

Culbertson neatly exploded this fallacy by carrying the bidding one round further:

West	East
1 ♡	1 ♠
1NT	3 ♣

comes to the same thing as

West	East
1 ♡	2 ♠
2NT	3 ♣

since even the minimum bidder could not dare bid only two clubs on the second round, and the same level would be reached.

What with one example and another, the warring camps managed to win arguments back and forth. All of this proved only one thing: that you can make up an example to support any side of a bridge dispute.

Now the war is over. All is quiet on the bridge front. In the United States, at least, there are no longer conflicting schools. The erstwhile minimum bidders decreased their requirements for a jump slightly. The erstwhile jump bidders slightly increased theirs. (And those who could not agree took up weak jump shifts!) Perhaps the main reason for this truce is that the hands on which jump shifts are made have been defined closely; more on that in a moment. There is no good reason to debate the subject any longer because a forcing jump shift so seldom occurs: no one has a good enough hand to make one anymore.

Things have improved during the eighties with the improved definition of what constitutes a jump shift, but it is still true that European players make jump responses on all hands that seem likely to go to game, and when they do so they often disgrace their American opponents who are minimum bidders according to our national custom.

From the meetings between teams from the United States and Europe in international competition during the 1960s, most of which ended disastrously for the Americans, it is possible to pick out at least five cases in which European use of the more liberal jump response resulted in a serious loss to the Americans, and no case in which American use of the minimum response can be held to have given them an advantage over the Europeans. And there would have been a sixth except that on one occasion Terence Reese dropped the ace of hearts on the floor. Not noticing that he had dropped the card, but still having a strong enough hand, Reese forced to game. However, a slam was not reached, and when Reese put down his dummy, his partner, Boris Schapiro, remarked in a monotone, "What a remarkable hand. Only twelve cards." The missing ace of hearts was then found and restored to the hand. As a result, the British pair missed a slam; but they still made a profit. The American pair, although seeing all their cards, bid a slam in the wrong suit and went down!

HOW A STRONG RESPONDING HAND IS BID

Just as taxi drivers adhere to the policy of always getting as far ahead as possible, even if they land behind a stalled moving van, American bridge experts always used to make the lowest possible bid, so long as it was forcing.

The decision about whether or not to jump shift has very little to do with the apparent strength of the hand, given a certain minimum. It is not necessary to have support for partner's suit. It is not necessary to have a solid suit of your own. A hand with 20 high-card points and good support for partner may be just right for a one-over-one, whereas a hand weak in playing strength and containing no more than 15 or 16 high-card points may be a good forcing take-out.

Few if any experts, holding either of the following hands, would make a jump response to partner's opening bid of one heart:

1. ♠ A K 8 4 3   2. ♠ 7 6 4
     ♡ Q 5   ♡ A 7 6
     ◇ A 7 5   ◇ A K 9 5 2
     ♣ A 8 2   ♣ A 7

The standard responses would be one spade on number one, two diamonds on the second. Yet experience indicates that a jump to two spades will work out better on number one, and a jump to three diamonds will work out better on number two.

The same players who consider the hands above far too weak for jump responses would consider the following hands strong enough:

3. ♠ Q J 9 7 5   4. ♠ 7 5
     ♡ A K   ♡ A 6
     ◇ A J 10 3 2   ◇ A K Q 10 5 3
     ♣ A   ♣ A J 4

The standard response to partner's one-heart bid is two spades on number three, three diamonds on number four. One spade and two diamonds, respectively, should produce better results.

The choice of responses should usually be governed by the answer to one question: Which partner will make the final decision as to the contract? This decision is usually made by the hand that is "solid"—has great trick-winning strength.

For example, hands one and two above have almost no trick-winning strength beyond their high cards. They are full of "holes." Hands three and four are each about four tricks better.

Consider hands one and three if partner does not open the bidding and if partner has an almost worthless hand containing nothing but four spades to the ten. Opposite such a hand, number one is likely to win only six or seven tricks; number three is a three-to-one shot to make game.

And consider numbers two and four if partner has an almost worthless hand including nothing of value except the king of hearts. Hand number two can barely make a part-score contract and will be hard put to win the contract from the opponents in the auction. Number four is odds-on to make game in notrump if spades are not led.

WHEN TO UNDERBID

Let us consider the hand designated above as number three. It is a beautiful hand—beautiful in more ways than one, as will be shown.

♠ Q J 9 7 5   ♡ A K   ◇ A J 10 3 2   ♣ A

Partner opens one heart. What should you respond?

There are nineteen points. A doubleton ace-king in partner's suit may not be the strongest support one would ask for, but you can be assured it's no misfit. Why not make a two-spade jump response on this hand? Well, a good rule, which is observed by almost all experts, is to avoid a jump shift with a two-suiter unless partner opened the bidding in one of the suits. Such hands need a slow approach.

It isn't a matter of rules, though. The best bid in bridge is the one that will work out best. On a hand like this a jump shift, suggesting a slam, will seldom work as well as a simple response. And when you go into the reasons why this is so, you discover the entire basis on which to make your choice between a jump and a non-jump suit response.

Suppose your response is one spade, as recommended in the previous paragraph. What happens then is:

North	South
1♡	1♠
3♠	?

Now South knows that North has a powerful hand and that a grand slam is virtually assured. North has given a jump raise in spades—and he has given it over a minimum one-over-one response that might have been made on a hand as weak as

♠ Q J 7 5   ♡ 4 3   ◇ K 3 2   ♣ 7 6 4 3

If North could take the responsibility for a contract of three spades opposite so weak a hand, and could urge a game contract if South's hand is any stronger, North must be very strong. Furthermore, North must have four spades and at least five hearts, so he probably has at least the king in one minor suit and the king or a singleton in the other. Even if North has a low doubleton in diamonds, South can expect to get enough discards in hearts and clubs to ditch his entire string of diamond losers. This is an unusual case in which South can go to seven spades over the three-spade bid and have about a ten-to-one chance of making it. Of course, in real life South will double-check about the top spade cards, but will be surprised if North does not have both.

What would have happened if South had made the less imaginative response of two spades over one heart? Every later bid would have lost some meaning; the following bidding would have been meaningless:

North	South
1♡	2♠
3♠	

North might readily have raised to three spades on a hand like the following:

♠ A 8 6 2   ♡ Q 10 9 5 3   ◇ Q 5   ♣ K Q

Three spades would be his best bid. Since his partner has forced to game, North is simply confirming the spade suit. South cannot tell whether North has such a bad hand, or whether he has A-K-x of spades, which would make the grand slam a reasonable gamble. On the supporting hand shown above, even the small slam—though the bidding of a small slam on South's hand was a foregone conclusion as soon as North opened the bidding—might in some circumstances fail to make.

The only way South can find out with any confidence is by letting North make a free, rather than a forced, rebid.

This is the great advantage of the one-over-one response: *It makes partner's rebids far more informative, because those rebids must allow for the possible weakness of the one-over-one.*

Does this mean that the one-over-one response is invariably superior to the immediate game-force? It most emphatically does not. In fact, the jump response is not used by Americans nearly as often as it should be. But the jump response should be made on a different type of hand from the one-over-one, and with a different object. The difference may be roughly stated in this way: *The one-over-one response is superior when the responder expects to have to make the final decision himself.* This occurs, usually, when his hand has great playing strength and very few "holes" (required key honor cards) in it, and when general information as to his partner's strength will be all he needs.

The game-forcing jump response is superior when the responder, despite his high-card strength, is missing so many key cards that he can hardly hope to find out about all of them in the course of a normal bidding sequence. In such cases it is better for the responder to make the jump response, revealing his abnormal high-card holding immediately. Given this information, his partner may be able to guide the combined hands into the best contract.

Most bridge players, including American experts, used to do exactly the opposite of what is right. They would make the game-forcing jump response only on hands strong in playing strength; they would make minimum responses (or occasionally jump notrump responses) on hands with little to recommend them except their high-card content. They demanded strong support for partner's suit, or a solid suit of their own, before they would make the jump response. To partner's one-club opening they would respond two diamonds, when it should have been one diamond, on the following hand:

♠ A　♡ K 6 2　♢ A K Q J 7 5　♣ 7 5 4

And they would bid one diamond, when they should have bid two, on this hand:

♠ 7 4 2　♡ A K J　♢ A K 6 5 2　♣ 8 6

The question to ask oneself, when holding a concentration of high cards but not a great deal of dependable playing strength, is, "Considering my partner's opening bid, am I willing to stop short of game?" If the answer is in the negative, then make the jump response of two diamonds.

JUMP-SHIFT RESPONSES IN LOWER-RANKING SUITS

Before the advent of the virtually game-forcing two-over-one response, exactly the same considerations prevailed when the choice was between a non-jump response at the two-level and a game-forcing jump to the three-level—that is, the question of whether to bid two or three diamonds over partner's one-spade opening. If you bid two diamonds, you would have found out more about partner's hand. Not so today. But if you bid three diamonds, you still tell him more about yours.

This is a good three-heart response to partner's one-spade bid:

♠ A 8 4   ♡ A K 7 6 3   ◇ 9 4 2   ♣ A 3

You are not going to stop short of game, but where do you go from there? Before the game-forcing two-over-one, if you bid only two hearts and partner rebid two spades, you could make no safe bid that would tell partner you have four tricks in top cards; yet that might be all he needed to know if he had something like this:

♠ K Q 9 7 6 3   ♡ Q 4   ◇ A 3   ♣ J 6 4

Even today, when you, the responding hand, can continue with a forcing three spades, does that really help your partner? Is he expected to cue-bid with four diamonds despite his minimum? How does he distinguish between a twelve-point hand and one containing seventeen points? The game-forcing two-over-one is not a panacea.

Your partner will never make a slam-try unless he is invited strongly and immediately. Yet you are not strong enough to make a slam-try that would risk passing the game level. Suppose partner is holding:

♠ K Q 10 6 3   ♡ 8 4   ◇ A Q 3   ♣ Q 10 4

You do not want to be any further along than four spades when the bidding ends.

The three-heart response solves the problem beautifully. You bid it and then relax. You can content yourself with absolute minimum rebids thereafter; if there is any chance of a slam, partner can bid it himself. After all, he knows what you have—and you couldn't very well have less.

THE DANGER IN THE MINIMUM RESPONSE

The great danger when one makes a minimum response on a hand with four top tricks in it, but little else, is that responder will always be doubtful that he has adequately shown his slam-going assets. He will try to make up later for his earlier underbidding and may find himself in a contract that has passed game but is not quite a slam—undertaking a risk out of all proportion to the possible gain.

Dlr: South
Vul: None

♠ A 8 3
♡ A K 7 5 4
◇ 7 6 2
♣ A 5

♠ J 5 4   ♠ 7 2
♡ 10 2   ♡ J 9 8 3
◇ Q 9 4 3   ◇ K 10 8
♣ K Q 9 2   ♣ 10 7 4 3

♠ K Q 10 9 6
♡ Q 6
◇ A J 5
♣ J 8 6

West	North	East	South
			1♠
Pass	2♡	Pass	2♠
Pass	3♣	Pass	3♡
Pass	3♠	Pass	4♠
Pass	5♠	Pass	Pass
Pass			

West led the king of clubs, dummy winning with the ace. Declarer cashed the king and queen of spades and the queen and king of hearts. South tried to ruff a low heart, but West overruffed.

West switched to a diamond and East's king fell to South's ace. Unable at this point to lead a club and establish a club ruff in the dummy (West would cash the queen of diamonds to defeat the contract), South led a spade to dummy's ace, discarded two clubs on dummy's hearts, and led a diamond. He lost two diamond tricks and was down one.

Granted that South played badly and could have made his five-spade contract in several different ways, there was no good reason for him to be at five spades in the first place. Contracts of five hearts and five spades are all futile, with nothing to gain and everything to lose.

Most bridge players do misplay hands occasionally. Why must they also be saddled with bad contracts?

Too often a player with a hand such as North's, having reached game, becomes fearful that he has not adequately shown his many high cards, carries on beyond game, and arrives at the unprofitable five-bid. An immediate jump response would relieve North of this fear. The bidding might go:

West	North	East	South
			1 ♠
Pass	3 ♡	Pass	3NT or 4 ♡
Pass	4 ♠	Pass	Pass
Pass			

Now South, with his minimum, might pass. Give him only a slightly stronger hand—for example, a six-card spade suit—and he would surely bid six, for North could not possibly have less for his jump response; and with a six-card spade suit in the South hand, the slam would be virtually laydown.

GOOD BIDDING, BETTER PLAY

Back now to the beautiful hand mentioned earlier, for the entire play of that hand should be given. It had a point that was missed by many a famous player.

```
Dlr: West              ♠ A K 8 3
Vul: None              ♡ Q 10 9 6 5 2
                       ◇ 6
                       ♣ K Q
      ♠ 6                            ♠ 10 4 2
      ♡ J 8 7 4                      ♡ 3
      ◇ Q 9 5                        ◇ K 8 7 4
      ♣ J 10 9 8 3                   ♣ 7 6 5 4 2
                       ♠ Q J 9 7 5
                       ♡ A K
                       ◇ A J 10 3 2
                       ♣ A
```

West	North	East	South
Pass	1 ♡	Pass	1 ♠
Pass	3 ♠	Pass	5NT (a)
Pass	7 ♠ (b)	Pass	Pass
Pass			

(a)   Grand Slam Force   (b) Two of the top three spade honors

West opened the jack of clubs. South won with the ace and laid down the jack of spades. So far, declarer and the various people who later essayed to make the contract all played the same.

The question concerns South's next lead. Declarer did not make the right play. He led the five of spades to dummy's king. Then, suddenly realizing that if the hearts did not break 3-2 he would not have enough entries to dummy to establish the heart suit and get back to run it, he tried to cash the ace and king of hearts. East ruffed the second round and declarer was one down. It didn't matter, anyway: South might just as well have gone down on the fifth trick as on a later one. Once he took the second round of spades he had thrown away the grand slam.

South was a good player, and his downfall should be attributed to carelessness in the face of an apparent abundance of wealth rather than to inability to figure out the proper line of play. After he took his licking, he showed the North-South cards to several of his expert friends, and only about half of them played so as to make the contract.

Yet the proper play is quite obvious when you stop to consider. If the hearts break no worse than 4-1, it is perfectly safe to cash a high heart. A 5-0 heart split is too remote a possibility to guard against. Therefore the ace of hearts should be cashed at trick three.

Having got this round of hearts through, South proceeds to take a second round of trumps, leading to the king. When the trumps do not break, he makes his contract absolutely safe by leading the king of clubs and discarding his king of hearts. Now he ruffs a low heart with the queen of spades, not caring whether the suit breaks or not, draws the last trump with a lead to dummy's ace, and ruffs another low heart with his last spade. Dummy is left with an established heart suit and the eight of spades as an entry. Thirteen tricks are in.

WEAK JUMP SHIFTS

The corollary of the strong-simple-response approach is adopted by those pairs who use weak jump shifts. In this style, a jump shift shows a respectable six-card suit and some 3-6 high-card points. For example, if partner opened one club, these players would respond two hearts holding something akin to:

♠4 ♡ K J 9 8 7 4 ◇ 7 6 5 ♣ 8 4 3

In this style, after an initial non-jump response, a simple rebid of his own suit on the second round by the responder becomes slightly encouraging, and a jump rebid of his suit is forcing.

There is a problem in this area whether or not weak jump shifts are being used. The simple response followed by a jump (e.g., 1♣–1♡–2♣–3♡) is sometimes needed for an invitational hand with about eleven points, and sometimes for stronger hands that can guarantee game. Either treatment leaves an awkward gap in the bidding structure.

7 Preemptive Bids

In addition to the idiosyncrasy we noted in discussing opening two-bids, P. Hal Sims did not believe in ever making a high shut-out bid. In this doctrine Sims was alone among bridge authorities, before and since. Every other authority advocates using the opening suit-bids of three and four to shut out the opponents, on hands that are weak defensively but have long trump suits. In no other department of the game has there ever been such unanimity among the experts.

Sims was wrong, the other authorities are right. Even though certain countermeasures have been developed against preemptive bids, the preemptive bid must be effective because there is no way for the opponents to recapture those lost rounds of bidding, in which they might have exchanged information to guide them to their best contract.

Dlr: South   ♠ Q 10 5 3
Vul: E-W   ♡ Q J 9 3
                    ◇ J 9 8 7
                    ♣ A

♠ A 9 7 4 2   ♠ K 8 6
♡ A K 10 8 6   ♡ 7 5
◇ K 6   ◇ A Q 4 3 2
♣ 9   ♣ 8 6 5

                    ♠ J
                    ♡ 4 2
                    ◇ 10 5
                    ♣ K Q J 10 7 4 3 2

Suppose South makes an opening bid of four clubs. (We will assume that North-South are not using the Namyats convention—see page 90.) West may suspect that his side can make ten tricks in whichever major suit East can better support. For West to show both his suits, however, would require two bids. This would necessitate undertaking a contract at the five-level, which might go down. For West to attempt, by guessing, to select the better suit would be equally dangerous. West may try a take-out double, but if East were to jump in diamonds, expecting support in his partner's hand, king doubleton will prove at best disappointing. Also, even if East responds only four diamonds, West will have to bid four hearts, which leaves his partner expecting only four spades. Finally, there is the danger that East can support neither suit, and that North can double and severely penalize any overcall.

STANDARDS FOR PREEMPTIVE BIDS

In stating the requirements for preemptive bids, the authorities show almost as complete unanimity as they do in accepting the principle.

One requirement is that the hand contain no more than 10 points in high cards.

The other requirement is that the hand be able to win within two tricks of the contract if vulnerable and within three tricks if not vulnerable, so that it will not go down more than 500 points (the approximate value of an opposing game) even if partner cannot add a trick.

Both of these rules are more honored in the breach than the observance. The experts may agree on pronouncing them but at the card table they do not often follow them.

Always, in setting the maximum of 10 high-card points, an outside jack and often a queen is disregarded. The following hand is an opening four-spade bid for anybody:

♠ A K Q J 8 6 3 2   ♡ 5   ◇ 6 5   ♣ J 4

If the jack were counted the hand would have 11 points, but the jack is treated no differently than a low card.

The theory of the 500-point limit, often called the Rule of Two and Three, is so plausible that perhaps it is no wonder the experts have all espoused it. But it is only plausible, not logical.

The 500-point rule applies, of course, only to bids that are made more or less blindly—that is, with no reasonable way of estimating the number of tricks the respective sides can win. After the bidding has progressed somewhat, no "rule" controls sacrifice bidding, except the scoring table.

West	North	East	South
			1 ♠
2 ◇	2 ♡	3 ◇	3 ♡

At this point, West has enough information to estimate, or at least to make an intelligent guess, as to how many points, if any, he should sacrifice to keep North-South from playing the hand. If in West's opinion North-South can make three hearts but not four, West will not deliberately go down more than 100 points. If West believes North-South can make a game, he will gladly go down 300 points at diamonds, and may risk as many as 500 points. But in any case he is measuring known risk against known gain.

But when the dealer picks up a hand like this:

♠ J   ♡ 4 2   ◇ 10 5   ♣ K Q J 10 7 4 3 2

(the South hand in the deal shown above) he has no real knowledge of where he wants the bidding to end up. Maybe the opponents can make game, but maybe if unmolested they will get in trouble. Maybe partner has a powerhouse and will be hindered by an opening preemptive bid. The possibilities both of gain and of loss are countless. It is necessary to choose the call that over a period of time will work out to South's advantage more often than not.

The true criterion of a preemptive bid is the same as for any other action, bid, pass, or double. If over a very large number of deals a certain call produces a better result than any other action, it is a good call. If it produces an inferior result, then it is a bad call.

Take the above hand, where South was holding eight clubs headed by the K-Q-J and nothing else. We say that the hand will win only seven tricks and may go down three in a four-club contract. The rule, then, will permit you to open four clubs if you are non-vulnerable, when your maximum loss is 500. If you are vulnerable, you are too weak for a four-club opening, as you might go down for 800.

But it is never the extent of your possible loss that really counts; it is the likelihood of your loss balanced against the extent and likelihood of your gain.

A bid that may go down for 1400 is not *ipso facto* a bad bid; what matters is how that bid will come out in the long run.

Most experts will open four clubs vulnerable or not, and some would even bid five clubs when non-vulnerable against vulnerable opponents.

NEW PRINCIPLES FOR PREEMPTIVE BIDDING

For those who wish to cast off their shackles and range anywhere from a Rule of 1 and 2 on down to a Rule of 4 and 5, there are some basic principles to be observed.

First principle: The harder the bid to overcall, the stronger the hand should be.

When you make a shut-out bid, it is quite obvious to your opponents that you do not want them to bid. They will react in a human manner and try to bid anyway. In a close choice between a bid and a penalty double, they will tend to favor the bid. If unable to bid and having a close choice between a pass and a penalty double, they will tend to double so as not to be shut out altogether.

If your preempt is four clubs, they are twice as likely to find a bid as if your preempt were four hearts, and even more likely to find a bid than if your preempt were four spades.

A four-spade bid must be strong because it is the most likely to be doubled, and because the double of four spades is clearly for penalties, while the double of a lower preempt is generally take-out or optional.

Second principle: Every defensive trick in your hand decreases the advisability of a shut-out bid. You might even say that every defensive trick calls for an extra playing trick, though that would be an oversimplification.

With this hand:

♠ Q J 9 8 7 5 4 3 2   ♡ 6   ♢ 9   ♣ 4 3

you have only seven winners, but not a prayer of a defensive trick; a vulnerable four-spade bid is justified. Add a defensive trick:

♠ A Q J 9 8 7 5 4   ♡ 6   ♢ 9 3   ♣ 4 3

and you have better than seven winners, but four spades stands to gain much less. One trick in partner's hand will probably stop an adverse slam, and if he has his fair proportion of the strength you may be able to stop a game. This is a good non-vulnerable four-bid but a doubtful vulnerable one. You'll never be shut out of the bidding on such a hand, anyway.

♠ J 9 8 7 5 4 3 2   ♡ 6   ◇ A K   ♣ 4 3

On this hand, with eight tricks, a four-spade bid would be "safe" in theory, but why bid it? You have some defense; you have some help for partner if he has a long suit, too. A four-spade bid would shut out your partner as well as your opponents, and if he has a good hand with a singleton in spades and perhaps solid hearts, your side may make four hearts when you couldn't make four spades.

Therefore a corollary to this principle is that a shut-out bid is best when you have nothing that will help partner if he plays the hand in his own suit.

Third principle: Vulnerability controls not only the number of points you will lose if doubled but also the probability that you will be doubled. If you are vulnerable and the opponents are not, they would rather double your preemptive bid than overcall it; therefore any preempt you make should be on the assumption that you will play the hand doubled. If you are not vulnerable and your opponents are, they will prefer to bid if possible and you will have a good chance to escape even if you run into one of those cases when they could double and beat you a million—if only they knew.

MORE DISREGARDED RULES

Nearly all the books advise one to avoid making a preemptive bid when holding four cards of a major suit outside the trump suit.

The idea is that the preempt may shut partner out with four or five cards of that suit, causing your side to miss a game.

The principle is logical but frequently an expert will feel that the chance of such a major-suit game is sufficiently remote to be disregarded. If a preemptive bid is indicated in the bidding situation, the chance of missing a game is just one more hazard to accept along with the principal risk, which is that the bid will go down more than you wish it to.

Such bugaboos are especially disregarded when a preemptive bid is used as a trap, which often occurs in third or fourth position after partner has passed and the chance for a slam is known to be remote or nonexistent.

In the following deal a high-ranking expert made the third-hand bid of four hearts. In almost every respect this hand violates the rules for preemptive bids, which of course is the principal reason he selected the bid. Such offbeat tactics are like bluffs in poker—they should be used sparingly.

Dlr: North
Vul: Both

```
                    ♠ J 10 5 4
                    ♡ Q J 6
                    ◇ J
                    ♣ A 10 7 3 2
    ♠ K 9 2                          ♠ A Q
    ♡ 7 2                            ♡ 5 3
    ◇ A Q 10 8                       ◇ K 9 7 5 4 3
    ♣ Q 8 6 4                        ♣ J 9 5
                    ♠ 8 7 6 3
                    ♡ A K 10 9 8 4
                    ◇ 6 2
                    ♣ K
```

West	North	East	South
	Pass	Pass	4♡
Pass	Pass	Pass	

When West led a low club, South was given an opportunity to make an unusual throw-in play.

The king of clubs won the first trick; and then South led the eight of hearts to dummy's jack, trumped a low club with the king of hearts, and led the nine of hearts to dummy's queen.

Now South cashed the ace of clubs and discarded not a spade but a diamond, though he could have ruffed his second diamond in the dummy after giving up the one trick he had to lose in that suit.

South trumped the seven of clubs, which made dummy's ten good. Finally, declarer executed his throw-in play by leading the diamond.

Whichever opponent won the diamond trick, after taking two spade tricks the defenders would have to lead another diamond, giving South a ruff-and-discard for one of his spade losers; the other would disappear on the ten of clubs. Only one diamond and two spade tricks were lost, and the contract was made.

This line of play brings home the contract if either defender has a singleton spade honor or two spade honors doubleton, and may make the contract even if the spade suit is not blocked but is misplayed. This can easily happen. For example, if West holds the K-Q-2 of spades, he might neglect to start by leading the two.

NAMYATS

In the early 1960s an English bid was adopted by Sam Stayman on this side of the Atlantic. It could not very well be called Stayman, so it became Namyats, an inversion of his name. The bid caught on, and is used by many tournament players. An opening four-club bid shows a strong four-heart opening, with some slam interest. Similarly, a four-diamond opening shows a strong four-spade opening. Partnerships need to agree on how partner signs off: by bidding the anchor suit shown by opener, or by bidding the next suit and allowing him to bid his suit. The obvious corollary is that openings of four hearts and four spades are clearly limited, with no interest in slam.

♠

♡

8 Overcalls and Doubles

♢

♣

Bridge authorities almost without exception used to counsel against overcalling an opponent's opening bid. It (almost) never pays, they would say.

Yet in a strong game, the auction was usually as hotly contested as it is today, and if these experts had followed their own advice strictly, it could not have been, for they would too seldom have got into the bidding. So what they meant in advising against overcalls was to caution against the average player's habit of making an overcall, particularly at the two-level, on a hand like this:

♠ 9 7 5   ♡ A Q 3   ♢ K Q 7 6 5   ♣ J 2

The average player will argue that he must bid because he has opening-bid values himself. But to bid two diamonds over an opponent's one-spade bid on such a hand is suicidal in a strong game. Even if two diamonds can be made, there is little to be gained, while if the two-diamond contract is doubled for penalties, it will probably be defeated by at least four tricks—700 (playing rubber bridge) or 800 points (playing duplicate) even if non-vulnerable.

High cards mean far less than playing strength in deciding whether or not to overcall, except in the case of a one-notrump overcall. How much playing strength is required depends on whether the player is vulnerable or not, and whether he can overcall with a one-bid or would have to go up to the two-level.

The expert overcalls quite freely when he need bid only at the one-level to do so. There are four reasons why a one-bid may be made on considerably less strength than a two-bid:

1. There is far less danger of being doubled. An overcall at the one-level is seldom doubled. An overcall at the level of two is almost always doubled if the opponents can easily defeat it.

2. Partner may be able to rescue if a one-bid is doubled and he has a fairly good suit; it is usually dangerous for partner to rescue a doubled two-bid, for he is almost certain to be doubled.

3. If you can overcall one spade, it keeps open the possibility of saving in the suit.

4. The very fact that a bid at the two-level is required means that the opponents have the higher-ranking suit. If the strength is evenly divided, the overcalling side will surely be outbid.

Therefore, despite the Rule of Two and Three, a vulnerable overcall at the two-level means the bidder is expecting to win eight tricks. Only with bad breaks or a very bad dummy will he win fewer.

♠ 6   ♡ K J 10   ♢ A Q 10 9 8 3   ♣ J 4 3

This hand is an acceptable bid of two diamonds over a one-spade opening bid, whether vulnerable or not. Remove the ten, nine, and eight of diamonds and replace them with three lower diamonds and the expert would pass if vulnerable, but would still bid two diamonds if non-vulnerable. Even if vulnerable, he would bid one diamond over an opponent's one-club bid.

The hand shown offers some incentive for overcalling: it has a six-card suit, and if partner has the king of diamonds and most of the high cards unaccounted for, there may be a game in notrump. It has strength in hearts, so if partner can bid hearts there may even be a heart game to be made. But with the side strength in clubs instead of hearts, some experts would pass over one spade, as there would be less to gain by overcalling, while the danger of a two- or three-trick penalty if doubled would still be there.

A hand with most of its strength in high cards is usually passed, unless it is strong enough for a take-out double.

♠ 10 6 3   ♡ K 3   ◇ A K J 5   ♣ A 6 3 2

Over an opening bid of one spade, most experts would pass this hand; there is too big a danger that partner will bid excessively in hearts. Over an opening of one heart, some experts would pass and some would double, the doublers being aware of the risk of partner's making a weak response in spades. Over an opening bid of one club, most experts would bid one diamond.

The reason to pass when holding high-card strength but no long suit is that no game contract is likely, and the opponents can probably be defeated if they overbid. This does not apply to a typical notrump hand, however:

♠ A Q 6   ♡ Q 7   ◇ K Q 10 4   ♣ K J 7 6

This hand is a typical one-notrump overcall of an opponent's opening bid of one club, diamond, or spade, whether vulnerable or not (and a take-out double over a one-heart opening).

To show how styles have changed, consider these two hands.

	1.		2.	
	♠	8	♠	10 9 7 6 5 3
	♡	9	♡	A Q J 6 5
	◇	Q J 10 7	◇	8
	♣	K J 9 8 7 5 3	♣	2

In the more conservative early days, most experts would make a two-club overcall with the first hand when non-vulnerable, but not when vulnerable. Now, almost everyone makes a weak jump overcall of three clubs whatever the vulnerability.

The second hand would have been a one-spade overcall regardless of vulnerability. Now, almost all experts would make a Michaels Cue-Bid to show both majors immediately (see page 241).

If the two-level overcall will be in hearts rather than a minor suit, you may take slightly greater chances, even when vulnerable, because a game is so much more likely.

Dlr: South
Vul: Both

```
                        ♠ J 8 7 4
                        ♡ 6 5 3
                        ◇ J 3 2
                        ♣ J 10 7
     ♠ 9                                    ♠ K 6 5
     ♡ K Q J 7 4                            ♡ 10 9 2
     ◇ K Q 10 8                             ◇ A 9 6 5 4
     ♣ 6 3 2                                ♣ K Q
                        ♠ A Q 10 3 2
                        ♡ A 8
                        ◇ 7
                        ♣ A 9 8 5 4
```

West	North	East	South
			1♠
2♡	Pass	2NT	3♣
Pass	3♠	4♡	Dble
Pass	4♠	Dble	Pass
Pass	Pass		

The four-spade contract could have gone down, but the defenders lost their way. West led the king of diamonds, and continued with the queen. South trumped and then cashed the ace of spades. Declarer continued with the ten of spades, overtaking with dummy's jack to force an entry to the dummy either on this round or the next.

East took his king of spades and could have assured the defeat of the contract by switching to hearts. But East saw no reason to discontinue the diamond attack, which was forcing out all of South's trumps.

However, South just ruffed the ace of diamonds with the queen of spades, led his low spade to dummy's eight, and played two rounds of clubs, unblocking dummy's ten and jack. After giving East his trick, declarer had the rest of the tricks, since he could discard two of dummy's hearts while running the clubs. He made four spades doubled; East-West could have made their four hearts.

THE QUESTION OF JUMP OVERCALLS

"Question" once was the right word. There used to be two schools among the experts, and they were irreconcilable: one group used single jump overcalls as weak shut-out bids; the other group used them as strong bids.

There is no question as to which is the larger group today. Almost everyone plays weak jump overcalls.

A jump overcall is a bid of one trick more than necessary over an opponent's opening bid, in such a situation as:

West	North	East	South
1 ♡	2 ♠ or 3 ◇		

North's bid in either instance is a jump overcall. The term is not applied to "double jump overcalls." If North had bid three spades or four diamonds, there would be universal agreement that his bid was preemptive: a weak bid suggesting that partner pass unless particularly strong and suitable for play in North's suit.

Among most of those who use the single jump overcall as a weak bid, the bid is a very weak one indeed. Either of the following hands would be typical:

♠ Q J 9 6 5 3   ♡ 6 3   ◇ J 9 8 2   ♣ 7
♠ Q J 9 6 5 4   ♡ 6 3   ◇ K 8 7   ♣ 7 5

If non-vulnerable, a player might make a jump overcall of two spades on either of these hands over an opposing opening bid. A vulnerable two-spade overcall would be one trick stronger:

♠ K Q J x x x instead of ♠ Q J 9 x x x

Almost always, the partner of the weak jump bidder will pass; when he raises, his purpose usually is to carry the preemptive principle further and shut out the opponents.

On this bidding:

West	North	East	South
1♡	2♠	Pass	?

South should pass the non-vulnerable two-spade jump overcall even with a hand as strong as this:

♠ A 7   ♡ K 5 2   ◇ A Q 6 4   ♣ J 8 4 2

If vulnerable, South might simply bid four spades. A jump to three notrump is dangerous because there is a risk of a club lead followed by a heart switch. And even if there is a heart lead, South can only see eight tricks: six spades, one heart, and one diamond.

Four spades would also be the bid with the following hand:

♠ 10 8 7 2   ♡ 9 8 4   ◇ 7   ♣ Q 9 8 6 2

Here the bid is a shut-out and an anticipated sacrifice bid. South is not only expecting but hoping for a double because the opponents may be able to make a slam and can surely make a game.

What does a two-notrump response over partner's weak jump overcall mean? Most experts play it as asking for further definition. Some use it as an Ogust inquiry (see page 147), but the majority use it to ask for a singleton. Normally, the two-notrump bidder will have a good fit for his partner's suit and interest in game if the hands fit well. For example, West opens one club, North bids two spades, and South holds

♠ A J 7   ♡ 7 6 5   ◇ K Q J 7   ♣ A 3 2

A singleton heart or club in the North hand would be welcome, justifying a shot at four spades. A singleton diamond would be most unwelcome, and if North has no singleton it is possible two spades will be the limit on the North-South cards, but the risk is worth taking.

THE QUICK RAISE

Those who do use the weak jump overcall and do not wish to miss some fortuitous notrump games must cultivate the quick raise of a minor-suit overcall made at the two-level. This raise promises a high honor (though not necessarily much length) in overcaller's suit and some interest in reaching three notrump.

The following is not an unusual bidding sequence:

West	North	East	South
		1♠	2♣
Pass	3♣		

In this instance, though, North's club raise was unusual in that he held this hand:

♠ 7 6   ♡ A J 7 5 2   ◇ Q 8 5 4   ♣ K 6

Only the North player who raised to three clubs got to the makable notrump game. South held

♠ K 5   ♡ 9 4 3   ◇ A 6   ♣ A Q J 7 5 2

Without the raise, South could not have dared to bid three notrump, vulnerable. A pass by North would have closed the bidding; a two-heart bid by North would have been raised to four hearts by South, and that would have been an inferior game contract. As the cards lay, it could not have been made, while three notrump could not be defeated.

TAKE-OUT DOUBLES AND RESPONSES

Probably the most widely practiced bidding convention in contract bridge has been the take-out double. The actual origin of the take-out double is in dispute, and can never be determined because the dramatis personae are all dead. Bryant McCampbell claimed the invention as of 1912 and called it (in his 1915 book) the McCampbell double. Major Charles L. Patton claimed it and called it the Patton double. Originally the double was used only over an opening bid of one notrump, which is now the only case in which it is no longer treated as calling for a take-out. Wilbur Whitehead may have adapted it first to suit bids. Ely Culbertson gave the take-out double its present name, but it seemed for many years that players could not be diverted from the names "informatory double" and "negative double"; only the present generation of bridge players have adopted "take-out double." But the basic idea remains the same as when it was first invented. A take-out double shows a good hand after an opponent has opened the bidding, and it asks partner to bid his best (longest) suit in response.

If an opponent opened with one heart, most experts would double with either of these hands:

1. ♠ A J 5 3	2. ♠ A Q J 5 3 2
♡ 8	♡ 8 2
◇ K J 6 2	◇ A Q 5
♣ A Q 7 4	♣ A Q

Everyone would double with the first hand; one or two experts would overcall one spade on the second. However, to most experts a simple overcall is limited in strength; they are more concerned with indicating first the extent of their strength than with showing its location, so they double first and bid the suit later, telling partner that they have a hand too strong for a simple overcall.

In recent years, the take-out double has become somewhat more vague. A good player would be unhappy at the thought of overcalling a one-spade opening bid with two clubs on the following hand:

$$\spadesuit 5\ 3 \quad \heartsuit K\ 9\ 8 \quad \diamondsuit A\ 10\ 7 \quad \clubsuit K\ Q\ 8\ 6\ 4$$

In two clubs he might be doubled for penalties and lose 500 points or more, and for what compensating gain? Perhaps no more than a partscore.

Nevertheless it is desirable to enter the bidding when possible in relative safety, and by doubling on the above hand a player can enter the auction fairly safely. His partner may be weak, but he may still have length in hearts or diamonds. A two-club overcall makes everything dependent on finding partner with support in clubs, but the take-out double leaves the way open to safety if partner has length in any of three suits.

Another advantage of getting into the bidding, even when the opening bidder's side seems sure to play the hand, is that information given by a defensive bid, including a double, may guide partner's defense and produce the setting trick. East's caution cost the contract in this deal:

Dlr: South
Vul: E-W

                          ♠ 9 3
                          ♡ A Q J 4
                          ◇ Q 10 7 6
                          ♣ K 10 5

    ♠ 10 8 7 6 2   ♠ A K 5 4
    ♡ 9 3 2   ♡ K 10 8 6
    ◇ 8 4   ◇ 3
    ♣ 9 8 3   ♣ J 7 6 2

                          ♠ Q J
                          ♡ 7 5
                          ◇ A K J 9 5 2
                          ♣ A Q 4

West	North	East	South
			1 ◇
Pass	1 ♡	Pass	3 ◇
Pass	5 ◇	Pass	Pass
Pass			

East did not have a good vulnerable take-out double of the
opposing non-vulnerable bid. Game is seldom bid or made
in a minor suit; East had much strength in the major suits; a
successful notrump game by North-South seemed to depend
on their having long and solid diamonds, which was not
more than an even chance. But when East passed, South
made his game because West, forced to guess an opening
lead, chose the nine of clubs.

   South won the first trick with the queen of clubs, drew
the opposing diamonds in two rounds, and cashed the other
two top clubs. Then South cast adrift in spades.

   East could win his two spade tricks, but then either he
had to lead into dummy's heart tenace or he had to concede
a ruff-and-discard. One way or the other, South would win
his eleven tricks.

   If East had doubled one heart, West might have led a
spade, as the double suggests strength there. However, with
five spades, West might still have led a club; it is not clear-
cut. After a spade lead, of course, East can take his high

spades, exit with a diamond, and await the setting trick with the king of hearts.

The responses to a take-out double are reasonably well standardized, and the principles governing them are sound enough in theory. The player must respond in his best suit, even if he holds a bust. To his partner's double of one heart, he must bid one spade on a hand like this:

♠ 7 6 3 2   ♡ 9 5 4   ◇ J 9 2   ♣ Q 8 5

Since a one-spade response may be made on so weak a hand, it would seem unreasonable to make the same one-spade response on a hand like the following:

♠ K Q 10 4   ♡ 9 5 4   ◇ A 9 2   ♣ 8 5 3

Therefore, the recommended response on such a hand is a jump to two spades, showing about 8-10 points in high cards.

THE CUE-BID RESPONSE

There is, finally, the cue-bid response to a take-out double. Once almost unheard of, this response has become standard. A typical situation is:

West	North	East	South
1 ◇	Dble	Pass	2 ◇

By his bid of the opposing suit, South may mean any of several things. Usually he is just announcing strength, and proposing that he and his partner look for their best fit. If no fit is found, they will play in notrump if that seems expedient. He may even have his own powerful suit but be too strong to make a limited bid.

Always remember that the doubler has shown considerable strength, and even a moderate number of high cards, if well positioned, are quite likely to produce a slam.

Dlr: East

Vul: N-S

```
              ♠ A Q 10 9 4
              ♡ 9 7 4
              ◇ A 6 3
              ♣ K 5
♠ 5                          ♠ 8 7 2
♡ 10 6 2                     ♡ A K Q J 8 5
◇ Q 10 9 4 2                 ◇ 7
♣ J 9 8 4                    ♣ Q 6 3
              ♠ K J 6 3
              ♡ 3
              ◇ K J 8 5
              ♣ A 10 7 2
```

West	North	East	South
		1 ♡	Dble
Pass	2 ♡	Pass	2 ♠
Pass	3 ◇	Pass	4 ◇
Pass	5 ♠	Pass	6 ♠
Pass	Pass	Pass	

When North bid diamonds at his second turn, South assumed that his partner had a real diamond suit. North's next bid, the jump to five spades, made it clear that he had been interested in playing in spades all the time, and that he was hoping his partner did not have two heart losers. Despite holding a minimum opening bid, South realized his cards were well placed, and that the singleton heart warranted risking the slam.

West opened the two of hearts, East took it with the jack and continued the suit. South ruffed with a high trump, led a spade to the dummy, ruffed another heart high, and drew trumps, discarding a low diamond from hand.

Declarer next cashed the high clubs and ruffed a club, hoping to drop the queen and jack. By this time, East had played six black cards. Since East was marked with a long heart suit, there was room in his hand for at most two diamonds. The diamond finesse, otherwise the simplest play for the slam, was therefore likely to fail.

A squeeze, however, was successful. Dummy's last trump was led. South released a diamond, but West had no good discard. If he threw the jack of clubs, South would win a trick with the ten. And if he came down to two diamonds, the top diamonds would clear the suit, establishing dummy's six.

THE CUE-BID OVERCALL—HOW IT HAS CHANGED

The term "cue-bid" has several meanings in bridge, but the original sense is still used: a bid in a suit previously bid by an opponent, as in the following bidding:

West	North	East	South
1♡	2♡!		

In the original sense, North's two-heart bid carried a multi-faceted message. It announced that North had a super-take-out double, requiring South to show his best suit; that he had first-round control in hearts, either the ace or a void; that North either had strong support for whichever suit South bid or had a solid suit of his own that required no support; and that he held enough values to force to game on his own.

    The traditional two-heart bid over one heart, as shown above, would have been made on a hand equivalent to one of the following:

1. ♠ A Q J 6	2. ♠ K Q 10 5
♡ A	♡ —
◇ A Q J 9 8	◇ A K Q J 8 6 3
♣ A K 5	♣ A Q

As this type of hand comes up once in a blue moon, a new meaning for the immediate cue-bid has been adopted. However, we will consider that two-suited approach in the next section, on page 231.

♠
♡

9 Doubling for Penalties

♢
♣

If there is one "greatest difference" between the strong bridge game and the average bridge game, it is in the use and frequency of penalty doubles. In the average game, moderate overbidding is seldom punished. The average player almost never doubles a low-level contract and rarely doubles anything on a weak-looking hand, but is apt to double a high-level contract on "general principles." In the expert game, unsound overbidding seldom goes unpunished, low-level contracts are doubled more often than high-level ones, and many a double is made on a hand that seems weak, at least in terms of high-card points. The negative double (see page 203) has tempered this somewhat, but it is still true to a great extent that the expert considers a double first before he thinks of bidding, and the average player tends to keep on bidding as long as he can, and to double only when he can no longer bid.

Ely Culbertson proposed certain basic situations in which a player should consider a double before he determines to bid. Briefly, these are: When your side has superior cards and the opponents outbid you; when your partner's opening bid is overcalled by an opponent; and when the opponents seem to stumble into a gambling contract and you have a fair hand.

Few players neglect the first opportunity.

The second of these situations has received much attention from bridge writers, yet is still overlooked by most players. And now, in the days of the negative double, it is becoming more difficult to extract penalties from bad overcalls. The best most players can do is to pass and hope that partner will reopen with a double, which they will pass, but there's no guarantee that partner will do his part. Still, most disciplined partnerships *do* collect most of the opportunities offered by overly aggressive opponents.

Less often analyzed in bridge literature, and more often missed in the casual bridge game, is the opportunity to double the opponents' gambling contracts. Said Culbertson, "The biggest invisible losses come when the opponents are defeated 150 points not vulnerable, or 300 points vulnerable, while doubling would have increased those scores to 500 and 800 points, respectively."

A British expert, the late S. J. Simon, in his book *Why You Lose at Bridge,* did give proper attention to these situations. In a rather startling but entirely convincing example, he proposed bidding like this:

West	North	East	South
	1♣	Pass	1♡
Pass	2♣	Pass	2NT
Pass	3NT	Pass	Pass
?			

Then he supposed that West held either of these hands:

	1.		2.	
♠	A 10 3		10 4 3	
♡	K Q 10		K Q 10	
◇	A K J 7 6		A K J 7 6	
♣	K 2		5 2	

If he must double three notrump on either of these hands, Simon said, he would far rather have the second hand. Number one is too strong; partner must have a totally worthless hand and North must have a six- or seven-card club suit lying over the king. The clubs will be run, squeezing West, and the contract will be made. When West holds the weaker hand, there is a good chance that East will have a high club or spade with which he can get the lead to play through South's queen of diamonds, and the contract goes down.

The moral implied by Simon is that the defensive strength must be divided between the two defenders' hands; and that the key to doubling is in recognizing that these two hands together have enough strength to defeat the contract. For example:

West	North	East	South
			1 ♡
Pass	1 ♠	Pass	1NT
Pass	2 ◇	Pass	2 ♡
Pass	2 ♠	Pass	2NT
Pass	3 ◇	Pass	3NT
?			

West held

♠ 4 3   ♡ K J 7 4   ◇ J 10 9 3   ♣ K Q 6

and he doubled. Obviously, North had only spades and diamonds, and could not support hearts even after they were rebid, so West's heart holding must be good for two tricks. South could not have risked three notrump in the face of North's refusal to raise without the A-J-10 of clubs; but West was sitting over this strength. South did not support spades, so East must hold a comfortable amount of spade strength, which would be properly placed over the dummy. South's first rebid, which was only one notrump, showed that he could not have a very strong hand; therefore, East must have a high card or two. It all added up to a strong probability that North-South could not win nine tricks in notrump.

The complete deal was as follows:

```
Dlr: South          ♠ A 8 6 5 2
Vul: None           ♡ 3
                    ◇ K Q 7 6 4
                    ♣ 7 5
    ♠ 4 3                            ♠ K 10 9 7
    ♡ K J 7 4                        ♡ 10 9 5
    ◇ J 10 9 3                       ◇ A
    ♣ K Q 6                          ♣ 9 8 4 3 2
                    ♠ Q J
                    ♡ A Q 8 6 2
                    ◇ 8 5 2
                    ♣ A J 10
```

Everyone passed West's double of three notrump. West led the four of spades, dummy's two was played, and East won with the king. He returned the ten of hearts.

South guessed (because of the double) that West held the king of hearts and a finesse would not work; and, also because of the double, he saw a good chance that West held the ace of diamonds. So South put up the ace of hearts, led a low diamond, and put up the queen when West played the three.

East won with the ace of diamonds and returned the nine of hearts, covered by the queen and king. Now West led the jack of diamonds, which was allowed to hold, and the ten of diamonds, which was won with dummy's king.

South was in trouble, and could not escape. He led a spade to his queen and exited with the two of hearts, hoping the jack would fall; but West won with the seven and cashed the nine of diamonds. On this, South had to let a heart go, so

West took a trick with the jack of hearts and still had to get a club trick. South was down four, and though he was non-vulnerable it was a clear gain of 700 points (in the days before the 1987 scoring change), 500 points more than they would have had if West had not doubled.

The North-South bidding was indefensible, but that is just the point: The big profits come from not letting the opponents get away with indefensible bidding.

THE DOUBLE DILEMMA

Nevertheless, the phase of the game most likely to produce ambivalent neuroses in bridge players is that of penalty doubles.

Any experienced rubber-bridge player knows that you cannot win without doubling the opponents when they over-bid. Against this indisputable fact there is the contrary fact that a double often gives the declarer information that permits him to save a trick or even to make a contract he could not have made without the double.

The following deal, from a game in a New York club, proved to be a lesson to the player who doubled unwisely.

Dlr: North
Vul: Both

```
                    ♠ A Q 4
                    ♡ 6 4
                    ◇ A K Q 10 6
                    ♣ 7 4 2
        ♠ K 10 9 3                    ♠ 2
        ♡ A 7 2                       ♡ 10 9 8 5 3
        ◇ 7 3                         ◇ 8 5 4
        ♣ K Q 9 8                     ♣ 10 6 5 3
                    ♠ J 8 7 6 5
                    ♡ K Q J
                    ◇ J 9 2
                    ♣ A J
```

West	North	East	South
	1 ◇	Pass	1 ♠
Pass	2 ♠	Pass	4 ♠
Dble	Pass	Pass	Pass

West opened the king of clubs and South took it with his ace. Declarer saw that he had a club loser, a heart loser, and a probable loser in spades.

If West had not doubled, South's play would have been quite simple. He might have made the percentage play of a spade to the ace, surrendering his best chance of getting an overtrick if the finesse won but guarding against a singleton king of spades in the East hand; or he might have made the usual play of finessing the queen of spades on the first round.

Whichever of these two plays South selected, he would have gone down. West would have been left with two trump tricks plus the ace of hearts and queen of clubs. But South was forewarned by West's double and figured West for a four-card trump holding, at least ♠ K 10 3 2 and perhaps (as was the actual case) ♠ K 10 9 x.

In either case, South could take advantage by leading the jack of spades from his hand at trick two. South did lead the jack, and West could only get one trump trick.

West covered the jack of spades with the king and dummy's ace won the trick. South reentered his hand with a diamond to the nine, and he continued with the eight of spades. West tried to save himself by playing the three, but South called for dummy's four and the eight won the trick. Dummy's queen drew another round of spades, leaving West with only one trump trick, the ten.

If West had covered the eight of spades, he still would have had only one trump trick, for dummy's queen would have taken the trick, another spade lead would have forced out West's ten, and South would have had the high spade to draw West's last trump, the lowly three.

West's double cost his side 890 points, the difference

between the 790 South scored by making four spades and the 100 East-West would have collected if West had kept quiet.

In the following deal a similarly overoptimistic double was even more costly because a slam was involved.

Dlr: South
Vul: N-S

```
                    ♠ 9 8 4 3
                    ♡ A 10 2
                    ◇ A Q 10 5
                    ♣ 9 7
    ♠ K Q 10 6                     ♠ 5
    ♡ K J 8 6                      ♡ Q 9 7 5 4
    ◇ J 4 2                        ◇ 9 8 6 3
    ♣ 5 4                          ♣ J 6 3
                    ♠ A J 7 2
                    ♡ 3
                    ◇ K 7
                    ♣ A K Q 10 8 2
```

West	North	East	South
			1♣
Pass	1◇	Pass	1♠
Pass	3♠	Pass	4NT
Pass	5♡	Pass	6♠
Dble	Pass	Pass	6NT
Dble	Pass	Pass	Pass

West's first double drove his opponents from a contract they could not make, six spades, to a contract they could not fail to make, six notrump.

Although West opened the six of hearts, his best lead, nothing could have affected the result, because South had twelve sure tricks when both minor suits behaved.

South properly ducked the first heart trick, which was won with East's queen. East returned his singleton spade and South won with the ace. This return made it necessary for South simply to run off his six clubs, stripping dummy down to the blank ace of hearts and four diamonds, and then cash the king, queen, and ace of diamonds, hoping the jack would drop. It did, and South made six notrump.

RESOLVING THE DILEMMA

To summarize the moral of the previous examples: If intelligent opponents have bid to a high-level contract under their own power, by standard bidding methods, it is unwise to double unless you have in hand enough sure tricks to defeat the contract—and to defeat any other contract to which the opponents may retreat. (See the four spades doubled contract on page 108 and the six spades doubled above.)

If the opponents' bidding indicates that they have a misfit and are groping for some safe contract—as when one opponent bids two of the four suits and the other opponent bids the other two suits—a gambling double may be justified; but against strong players there is no assurance that such bidding shows a misfit. (See the three-notrump doubled contract on page 107.)

If the opponents apparently have the weaker cards and have outbid a game or higher contract that your side can almost surely make, it is essential to double. Occasionally the opponents will have freak hands and will make their intended sacrifice contract, but this should not happen often enough to affect your doubling habits.

PART II

Bidding
Conventions

♠
♡
1 What Is a
Convention?
♢
♣

The natural meaning of any bid is that the bidder is prepared to play in the contract named. When a player bids two spades, the natural meaning of the bid is that the player wishes spades to be trumps and expects to win at least eight tricks.

If a bid carries any additional meaning that can be fully understood only by agreement between partners, in bridge terminology it is a convention.

A conventional bid may be either natural or artificial. The opening two-spade bid used as a game-forcing bid is conventional because it demands a response from partner—something not implicit in the bid itself—but it also is natural because the two-spade bidder does have a spade suit and a hand strong enough to make the contract he undertakes. A one-club bid used to show a certain number of high-card points, without any representation as to the bidder's club suit, is artificial as well as conventional. The bidder may not be prepared to play at a club contract.

In the 1950s it was true to say that the expert player disliked artificial bids. He viewed them with suspicion and was slow to adopt them; he considered them theoretically unsound, because they gave too much information to the enemy. He considered them dangerous, because partner may forget their meanings.

Now, almost forty years later, almost exactly the opposite is true. Most of the world's bridge experts have joyously espoused the principle of artificial bidding and vie with one another to devise the newest and fanciest bidding conventions.

ETHICAL AND PRACTICAL CONSIDERATIONS

A convention is a signal. The idea of signals is controversial in bridge ethics, and there are still players—especially in England—who cling to the doctrine of Admiral Burney, one of the ancients, who wrote in 1821 that signals "impinge on the integrity of the game." Even the most hidebound proponents of natural bidding use some conventions, for example forcing bids and the take-out double, but they agree with the rank and file of players when they oppose the unrestricted use of bidding conventions.

To the serious bridge player, and especially to the minority who play tournament bridge, there is no current topic of greater importance. The Italian Blue Team, whose pairs used many special conventions, won sixteen world championships in the period 1957–75. The team from the United States that won the 1970 and 1971 Bermuda Bowls included two pairs playing complicated systems that employed many conventions.

A multiplicity of conventions may increase a bridge player's effectiveness, but it can also be self-defeating. Literally hundreds of fancy bids have been proposed and new ones appear every week or month. If casual players began to use more than a few of these, it would become impossible to sit down in a bridge club or at a bridge party with three comparative strangers and play an enjoyable game. Furthermore, there would be so many partnership misunderstandings that the standard of play would go down.

A most unenviable job falls to directors of the American Contract Bridge League and to tournament and club committees. They have the power and duty to decide which conventions may and may not be used. However they decide, there is always turmoil. Should they rule in favor of the experts, who like conventions? Or is their duty to the rank and file, who, if given full democratic control, would bar most of the conventions and all psychic bids?

Nearly all authorities agree that such restrictions would hurt the game, by reducing the element of skill. So the committees thread their way gingerly between the conflicting points of view, yielding to majority pressure enough to bar the fanciest bidding conventions but being paternalistic enough to admit some that are unpopular but that seem good for the game.

Inevitably, the committees commit some errors of judgment and some abuses of power. During an Eastern States tournament in New York City many years ago, the tournament committee barred the limit raise of an opening one-heart or one-spade bid—a feature of the Acol system that is popular in England but was rarely played in the United States. Since then, of course, virtually every expert pair has adopted the limit raise. It came up on the following deal.

Dlr: South   ♠ 10 8 6 5 2
Vul: None   ♡ Q 4
                    ◊ A K 8 3
                    ♣ 6 2

♠ K 9   ♠ J
♡ 9 7 3 2   ♡ A 8 6 5
◊ Q J 10   ◊ 9 5 2
♣ Q J 4 3   ♣ A 9 8 7 5

                   ♠ A Q 7 4 3
                   ♡ K J 10
                   ◊ 7 6 4
                   ♣ K 10

West	North	East	South
			1♠
Pass	3♠	Pass	Pass
Pass			

North's bid was the limit raise. Under the old-fashioned American methods, a jump to three spades by North would show a stronger hand and would be forcing to game. To these players, North's three-spade bid on the above hand seems odd and "conventional." Yet North's hand is somewhat too strong for a simple raise to two spades, and the alternative, which is to respond two diamonds and suppress the strong spade support, is artificial and unnatural.

    The fact is that the laws of contract bridge do not permit a committee to bar a bid such as North's three-spade response. A bridge player cannot be forbidden to bid what he thinks he can make. Committees often misunderstand this and rule against a natural bid simply because it is unfamiliar, while an artificial bid is permitted on the grounds that "everybody understands it"; and such rulings are popular.

    Incidentally, the deal shown above did not result in a protest and the committee at the Eastern States tournament soon rescinded its ruling. The three-spade bid was very successful because South lost one trick in each suit and made exactly his contract.

Usually the problem of deciding which conventions to admit, and which to exclude, is attended by so many complexities and delicacies and conflicting interests that no committee can be expected to judge wisely at all times. Both philosophically and practically, the bidding and playing conventions of bridge are the major issue of the game, and they are likely to continue to be so.

The American Contract Bridge League has recently revised the list of permitted conventions. Now there is a limited group for players in games with an upper limit of ten masterpoints. The major classification is for all other events except national championships. All well-known systems and conventions are permitted as long as they are constructive in nature. For national championships, anything is permitted except destructive methods and "pass" systems: those involving an initial pass (either in the first seat or in the second position after a normal pass by the dealer) that promises positive values. (These methods started in Poland, and made a brief sortie into Italy in the form of the Marmic System, but the present wave is from Australia and New Zealand.)

Every player is required to fill in a convention card; the two cards for a pair must be identical—you are not allowed to play different methods from your partner. (This is to stop an expert who is playing with a student from monopolizing the declarer play by, for example, not using transfer bids while his partner does.)

The front and back of the card is reprinted on pages 120 and 121 with the permission of the American Contract Bridge League. (Items in italics are in red on the actual card.)

All conventions marked in red (italics) and all non-standard partnership agreements must be alerted.

Date _____

Names _____ **Section** _____

General Approach _____ Pair # _____

Strong Forcing Opening: 2 ♣ ☐   2 bids ☐   1 ♣ ☐   *Other*_____

NOTRUMP OPENING BIDS

1NT _____ to _____   2 NT _____ to _____ HCP

1 NT _____ to _____   3 NT _____ to _____ HCP

2 ♣ Forc. ☐ Non-Forc. ☐ Stayman   *Solid Suit* ☐: _____

2 ◇ *Forc.* ☐ *Non-Forc.* ☐ *Stayman*   _____

Transfers: Jacoby ☐ *Texas* ☐ *Other* ☐   _____

1NT - 3 ♣ /3 ◇   **Is** *Invitational* ☐   *Preemptive* ☐   *Forcing* ☐

MAJOR OPENINGS

1 ♡ -1 ♠ Opening on 4 Cards

	Often	Seldom	Never
1st-2nd	☐	☐	☐
3rd-4th	☐	☐	☐

RESPONSES

Double Raise Forcing ☐ Limit ☐

Preemptive ☐   Limit in Comp. ☐

Conv. Raise: *2NT* ☐   *3NT* ☐

Swiss ☐   *Splinter* ☐

Conv. Responses: *1NT Forcing* ☐

Drury ☐   *Single Raise Constr.* ☐

Other_____

MINOR OPENINGS

Length Promised

	4+	3+	Shorter
1 ♣	☐	☐	☐
1 ◇	☐	☐	☐

RESPONSES

Double Raise

Forcing ☐ Limit ☐ *Preempt* ☐

Single Raise Forcing ☐

1NT/1 ♣ _____ to _____ HCP

1 ◇ *Resp. Conv.* _____

Other_____

2♣ WK ☐ ☐ _____ to _____ HCP. Describe _____
     INT ☐ ☐ *Conv. Resp. & Rebids* _____
     STR ☐ ☐ _____ 2 ◇ Neg. ☐ 2 NT Neg. ☐

2◇ WK ☐ ☐ _____ to _____ HCP. Describe _____
     INT ☐ ☐ *Conv. Resp. & Rebids* _____
     STR ☐ ☐ _____ 2 NT Force ☐ 2 NT Neg. ☐

2♡ WK ☐ ☐ _____ to _____ HCP. Describe _____
     INT ☐ ☐ *Conv. Resp. & Rebids* _____
     STR ☐ ☐ _____ 2 NT Force ☐ 2 NT Neg. ☐

2♠ WK ☐ ☐ _____ to _____ HCP. Describe _____
     INT ☐ ☐ *Conv. Resp. & Rebids* _____
     STR ☐ ☐ _____ 2 NT Force ☐ 2 NT Neg. ☐

OTHER CONVENTIONAL CALLS

_____

_____

_____

SPECIAL DOUBLES (Describe)

Negative _____

_____

Responsive _____

Other _____

_____

DIRECT NT OVERCALLS

1 NT _____ to _____ HCP

Jump to 2NT: _____ to _____ HCP

Unusual for Minors □

2 Lower Unbid □

Other _____

SIMPLE OVERCALL

____ to ____ HCP (occ. light □)

Responses: New Suit Forcing □

Cuebid Is: One-Round Force □

Game Force □ Limit Raise □

Other _____

Vs. Wk. □ Strong □ NT Opening

Direct □ Balance □

2 ♣ shows	♣	♦	♡	♠
2 ♦ shows	♣	♦	♡	♠
2 ♡ shows	♣	♦	♡	♠
2 ♠ shows	♣	♦	♡	♠

Other _____

JUMP OVERCALL

Strong □ Interm □ Preempt □

Special Responses _____

_____

OVER OPP'S TAKEOUT DOUBLE

New Suit Force 1-level □ 2-level □

Jp. Shift Force □ Good □ Weak □

Redouble Implies No Fit □

Other _____

OPENING PREEMPTS

	Sound	Light	Solid Minor
3-bids	□	□	□

Other _____

Vs. Opp's Preempts Dbl. Is

	Takeout	Opt.	Penalty
Wk. 2's	□	□	□
3 Bids	□	□	□

Conv. takeout _____

PSYCHICS

Never	Rare	Occ.	Frequent
□	□	□	□

Describe: _____

DIRECT CUEBID

Strong Takeout: Minor □ Major □

Natural: ♣□ ♦□ Artif. Bids □

Two Suits □ _____

_____

SLAM CONVENTIONS

Gerber □ _____ 4NT Var. □ _____

Interference over 4 ♣ or 4NT □ *[Describe]* _____

DEFENSIVE CARD PLAY

Opening lead vs. SUITS: 3rd best □ 4th best □ 5th best □ Other _____

Mark card led: x x x A **K** x **K Q** x Q J x J 10 x **10** 9 x

K **J** 10 x K **10** 9 x Q **10** 9 x x x x x

Opening leads vs. NT: 3rd best □ 4th best □ Other _____

Mark card led: x x x A **K** J x A **Q** J x A J 10 9

(Red Dot) A **10** 9 8 **K** Q J x **K** Q 10 9 K J 10 9 K **10** 9 8

Q J 10 x Q **10** 9 8 J 10 9 x **10** 9 8 x x x x x x

Special Carding _____ Frequent Count Signals □

If in doubt as to the meaning of a conventional call—ASK AT YOUR TURN!

♠
♡
2 # The Forcing One-Notrump Response
♢
♣

When the idea of requiring at least a five-card suit to open one heart or one spade was proposed, it did not gain much support. Now, however, the majority of the world's experts do play five-card majors. Why the difference? Arguably, the answer to that question is the forcing one-notrump response.

Like so many other bidding developments, the forcing-notrump response is a Roth-Stone innovation. It is probably the most brilliant idea bridge has seen since the days of the pioneers, back in the 1920s and early 1930s. Like almost all the best ideas, it is simple in concept, yet when it was introduced it seemed like heresy even to experts.

The forcing-notrump response occurs in the following situation:

West	North	East	South
	1♡/♠	Pass	1NT
Pass	?		

Now North must bid again.

Theoretically, this is unsound. In pure bridge theory, every notrump bid (unless used artificially, like the Blackwood convention) is limited and passes captaincy (control of the level of the auction) to partner. A bid that is forcing *ipso facto* retains captaincy. But in practice the forcing one-notrump response to a major works perfectly, especially in harness with the two-over-one game-force approach. Furthermore, it has succeeded in resolving a dilemma that for many years had seemed unsolvable.

The predicament arose principally with hands such as this:

♠ 6   ♡ A 9 8 6 3 2   ◊ 10 4   ♣ J 7 5 2

Partner opens with one spade and the next player passes. What do you do?

Any action taken on this hand could work out badly. A pass might leave the partnership to play in a spade contract when one in hearts would be much better; and a pass might even cost a game if partner has a very strong or unbalanced hand that fits hearts. A non-forcing one-notrump response gives the desired message of weakness, but with a minimum partner may pass one notrump, which is the last place that responder wants to be. The aim is to get to two hearts and stop there if partner is not very strong, without restricting partner's license to go on if his hand warrants it.

The problem is solved by making the one-notrump response forcing.

The above hand was a part of the following deal:

Dlr: North
Vul: None

        ♠ A K 7 5 2
        ♡ 10 7
        ◇ 6 5 2
        ♣ A K 6

♠ 9 4 3   ♠ Q J 10 8
♡ Q 5   ♡ K J 4
◇ A K J 7   ◇ Q 9 8 3
♣ Q 10 9 3   ♣ 8 4

        ♠ 6
        ♡ A 9 8 6 3 2
        ◇ 10 4
        ♣ J 7 5 2

West	North	East	South
	1♠	Pass	1NT
Pass	2♣	Pass	2♡
Pass	Pass	Pass	

To allow the responder to show which hand type he has, the opener tries to keep the bidding as low as possible when he lacks considerable extra values. He normally shows his second suit, but when he holds a 5-3-3-2 shape and strength below that of a one notrump opening, he rebids in his lower-ranking three-card suit. That occurred above when North bid two clubs.

South could have passed the two-club rebid, since he held four-card support. No great damage would have been done if South had passed, for North would probably have wangled out eight tricks. But two hearts, which South decided to bid, proved better.

West started with the king, ace, and a third round of diamonds, ruffed by declarer.

South's technique was good. He wished to establish a long spade, so he led his singleton to dummy's ace and trumped a low spade in his hand. If South had started leading trumps too early, a club lead by East would have driven out one of the club entries South would need later to reach the established spade winner.

After trumping the spade, South led a low heart. Just in case one opponent had ♡ K Q J x, he played to keep a trump in the dummy in case the defense played another diamond, and also to retain the ace of hearts in hand to control the trump suit.

West put up the queen of hearts and led the nine of spades. South played low from the dummy and ruffed in hand. South cashed the ace of hearts, played a club to dummy's king, and discarded his two club losers on the king and seven of spades, which East trumped. South had the rest of the tricks and had made an overtrick. He would have made his contract, two hearts, even against a bad trump break.

What hand types will the responder have when he makes the forcing one-notrump bid? Normally, he will not hold enough points for a two-over-one response: usually a maximum of 10 high-card points. In this case, most of the time he will have a hand that would have made a non-forcing one-notrump re-sponse in pristine methods. The only difference is that one notrump cannot be the final contract.

There are two stronger possibilities: a balanced 11 or 12 points, with which the responder plans to rebid two notrump; or a (probably) balanced hand with three-card support for the opener's major suit and about 11 points, with which the responder will rebid three of his partner's suit (in other words, a limit raise with three-card support).

One other agreement is common among American ex-perts: if the responder raises the opened major suit directly to the two-level with only three-card support, he will not have a minimum 6 or 7 points, he will have 8 or 9. With the weaker hand he will start with one notrump and then sup-port partner's suit on the next round.

If the responder returns to the opener's major on the second round, it is not certain that he has three-card support. If he does not have a fit for opener's second suit, he may return to the major when holding only a doubleton. So, if the opener bids one spade and responds, say, two clubs over the forcing one-notrump bid, the responder would bid two spades with either of these hands:

♠ J 7 6   ♡ K 6 5 4   ◇ Q 9 7   ♣ 9 5 4
♠ Q 4   ♡ K 7 6 5   ◇ Q J 8 7 6   ♣ 4 3

In any of these limited auctions, the opener is not forced to pass the responder's two-level rebid. However, he would only bid on with extra values. For example, after the two-heart rebid considered on the hand above (page 124), the opener may raise with some heart fit. Perhaps he might hold

♠ A K 7 5 2   ♡ K Q 5   ◇ 3   ♣ K 10 9 8

It should not be inferred that the forcing one-notrump response is perfect. Some hands appear, especially misfits, that are bound to get too high and this device is powerless to prevent it. But weak hands seldom get more than one trick higher than necessary when the forcing one-notrump response is used. For example, if the responder has a weak hand with a long diamond suit and the opener rebids two hearts or two spades, he will be forced to rebid three diamonds.

♠
♡
3
♢
♣

The Stayman Convention

Next to Blackwood, the bidding convention most used around the world is Stayman, which is a response of two clubs to an opening bid of one notrump, asking opener to bid a four-card major if he has one.

The basic purpose of this convention, which was devised independently by players in the United States and England, is to reach game in a major suit rather than in notrump when a player opens one notrump and his partner has a hand like this:

♠ K J 7 6   ♡ K 7 4 3   ♢ 9 2   ♣ K 6 5

Opposite a strong notrump, this hand gives promise of game. And if a 4-4 fit can be uncovered in either major suit, game in that strain might be better than three notrump.

ORIGIN OF THE CONVENTION

In 1945, George Rapée of New York suggested the idea to his partner, Samuel M. Stayman, and they experimented with it. They found it effective, and adopted it for regular use. Stayman wrote an article about it, which was published in *The Bridge World* magazine in the United States and was translated and published in the bridge magazines of several other countries. Bridge players throughout the world liked this convention, and by 1948 it was in general use. (It is doubtful if any other bidding convention had ever won favor so quickly.) Those who adopted the bid called it the Stayman convention.

Having thus had international fame thrust upon him, Stayman engaged in a continuing and exhaustive study of the convention that bore his name and he has become the unchallenged authority on it.

STAYMAN VARIETIES

There are three varieties, which focus on the meaning of the two-heart or two-spade rebid by the Stayman bidder:

Opener	Responder
1NT	2♣
2♦	2♥ or 2♠

a. Forcing Stayman
The bid is forcing, allowing the auction to develop slowly when the responder is strong. This treatment, popular in the fifties, has gradually become obsolete. The use of transfers (see below) or Two-Way Stayman makes it unnecessary.

b. Non-forcing Stayman
The bid is invitational, suggesting a five-card suit. The strength will be 8 or 9 high-card points opposite the standard strong notrump.

c. Weak Stayman

Many experts use the two-of-a-major rebid with a weak, unbalanced hand which is escaping from notrump. A two-spade rebid would announce 5-4 in the majors. A two-heart rebid implies 4-5 or 5-5 in the majors (though 4-4 with a minor-suit singleton is possible). The opener will pass with three hearts, or correct to two spades when 3-2 in the majors.

A few experts use the two-spade rebid to show a four-card suit and a weak, unbalanced hand. If the opener does not like spades, he continues with three clubs (if he has clubs) or two notrump (without clubs).

An example:

♠ A J 5 4	♠ K 9 3 2
♡ J 3	♡ 10 6 5 4 2
◇ A J 5	◇ 10 9 6
♣ K Q 7 6	♣ 5

These hands would be unlikely to make one notrump, but will usually make two spades. They were bid, using weak Stayman, as follows:

West	North	East	South
1NT	Pass	2♣	Pass
2♠	Pass	Pass	Pass

East was delighted to pass two spades. And if instead West had rebid two diamonds, East would have bid two hearts, indicating a weak major two-suiter and asking partner to pass (with three hearts) or to correct to two spades (with three spades and two hearts).

However, if East and West were using forcing or non-forcing Stayman, East could not afford to risk a two-club response. What would he do if West rebid two diamonds? Instead, he would have to respond two hearts and thus miss the spade fit.

It is implicit in the Stayman convention that, unless transfer bids are being used, a direct response of two spades, two hearts, or two diamonds shows a one-suited hand so weak that game is impossible and the notrump bidder must pass. A two-spade response to one notrump might be made on the following hand:

♠ J 8 6 5 3 2   ♡ 10 6   ◇ 8 2   ♣ J 8 4

From the weakness of this hand it is apparent that the bid requires partner to pass it automatically. Two spades is almost certain to be a better contract than one notrump.

TWO-WAY STAYMAN

A prevalent variation of the Stayman convention is called "two-way Stayman" or "double-barreled Stayman," which means that a two-club response to one notrump asks for a four-card major but shows a weak hand, at best enough to invite a game contract, while a two-diamond response to one notrump also asks for a four-card major but shows a strong responding hand and is forcing to game.

The main advantage of two-way Stayman is that after the forcing two-diamond response the possibility of slam can be explored at the three-level because the partnership is already committed to game. There are, however, disadvantages.

In addition to giving the opponents perhaps too much information, this use of the two-diamond response shuts off the weak two-diamond response to get out of a dangerous notrump contract, but proponents of extended Stayman contend that this is unimportant.

If the responder has a hand such as

♠ 65   ♡ 73   ◇ J 9 7 6 5 3   ♣ 8 5 2

he responds by jumping to three diamonds, a preemptive bid demanding that partner pass.

It is true that the responding hand has pushed himself up to three diamonds on a hand he might have played in two diamonds, but he has also made it harder for the opponents to find a major-suit fit.

As an addendum to this, if the responder first bids two clubs, non-forcing Stayman, and then bids three of a minor, it is usually treated as a game invitation showing a good six-card suit and asking the opener to bid three notrump with some fit for the minor and stoppers on the side (though some pairs do play it as weak with a four-card major and a longer minor).

4 Transfer Bids

Transfer bids have become very popular with tournament players; but as with most things in life, there are many varieties. However, the basic purpose is the same. It transfers play of the contract from the weak hand into the strong hand. For example, South opens one notrump and North holds a hand such as this:

♠ 7 6   ♡ Q 10 8 7 6 2   ◇ 8 4 3   ♣ K 8

It is almost sure that the North-South hands will play best with hearts as trumps, but since South has a strong hand in high cards and North a weak one, it will be better if South is the declarer so that the opening lead will be made around to his hand, not through it, and so that the exact nature of his high cards will be concealed. The North-South object, therefore, is to reach a heart contract with South as the declarer, and the transfer bid achieves this.

A transfer bid is a response in a suit lower in rank than one's real suit; usually the suit directly below the one held. On the hand shown above, for example, the real suit is hearts, and the holder of the hand would bid two diamonds to show hearts. That allows the notrump opener to bid hearts first and become the declarer.

The invention of transfer bids is generally credited to David Carter, a Missouri man. The bids were developed by Oswald Jacoby, and so have come to be known as Jacoby transfers in North America. As with most good ideas, though, transfer bids were independently devised elsewhere—in this case by Olle Willner of Stockholm, Sweden.

In their simplest and original form, transfer bids were made only at the four-level. If South opened one notrump and North responded four diamonds, South had to bid four hearts; if North responded four hearts, South had to bid four spades. These are known as Texas transfers. (There is also a version called South African Texas in which responder bids four clubs to show hearts and four diamonds to indicate spades.)

For a four-heart response North may have a hand such as this:

♠ K J 9 7 6 5 2   ♡ 8   ◊ Q 6 4   ♣ 8 3

Opposite a hand strong enough for an opening one-notrump bid, this will almost surely produce a game but not a slam. The combined hands may play one trick better if the stronger hand is the declarer.

The heart hand shown earlier:

♠ 7 6   ♡ Q 10 8 7 6 2   ◊ 8 4 3   ♣ K 8

is not strong enough to insist on game if the notrump hand is a minimum and lacks a fit with hearts. The Jacoby transfer bids were designed for such hands.

THE JACOBY TRANSFER BIDS

The Jacoby transfer bids apply at the two-level. A response of two diamonds shows hearts; a response of two hearts promises spades; and a response of two spades indicates a minor two-suiter, the notrump opener bidding whichever minor suit he prefers.

Three-level responses are traditionally strong and forcing, promising the values for game and at least a five-card suit. However, modern bidding developments have had an impact. Responses of three of a minor require partnership agreement.

Opener	Responder
1NT	3♣ or 3♢

As with Stayman, there are three common interpretations:

a. Forcing, and hinting at a slam.
This is standard in social games, but relatively rare in tournament play.

b. Invitational
A six-card suit with some hope of three notrump or five of the minor.

c. Weak
A sign-off in a six-card suit; the equivalent of a standard two-heart or two-spade response, except that the responder will often make these major-suit bids with only five-card suits.

Players who use transfer bids, or two-way Stayman as described in the previous chapter, have little need for a jump response of three hearts or three spades. Some use the former to show an invitational 5-5 major-suit hand, with three spades for stronger hands of that type. Others use them as preemptive jumps, indicating a weak hand with a long suit. There is a third group who like to be able to show a shortage in the responder's hand; they play that the jump shows either a three-suited hand with a given singleton, or a powerful suit, slam interest, and a void somewhere. In the latter case, the opener can bid one step up to locate the void. The aim is for the opener to be able to assess slam capabilities based on how well the hands fit.

An immediate response of four clubs is Gerber; four diamonds and four hearts are again transfer bids showing hearts and spades, respectively.

Use of transfers at both the two- and four-levels gives the partnership a great deal of flexibility in describing hands with slam interest, without slam ambitions, two-suiters, and relatively balanced hands. For example, game-going hands without slam interest can be shown by making the transfer at the four-level, with slam interest being shown by transferring at the two-level and then raising to four. Thus

North	South
1NT	2♦
2♡	4♡

shows a much better responding hand than

North	South
1NT	4♦

In the former auction, the opener may bid again; in the latter, he must just honor the transfer.

After a two-level transfer, if the opener's partner "raises" his real suit (e.g., 1NT–2♡–2♠–3♠), it is a simple game invitation in the suit. If the responder rebids two notrump (e.g., 1NT–2♦–2♡–2NT), he suggests 5-3-3-2 shape and gives the opener the option of playing in a partscore or game in either notrump or the major. Responder might hold a hand such as:

♠ K 5   ♡ K Q 10 7 3   ♦ 7 4 2   ♣ 9 8 6

Similarly, 1NT–2♦–2♡–3NT offers the opener a choice of

games: three notrump (without heart fit) or four hearts (with fit). The responder will have a hand like this:

♠ 7 6 4   ♡ A Q 10 8 4   ◇ K Q 7   ♣ 8 3

In the original Jacoby methods, a new-suit rebid by the responder after a transfer bid is natural and forcing to game. However, some regard this as only a one-round force. For example, holding

♠ 6   ♡ K Q 10 7 3   ◇ A 7 4 2   ♣ Q 8 6

responder bids first two diamonds, showing five or more hearts, and then continues with three diamonds.

EXAMPLE OF THE JACOBY TRANSFER BID

The Jacoby transfer bids led to a very pretty result on the deal that included a hand shown earlier. The full layout was:

```
Dlr: South        ♠ 7 6
Vul: E-W          ♡ Q 10 8 7 6 2
                  ◇ 8 4 3
                  ♣ K 8
  ♠ A 10 4                      ♠ Q J 9 5 3
  ♡ A 9                         ♡ 5 4 3
  ◇ K 9 6 2                     ◇ 10 5
  ♣ J 7 4 2                     ♣ Q 9 6
                  ♠ K 8 2
                  ♡ K J
                  ◇ A Q J 7
                  ♣ A 10 5 3
```

West	North	East	South
			1NT
Pass	2◇	Pass	2♡
Pass	3♡	Pass	4♡
Pass	Pass	Pass	

Jacoby held the North cards, and his partner was his son, James Jacoby, who followed in his father's footsteps by winning several national titles while still in his twenties, and has been a world champion three times.

North's three-heart bid, as we just saw, was a game invitation showing at least a six-card heart suit. Jim Jacoby had an exceptionally strong notrump hand; he had 18 high-card points, and the best players today seldom open one notrump with more than 17 points. Therefore his acceptance of the game invitation was automatic.

West played safe by leading the ace of hearts and continuing with the nine. Any other lead from his hand seemed dangerous, and although as it happened he could have opened diamonds or clubs with impunity, a spade lead would have wrecked the defenders' chances from the start.

South, who had unblocked by throwing his king of hearts on the first trick, won the second trick with dummy's queen of hearts and drew the last outstanding trump with dummy's ten, on which he discarded a spade, as did West. Then South took the king and ace of clubs and trumped a club in dummy, on the bare chance that both the queen and jack would fall. They did not, and South tried a diamond finesse, leading low from dummy and playing the queen. West could not dare refuse this trick, so he won with his king and exited with the jack of clubs, which dummy trumped.

Dummy now had one trump left, and South led it, discarding his remaining low spade. West could not part with a diamond, for that would establish South's low diamond; so West blanked his ace of spades. South led the eight of diamonds from dummy, won with the ace and threw West in by leading the king of spades. West had to lead from the 9-6 of diamonds into South's J-7, and South made his game contract.

FOUR-SUIT TRANSFERS

A method that has gained great popularity in recent years permits a player to transfer into *any* suit. Over the opener's one notrump, two diamonds and two hearts are transfers showing the major suit as in the Jacoby style. But the transfers do not stop there: two spades shows a club suit and two notrump indicates diamonds.

This has one immediate effect: the responder may no longer invite game in notrump with a raise to two notrump. He must start with two clubs, Stayman, and rebid two notrump, not promising a four-card major. This is not as serious as it sounds. If the opener responds two diamonds over the Stayman inquiry, the responder just bids two notrump and the defenders do not know whether there will be one or two majors coming down in the dummy. And if the opener responds two spades, denying four hearts, the responder again bids two notrump, at the same time leaving the opponents temporarily in the dark over hearts. The only difficult auction occurs when the opener bids two hearts, showing that suit and perhaps having spades as well. Now if the responder bids two notrump and the opener has a minimum with four spades, he will not know whether to pass or bid three spades. The answer is that the responder bids two spades over two hearts to show exactly four spades and at least the values for two notrump. So the auction 1NT–2♣–2♡–2NT denies holding four spades.

The other effect of four-suit transfers is that the opener may express some suitability for the indicated minor. If the responder bids two spades to indicate clubs, the opener can bid either two notrump or three clubs. The normal method is that bidding the shown suit expresses an interest in that suit: the opener usually holds at least three cards in the suit and one or more of the top three honors.

Suppose the bidding has begun 1NT–2♠. Holding

     ♠ K J 7 6   ♡ A J 4   ◇ A Q 4 3   ♣ J 7

the opener bids two notrump, denying any interest in clubs. However, with

     ♠ K J 7 6   ♡ J 7   ◇ A Q 4 3   ♣ A J 4

he rebids three clubs, announcing a good fit for clubs. This will sometimes allow the responder to decide whether or not to take a shot at three notrump on the basis of a running minor suit.

If the responder bids a new suit after transferring into a minor, it is natural and forcing to game. Holding

♠ K J 7 6   ♡ 2   ◇ K 4   ♣ A J 10 7 6 5

the responder first bids two spades to show his clubs, and then continues with three spades to indicate his second suit and high-card values for at least game.

One final point: Some players do not use the recommended style given above. After, say, 1NT–2♠, a transfer to clubs, they use opener's rebid of two notrump, not three clubs, to show a fit for clubs. This is wrong.

Suppose the responder holds a hand of this type:

♠ 6   ♡ 7 4   ◇ J 8 7 4 3   ♣ J 9 5 4 2

What does he respond to a one-notrump opening bid?

It would be wrong to pass, and using the method just mentioned, he will have to guess correctly which minor his partner likes. However, using the recommended style, no guesswork is necessary. The responder bids two notrump, a transfer to diamonds. If the opener rebids three diamonds, guaranteeing a diamond fit, the responder passes and the best contract has probably been reached. If instead the opener rebids three clubs, denying a diamond fit, the responder again passes! If the opener does not like diamonds, he surely has support for clubs. Once more, it is probable that the best resting place has been found.

♠

♡

5 The Weak
Two-Bid

♢

♣

The weak two-bid is used throughout the world. Its adherents were once far more numerous among experts; the average player was reluctant to make a high bid on a weak hand. Now, in the United States at least, virtually all tournament players use the weak two, and even some social players have deserted the strong two-bid in favor of its weaker cousin.

The object of the weak two-bid is to interfere with the opponents' bidding. Opening three- and four-level preempts are universally used as shut-out bids, of course, but they have two disadvantages. First, hands of the proper type for such bids are rare. Second, so high a bid will shut out partner as well as opponents.

The weak two-bid has neither of these disadvantages. Ideally it is made on a hand with a fairly strong six-card suit and a total high-card strength of about a trick and a half, and such hands are frequent. An example for a two-heart bid might be:

♠ 8 3   ♡ Q J 10 8 7 4   ◇ A 7 6   ♣ 6 5

Provided the bid is never made on a hand materially stronger or weaker than this, partner's bidding is not affected, because he is given quite precise information. Necessarily, the opponents have this information too, but they will still find it dangerous and therefore difficult to enter the bidding at so high a level. For example, the following case from a rubber-bridge game:

Dlr: South   ♠ A 7 5 2
Vul: E-W   ♡ Q 7 6
        ◇ A 8 7 6
        ♣ 10 4

♠ K Q 9 4   ♠ J 10 8 3
♡ 9   ♡ A 4 2
◇ J 9 3   ◇ Q 2
♣ K Q 9 5 2   ♣ A J 7 3

        ♠ 6
        ♡ K J 10 8 5 3
        ◇ K 10 5 4
        ♣ 8 6

West	North	East	South
			2♡
Pass	3♡	Pass	Pass
Pass			

North's raise to three hearts was intended to make it even more difficult for the opponents to enter the bidding—North would have bid two notrump if he had wanted to invite game. North's bid had the desired preemptive effect, for West did not feel strong enough to bid over two hearts, nor East over three, since they were vulnerable.

  As a result South made three hearts easily, losing one heart trick, one diamond, and two clubs. West could as easily have made three spades, and might have made four if the defense was not very careful.

Experience from this type of result has shown that an opponent should strain to enter the bidding when short in the preemptor's suit. Here, West should have made a take-out double over two hearts. Admittedly, East would probably drive to game, but it is better to play in four spades than to sell out to three hearts on these cards.

The weak two-bid applies only to bids of two spades, two hearts, and two diamonds. The opening bid of two clubs is reserved as an artificial forcing bid, which will be discussed in the next chapter.

The weak two-bid was introduced by Howard Schenken and incorporated in the system of his team, the Four Aces, about fifty years ago. Harold Vanderbilt's original club system, the first contract bridge system, had incorporated a weak two-bid but it had so wide a range that it resulted in the occasional loss of a game. The Schenken development put the weak two-bid in a straitjacket and greatly increased its effectiveness.

Despite Schenken's great prestige among bridge experts, many qualified bridge theorists disliked the weak two-bid. They admitted it was hard to play against when used by good players, but they added that "anything is hard to play against when used by good players." They indicted the weak two-bid principally on the ground that it seldom kept the opponents out of game.

This may be true enough, but it does not mean the weak two-bid is ineffective. The great value of the bid is (as in the deal shown above) when the strength is fairly well divided and either side can make a partscore. On game-going hands the opponents may get into the bidding without too much trouble; on partscore hands they do not dare.

Furthermore, the weak two-bid does occasionally keep the opponents out of a game. It did in this deal:

Dlr: North   ♠ J 6
Vul: E-W   ♡ K Q 8 6 4
                    ◇ Q J 6
                    ♣ 10 9 3

♠ Q 8 2   ♠ A 4
♡ 10 3   ♡ A J 7 5
◇ A K 10 9 3   ◇ 7 2
♣ K J 5   ♣ Q 8 7 4 2

                    ♠ K 10 9 7 5 3
                    ♡ 9 2
                    ◇ 8 5 4
                    ♣ A 6

West	North	East	South
	Pass	Pass	2♠
Pass	3♠	Pass	Pass
Pass			

North's raise was a shut-out bid in its own right. Many of those who use the weak two-bid give a single raise on the sort of hand with which they would raise a one-bid (except that less trump support is needed, because the opener is known to have a six-card suit).

In this case West was not strong enough to risk a bid of three diamonds. East might have summoned up enough courage to bid if North had passed, but the three-spade level was too much for him. North's raise was known to be pre-emptive, but South, bidding third hand, might have been trapping with a good hand.

A double of three spades would have given East-West a fair score, because South went down three, but South got bad breaks. West opened the king of diamonds and continued with the ace and a low one. East trumped, cashed his ace of spades, and led a club. South had a club, a heart, and another trump to lose.

The loss of 150 points was of course a big profit for North-South, because their opponents had an easy game in notrump. At worst they would win four club tricks, two spades, two diamonds, and a heart.

How could East-West get into the bidding and reach their game? The only answer is that in expert play they usually do, by intuition or inspiration or whatever unusual quality it is that experts have. Since most bridge players are not so gifted, the weak two-bid is likely to be a most effective tool when used by the best players against weaker players. In fact, opponents of the weak two-bid have called it an intentional "sucker-killing" device.

The average player would be wise to use the weak two-bid only on classic hands such as are shown above. He should confine himself to six-card suits, and not make the weak two-bid (as Schenken himself was known to do) on a hand like this:

$$\spadesuit 6 \quad \heartsuit K Q 10 7 4 \quad \diamondsuit K J 8 3 \quad \clubsuit 7 5 2$$

Perhaps the principal pitfall to avoid is bidding two hearts on this kind of hand:

$$\spadesuit 9 6 5 3 \quad \heartsuit A Q 10 9 6 5 \quad \diamondsuit 8 2 \quad \clubsuit 6$$

Partner might have a fair hand with a spade suit and game might be missed. A hand with four spades or four hearts is seldom suitable for the weak two-bid. Exchange the spade and club holdings and this hand would fit the weak two-bid standard.

VULNERABILITY AND MATCHPOINT CONSIDERATIONS

Like any preemptive bid, the weak two-bid anticipates a possible double, so a weak two-bid is usually stronger when the bidder is vulnerable than when he is not vulnerable, but there are some respects in which the considerations applying to a weak two-bid are exactly the opposite of those applying to a three- or four-bid.

For example, a three-spade bid is far more likely to be doubled for penalties than a three-diamond bid, so a vulnerable player will bid three diamonds on a weaker hand than he requires for a three-spade bid.

But a weak two-bid may be made in spades with a hand that would be passed if the suit were diamonds. On the following hand two spades might be bid, first hand, non-vulnerable, against vulnerable or non-vulnerable opponents:

♠ Q 10 9 8 6 3   ♡ 8 6   ◇ 7   ♣ K 10 9 8

Change the suits, leaving the cards the same:

♠ 8 6   ♡ 7   ◇ Q 10 9 8 6 3   ♣ K 10 9 8

On this hand it is hardly worthwhile to bid two diamonds. The opponents are less likely to be shut out, so there is the same risk with less to gain; if partner should have great strength it will avail much less, because five diamonds will be so much harder to make than four spades would be on the preceding hand; and if partner wishes to sacrifice against a major-suit game he must go one trick higher than would be necessary on the spade hand.

The weak two-diamond bid, for these reasons, is seldom heard in rubber bridge. In duplicate games with matchpoint scoring it is used more often when non-vulnerable against vulnerable opponents, but largely because it avoids one danger of a heavily shaded one-diamond bid: partner is immediately warned of weakness and will not be likely to overbid on a very strong hand.

Generally it is best to adhere to the classic requirements, a good six-card suit with a trick and a half (7-9 high-card points) in the hand.

RESPONDING TO THE WEAK TWO-BID

There are two possible objectives in responding to a weak two-bid: one is defensive, the other offensive. As suggested earlier, the partner of the weak two-bidder may increase the level of the preempt by making a simple raise. He may also raise to game, either as a preempt or with the expectation that game will be made. The ambiguous character of the game raise makes it doubly difficult for the opponents to know when to enter the auction, since the responder could raise a weak two-heart bid to game with any of these hands:

1. ♠ 7
   ♡ K 8 7 5
   ◇ 9 6 2
   ♣ K 8 6 4 2

2. ♠ A K 7
   ♡ J 8 7 5
   ◇ K Q 6
   ♣ K Q 4

3. ♠ A 8 6
   ♡ A
   ◇ A 9 8 6 5
   ♣ A Q 4 3

When the responder has an in-between hand and does not know whether to bid or which game to bid, he can make a forcing bid to request more information from the opener. A new-suit bid is generally considered natural and forcing, although many players treat it as non-forcing, especially if they adopt a freewheeling style for opening weak two-bids.

The response of two notrump is conventional and forcing. Most pairs play that it requests the opener to rebid his suit if he has a minimum, to rebid three notrump if his suit is solid (at least A-K-Q-x-x-x), or to show a feature if maximum. A feature is usually the ace or king in the side suit, but might be Q-J-x if maximum but holding no ace or king outside the weak-two suit.

For example, after 2♡–2NT, bid three hearts to show a minimum holding

♠ 5 4   ♡ K J 10 6 5 4   ◇ Q J 6   ♣ 8 3

Bid three notrump with

♠ 7 3   ♡ A K Q 10 8 7   ◇ 7 6   ♣ J 3 2

And bid three clubs if clutching

♠ 6   ♡ K Q 10 8 7 4   ◇ 6 5 4   ♣ A 5 3

THE OGUST TWO-NOTRUMP RESPONSE

In practice, contrary to the classical requirements, there is considerable variation both in the high-card content of weak two-bids and in the location of the high-card strength. To cope with the wide range of hands that the weak two-bidder may hold, the late Harold Ogust developed a convention to codify the opener's answers to his partner's two-notrump inquiry.

For example, when opener bids two hearts responder may have a rather ordinary hand such as

♠ A K 7 3   ♡ 8 7 5   ◊ A 6   ♣ Q J 8 4

There are many correct weak two-bids opposite which responder's hand will produce game. Using the Ogust convention, following a two-notrump response the opener has four bids available to announce whether his suit is "good" or "bad," and whether his hand is minimum or maximum.

Opener rebids three clubs to show a bad hand with a bad suit, perhaps:

♠ 8 4   ♡ Q J 10 4 3 2   ◊ K 4   ♣ 7 3 2

A three-diamond rebid shows a good hand with a bad suit; for example:

♠ 8 4   ♡ Q J 9 4 3 2   ◊ K 4   ♣ A 7 3

A three-heart rebid shows a bad hand with a good suit; maybe:

♠ 8 4   ♡ A K J 4 3 2   ◊ 5 4   ♣ 9 5 3

(If opener's heart suit were solid, of course, he would rebid three notrump. Also, note that some partnerships reverse the meanings of the three-diamond and three-heart responses.)

A three-spade rebid shows a good hand with a good suit, such as:

♠ 8 4   ♡ A K 10 4 3 2   ◊ 5 4   ♣ K 10 7

With the information provided by the Ogust rebids the responder should be able to make a reasonably intelligent decision whether or not to bid a game, and if so, where.

In conclusion, whatever one's views about the weak two-bid, it is true to say that most experts worldwide now use it in one form or another.

♠
♡
6 **The Forcing Two-Club Opening Bid**
◇
♣

Use of the weak two-bid virtually demands that an opening of two clubs be a very strong, usually game-forcing, bid; but the popularity of the two-club bid is not exclusive to those who use weak two-bids. Many of the world's most successful players combine the forcing two-club bid with strong two-bids in the other suits.

The two-club convention is this: An opening bid of two clubs is forcing to game (with occasional exceptions that will be noted later). The two-club bid does not necessarily show a club suit. The bidder may even be void in clubs. It does show an unusually strong hand, especially in aces and kings.

The partner of the two-club bidder must make an artificial response of two diamonds if he wishes to deny strength. If he bids another suit, or two notrump, he shows some strength of his own and the rest of his bidding is likely to be pointed toward a slam.

The history of the two-club convention is obscure. It was originated in the early days of contract bridge, in 1929, by David Burnstine, then a member of the Four Horsemen and later of the Four Aces. Milton Work, the senior prophet of the predecessor game of auction bridge, espoused the bid, but temporarily it lost favor as Ely Culbertson and his forcing two-bid (in every suit) became ascendant.

The advantages claimed for the two-club bid are twofold. First, it often saves a round of bidding, especially when the bidder's principal strength is in spades or hearts and not in the minor suits. Second, it frees the bids of two spades, two hearts, and two diamonds for other uses.

The most popular use of these other two-bids today is in the weak two-bid, a mild shut-out bid, described in the preceding chapter.

Burnstine's original two-club bid was combined with other two-bids (spades, hearts, diamonds) that were strong but not game-forcing. By this interpretation a strong but non-forcing two-spade bid might be made on

♠ A K Q 10 6 5   ♡ 9 5   ◇ A Q 10   ♣ K 5

This hand might make game opposite any hand that has a small amount of spade support or high cards insufficient for a response to a one-bid, for example:

♠ J 8 2   ♡ 10 8 7 3   ◇ 5 4   ♣ Q 9 6 2

On these combined hands game might be made by a winning finesse or a favorable lead, and such games should be bid.

With no support in trumps or outside high cards the responder may pass the strong but non-forcing two-bid or may drop it short of game.

The advantage of the strong, non-forcing two-bid is largely negative. It permits one-bids to be made on weaker hands and it permits the one-bidder's partner to pass more readily without fear of missing game, since the range of the one-bid is more limited.

A variation of these methods—with the strong two-bid forcing for one round but not forcing to game—is part of the Acol system used by many of the leading British players.

The disadvantage of the forcing two-club bid is a practical one: the average player hates artificial bids. If he bids clubs, he wants to have clubs, not spades or hearts or diamonds. However, this consideration does not bother the expert.

HOW THE TWO-CLUB BID WORKS

Requirements for the two-club bid can hardly be expressed in points, or at least not in high-card points. A hand that qualifies for the forcing two-bid is a proper hand for a two-club bid, but an advantage claimed for the two-club bid is that some hands that do not qualify as forcing two-bids are safe two-club bids.

The typical two-club hand will be either balanced with at least 23 high-card points or strong and distributional. In the latter case, how do you decide whether a hand is worth a two-club opening bid? First of all, the hand should contain defensive tricks. This hand:

$$\spadesuit \text{ A K Q J 10 9 8 7 6 5} \quad \heartsuit 2 \quad \diamond 2 \quad \clubsuit 2$$

is not a two-club opening. It will make a game in spades, to be sure, but it will be lucky to score one defensive trick. A two-club opening should contain at least four defensive tricks. Second, if you open with a one-bid, is there a risk that it will be passed out and a game missed? If so, assuming partner holds one key card, the hand is worth two clubs. Partner may not have the necessary card and game may go down, but it is always worth the risk in an effort to collect the lucrative game bonus.

Any of the following hands would be a two-club bid for

the majority of present-day experts, who, it should be noted, do not demand nearly so much as the previous generations of experts for the bid:

1.	♠ A 6	2.	♠ A Q J 8 5	3.	♠ A K 6 4 3
	♡ K J 4		♡ A K Q 10 4		♡ 6
	◇ A 3		◇ A 8		◇ A K 5
	♣ A K Q J 7 5		♣ 7		♣ A K 8 7

The partner of the two-club bidder must respond; and it has been normal to bid two diamonds unless he has, in high cards, at least an ace and a king or the equivalent: a king and a king-queen, or three kings, or at least a five-card suit headed by two of the top three honors with a queen outside. Two diamonds was known as the negative response; and all other bids were positive responses.

However, it has become common practice that a positive response in a suit promises a good holding: usually at least two of the top three honors. This is in line with the excellent principle of not bidding bad suits in potential slam auctions.

Similarly, the two-notrump response to show a balanced positive has become scarce, as it caused too many high-level notrump contracts to be played from the wrong side.

Lacking the values for a positive response under these more rigid guidelines, the responder makes the "waiting bid" of two diamonds, planning to show any extra values later in the auction.

Here are some possible responding hands:

4.	♠ 8 7 5 4 3 2	5.	♠ 8 6
	♡ 4		♡ J 9 8 7 5
	◇ 7 6 2		◇ A 3
	♣ J 8 6		♣ K 6 5 4

6.	♠ A Q 6 5	7.	♠ K Q 10 8 7
	♡ K J 5 4		♡ 6
	◇ 7 5 3		◇ A 8 5
	♣ 8 2		♣ 9 6 4 3

Hand four is the classic two-diamond negative response. Hand five should make the waiting bid of two diamonds. It has the values for a positive response, but that heart suit is too weak to show immediately. Similarly, hand six should bid two diamonds. It is possible to bid two notrump, but with all the points in two suits, it is wiser to settle for two diamonds. Finally, hand seven makes an ideal two-spade response: positive values and a good suit; opener will find responder's high cards where he expects them to be.

Once the opening bid and first response are out of the way, both partners bid normally. The opener's first rebid shows his real suit. Traditionally, any rebid in a suit by opener, such as

North	South
	2♣
2♦	2♠

indicates that the opener has a good enough hand to make game all by himself, and North is required to bid again, and keep on bidding, until game is reached. The responder, if he started with two diamonds, shows his own suit or supports the opener's suit, if he can; or with abject weakness makes a bid that is called a double negative—emphasizing the nature of his hand. Traditionally, the second negative is two notrump, but most experts now prefer to bid three clubs so that if the hand is to be played in three notrump, the strong hand will be the declarer.

When the opener rebids in a minor, the situation is a little more complicated.

North	South
	2♣
2♦	3♣ or 3♦

Many pairs use three diamonds as a second negative over three clubs. Over three diamonds, though, most pairs have no second negative (except three notrump). A few pairs use three hearts to show either abject weakness or a balanced hand, and then three notrump indicates a heart suit and some values.

According to modern expert practice, the two-club opening bid ceases to be forcing if the opener merely rebids the same suit over a double negative:

North	South
	2♣
2◇	2♠
2NT or 3♣	3♠

This procedure increases the number of hands that can be opened with two clubs to include some that are similar to the intermediate hands discussed on page 150.

LATER BIDS BY THE RESPONDER

There is no doubt that these restrictions often serve to clarify the meanings of rebids. For example, here is a hand bid to a slam in a New York tournament.

Dlr: North
Vul: Both

♠ A K Q 10 8 4
♡ A Q 5
◇ A Q 6
♣ 8

♠ J 9 7 6 2   ♠ 3
♡ 4   ♡ 9 2
◇ K 9 5   ◇ J 10 7 2
♣ K J 7 3   ♣ A Q 10 5 4 2

♠ 5
♡ K J 10 8 7 6 3
◇ 8 4 3
♣ 9 6

West	North	East	South
	2♣	Pass	2◇
Pass	2♠	Pass	3♡
Pass	4NT	Pass	5◇
Pass	6♡	Pass	Pass
Pass			

South showed some values with his three-heart bid as he had not employed the second negative. Four notrump was Roman Key Card Blackwood (see page 191); and the five-diamond response indicated one key card: from North's point of view, the ace of clubs or, more likely, the king of hearts. North decided that the slam would be at worst on the diamond finesse.

Because of South's extra heart length, the contract was laydown, despite the bad spade break. West led a low club, and after taking his ace East shifted to a trump. South had only to draw trumps, ruff his losing club in the dummy and discard his diamonds on the high spades.

A diamond lead by West would have made greater demands on South's skill, but a good declarer should have made his contract with no greater difficulty.

Of course, the first-round diamond finesse could not be taken by anyone who does not peek. If the finesse lost, a club switch would defeat the contract. So the ace of diamonds would be put up.

The ace of spades would be cashed next, for a 6-0 break in a suit is sufficiently unlikely to be disregarded in nearly all cases. The ace of spades would win, and a low spade would be led from the dummy, with South prepared to ruff with the ten of hearts if East followed; but he would have to discard or ruff, so South could safely ruff with any heart sure to win.

There would follow a heart lead to the queen, another low spade ruffed in hand, and a second heart lead to the ace. This would draw trumps and allow declarer to cash three spade tricks, discarding three of his four minor-suit losers. South would surrender a trick, taking the rest and making his contract. The 2-1 break of the opposing trumps made the establishment of the ten of spades unnecessary, since declarer could have ruffed his second club in the dummy, but this line of play might have been needed if the hearts had broken 3-0.

TWO CLUBS AS A TWO-NOTRUMP BID

The two-club forcing opening bid in its most popular application is not necessarily forcing to game. It may be made either on a typical two-notrump hand or on a game-going powerhouse, and no one but the opener himself knows which it is until he rebids. Sometimes not even then.

West	North	East	South
			2♣
Pass	2◇	Pass	2NT

South holds just what a traditional two-notrump opening used to show: about 23 or 24 high-card points. Responder is not forced to bid over this rebid, but he should bid again if he has as much as a queen and a jack or a couple of queens.

The great value of using the two-club/two-notrump sequence to show a hand of 23 or 24 points is that the two-notrump opening can be made on a slightly weaker hand, about 21 or 22 points. This permits the opener's hand to be described with greater precision, which is more and more desirable as the bidding approaches the game level.

Of course, if the opener has a balanced hand containing even more than 24 high-card points, he must jump in notrump over the responder's negative response. A jump to three notrump would indicate about 25-27 points; a leap to four notrump some 28-30 points. As these calls take up so much room, bidding accurately is difficult; the only saving grace is that they are very rare.

A positive response by the responder creates a game-forcing situation, even if South's rebid is two notrump:

West	North	East	South
			2♣
Pass	2♡	Pass	2NT

North must bid again, and both North and South must continue bidding until game is reached. The values shown by North's two-heart response must produce a play for game, even if South has a minimum for his two-club bid. Here, South may rebid two notrump with more than the usual 23 points in order to learn more about his partner's hand at a lower level, proposing to drive to at least a small slam.

THE STRONG CLUB

The first important book on contract bridge was by Harold Vanderbilt, the millionaire yachtsman who gave the contract idea its modern form. Three years after his famous 1925 cruise through the Panama Canal on the SS *Finland,* he published *Contract Bridge: Bidding and the Club Convention.*

His idea was to use an opening one-club bid for nearly all strong hands, and therefore place an upward limit of about 15 points on opening bids of one diamond, one heart, one spade, and two clubs. In addition to defining these four openings more precisely, a strong one-club system preserves bidding space on the strong hands by starting with the lowest possibld bid.

Vanderbilt had considerable success with this system. Playing in four-man teams with the late Waldemar von Zedtwitz he twice won his own trophy, the Vanderbilt, defeating the greatest players of the day.

As an amateur, Vanderbilt had little chance of converting the bridge public to his method; the professional organization of Ely Culbertson, who hired among others the original author of this book, dominated the scene. But he lived to see his system vindicated. In 1957 the Italian Blue Team began a string of world-championship successes relying considerably on a strong club, originally named Neapolitan and later called the Blue Team Club. This provoked Vanderbilt into producing, in 1964, a modern version of his original book, hoping it would regain international supremacy for the United States. One of his example hands was this:

♠ A K Q J 2	♠ 10 6
♡ A 10 9 8	♡ Q 5 4
◇ 9	◇ 7 4 2
♣ K Q J	♣ A 10 9 8 3

All the pairs asked to bid this hand in 1964 landed in four hearts or four spades, failing completely to mention the club suit. Few would do better today.

Playing a strong club, it is easy for East to show clubs at his second turn after giving a negative response of one diamond. Vanderbilt's sequence was:

West	East
1♣	1◇
1♠	2♣
3♡	4♡
4NT	5◇
6♣	Pass

West intends to pass five clubs if East shows that he is aceless. The slam is, of course, easy. If a heart is led, trumps are drawn; and on another lead a diamond ruff is taken in the West hand.

The Italian successes prompted two other American developments in the sixties. In 1963 the late Howard Schenken, regarded by some as the world's greatest player, published his Big Club method, which he had already used in a world championship. And in the following year a Chinese-American ship owner experimented with a strong club using the five-card-major principle and a weak notrump.

This was the late C. C. Wei, and he asked the senior author of the present book for assistance. He got some help but a gloomy prediction: "New systems have little chance of success," he was told, "and new systems by unknown players have none at all." This forecast proved about as prescient as Culbertson's famous rejection of the Blackwood convention. Within a decade, Wei's system named Precision, spread around the world and was the subject of many books. It probably has more adherents than all other strong-club methods combined, and has been used in every world championship from 1969 on. In some world events the number of strong-club partnerships have outnumbered those using natural methods.

The basic framework of Precision is:

(1) One club: almost any hand with 16-plus points. (Some prefer 17-plus.) The one-diamond response is negative. Minimum suit responses show at least a five-card suit and are (in most versions) game-forcing.

(2) One diamond: in most versions, a catch-all for minimum openings unsuitable for other actions. (The hand contains perhaps as few as two diamonds.)

(3) One heart and one spade: five-card suits, 11-15 points, and continuations similar to the modern style described elsewhere in this book.

(4) One notrump: 13-15 (or 12-15 in the original version). Many experts now prefer a 14-16 range, using one diamond followed by one notrump to show 11-13.

(5) Two clubs: club length, usually six or more, and 11-15 points. A response of two diamonds is strong and artificial, asking for a further description.

(6) Two diamonds: A three-suiter short in diamonds. Exactly four cards in one major with three or four in the other, a singleton or void in diamonds, and four or five clubs. A two-notrump response asks for clarification.

(7) Other openings are standard, although two notrump can be used to show a moderate hand with length in both minor suits.

HYPERMODERN DEVELOPMENTS

A strong-club method is often used with relay structures, in which one hand makes minimum bids to request more information and the other hand describes itself. At the end of the auction one hand is fully portrayed, often in great detail, while the other, totally undescribed, makes a final decision for the partnership. The use of relays is restricted by the American Contract Bridge League.

The ACBL totally bars some weird methods used by a handful of experts in other parts of the world. These all involve taking the principle of starting low even further by giving an original pass a special meaning. It may show a strong hand (the equivalent of a strong-club opening bid, or any hand with at least 13 high-card points), or a hand of moderate strength (the equivalent of a Precision one-diamond opening). It follows that if a pass promises positive values, very weak hands must be opened, and such openings are called Ferts—they "fertilize" an unusual auction.

These Funny Pass (or Weak Opening) systems present their opponents with unfamiliar problems. (For example, how do you double a pass to show a good hand?) As a consequence, they tend to be frowned upon by the game's governing bodies, except in games restricted to players at the highest levels. Everybody strives to be as effective as possible at the bridge table; if strange methods work better than more traditional ones, so be it. But the methods should not be effective just because of the opponents' lack of familiarity. Where these systems are permitted, the opponents need to be given full details of the systems well in advance so that they may prepare their defenses. But, at the club level, bidding should be kept as simple as possible; near-beginners prefer to play against pairs using the same methods they employ for greater comfort.

The juggling necessary to balance the aims of experts and the masses requires the skill of circus performers.

♠
♡
7
◊
♣

The Flannery Two-Diamond Opening Bid

One type of hand bridge players have found difficult to bid contains four spades, five hearts, and minimum opening-bid values. For example, West holds

♠ A Q 10 6   ♡ K Q 8 5 3   ◊ K 7   ♣ 9 7

West cannot open the bidding with one heart and rebid two spades over North's two-of-a-minor response because that would be a reverse showing extra values. It is equally problematical if partner makes a forcing one-notrump response (see page 122). Again, two spades would promise reversing values, and a two-heart rebid would normally indicate at least a six-card suit. Also, suppose these are the two hands:

♠ A Q 10 6	♠ K 4 2
♡ K Q 8 5 3	♡ 6 2
◊ K 7	◊ A Q J 6 3 2
♣ 9 7	♣ 8 4

On this hand the only plausible game for East-West is four spades. Yet most pairs would fail to reach this spot.

One solution to this problem is the Flannery two-diamond opening bid, devised by William Flannery. An opening bid of two diamonds shows a hand of 11 to 15 points with four spades and five hearts. (A few players permit a six-card heart suit.)

The responder knows the exact distribution of opener's major suits and can often place the final contract immediately. Otherwise he can invite game by jumping to three of the major he prefers, or can ask for further information about the opener's distribution and strength by bidding two notrump. A response of three clubs is usually treated as a sign-off, but three diamonds is a game-try because the responder could pass with a weak hand and a long diamond suit. Jumps to four clubs and four diamonds by the responder are normally treated as transfer bids to hearts and spades, respectively.

Over the forcing two-notrump response, the opener's usual rebids are:

3♣: 4-5-1-3 shape
3♢: 4-5-3-1
3♡: 4-5-2-2 and a minimum: 11–13 points
3♠: 4-5-2-2 and a maximum: 14–15 points
3NT: 4-5-2-2, a maximum and a lot of points in the minors
4♣: 4-5-0-4
4♢: 4-5-4-0

The Flannery convention was almost too good for the following hand:

♠ A 9 6 3	♠ K 8 7 5 4 2
♡ A 10 8 5 3	♡ K 6
♢ 4	♢ A 9 5
♣ A 7 4	♣ K Q

These cards were dealt in the Spingold Teams at the 1971 Summer Nationals in Chicago. At one table, the defending champions, a team of young New York experts, used Flannery, which seemed ideally suited for this hand, to reach the fine contract of seven spades. The auction was:

West	East
2♦	2NT
3♣	4NT
5♠	7♠
Pass	

Two notrump asked for clarification; three clubs showed 4-5-1-3 distribution; four notrump was Blackwood; and five spades showed three aces.

Assuming no side suit could be ruffed at trick one, this contract depended only on a 2-1 trump break: better than a 77 percent grand slam. Unfortunately for the defending champions, the spades broke 3-0 and the contract failed.

At the other table, their opponents were not using Flannery and had little chance to reach the grand slam; in fact they bid conservatively to only four spades, reaching an inferior contract but gaining eleven IMPs (International Match Points). Had they bid the virtually assured small slam, they would have collected fourteen IMPs.

In spite of the loss on this deal, the defending Spingold champions, playing Precision Club, won the match by just one IMP, and went on to retain their title.

8 ♠ ♡ Trump Raises ◇ ♣

Until about thirty years ago Standard bidders had almost no way of making an immediate forcing raise of partner's opening bid of one in a suit except by bidding three of the suit. This standard response revealed that responder's hand was worth about 13 to 15 points, but did little to clarify his distribution or the texture of his trump holding.

Similarly, when many experts adopted limit jump raises as part of their methods, some substituted three notrump as their forcing raise of opener's suit, which gave no better description of the responding hand than did standard methods. Other experts who adopted limit raises elected not to have any immediate forcing trump raise but to manage such hands by indirect bidding.

After the Italian Blue Team started winning one world championship after another and enjoyed superior results on their slam decisions, American bridge writers began to take a closer and more critical look at the slam bidding of the American experts. One of the principal places needing improvement was trump raises.

To facilitate good slam bidding a partnership needs to be able to fix the trump suit in a way which both forces game and suggests slam interest; to determine whether or not the trump suit is reasonably solid; a way to ferret out slams that depend more on "fit" than on raw power—and, conversely, a way to discover when too much of the partnership's power is wasted.

With these goals in mind, a variety of conventions have been developed which at once establish the trump suit and either give or solicit additional specific information. Among these, the most widely used are the Swiss convention, the Jacoby two-notrump response, and splinter bids.

The first of these retains popularity primarily in England. It features a jump to four clubs or four diamonds over an opening bid of one of a major. Because it uses up so much space, it makes the auction difficult to resolve accurately, and so has almost no adherents here in the United States.

THE JACOBY TWO-NOTRUMP RESPONSE

This convention was devised by Oswald Jacoby for use in conjunction with limit raises, and is designed to create a game-forcing situation while requiring the opening bidder to clarify his distribution and/or strength.

After an opening bid of one of a major suit, a response of two notrump is a forcing raise, unlimited in strength but usually denying a singleton (since if he held one the responder would normally make a splinter bid—see below). Opener shows his distribution as follows: with a singleton (or perhaps a void), he bids that suit at the three-level; with no short suit, opener shows the strength of his hand by bidding his suit at the four-level with a minimum and no slam interest, or at the three-level to show strong slam interest, usually with at least 16 points; or bids three notrump to indicate a sound minimum opening bid, some 14 or 15 points.

There are two schools of thought about a jump to four of a new suit over the Jacoby two-notrump. In its original form, this showed a void in the bid suit. However, the chances of holding a void are slim, and now a lot of experts play that this jump shows an additional concentrated five-card or longer suit, the second one usually being headed by at least two of the top three honors.

Here is a hand cited by James Jacoby as an example of the effectiveness of this convention:

♠ A	♠ 8 4 2
♡ A 6 4 3 2	♡ K Q 10 8 5
◇ K 7 5 2	◇ A Q 6
♣ K 5 4	♣ A 6

West	East
1♡	2NT
3♠	4NT
5♡	5NT
6♡	7♡
Pass	

West shows a singleton (or void) in spades with his three-spade rebid. Now it is safe for East to use Blackwood, since he knows the partnership does not have two quick spade losers. West's five-heart response reveals that his singleton spade is the ace. Finally, East learns about the two minor-suit kings and can count thirteen tricks. He bids a virtually assured grand slam in a hand on which many pairs would not even reach six.

Here is a second example:

Dlr: East
Vul: None

	♠ A 5
	♡ A 10 9 5 2
	◇ K 3 2
	♣ J 8 3

♠ K Q 7 4 2		♠ J 10 9 6 3
♡ Q 6		♡ K
◇ 9 6		◇ J 10 7 4
♣ 10 5 4 2		♣ Q 9 7

	♠ 8
	♡ J 8 7 4 3
	◇ A Q 8 5
	♣ A K 6

West	North	East	South
		Pass	1♡
Pass	2NT	Pass	3♠
Pass	4◇	Pass	4NT
Pass	5♡	Pass	5NT
Pass	6◇	Pass	6♡
Pass	Pass	Pass	

When South indicated a singleton spade, North had an awkward bid. To sign off in four hearts would make South think there was duplication in spades. So North cue-bid a second-round control in diamonds, hoping his partner would use Blackwood before committing the partnership to a slam. South did use the ace-asking convention, and moved on to the slam over the two-ace reply. He knew that North had cue-bid a king—it could not be a void or a singleton because, as mentioned above, North would have made a splinter bid, instead of using the Jacoby two-notrump convention. North would do that only with a hand suitable for a slam, so South told his partner they had all the aces and seven was still a possibility. However, when North admitted to holding only one king, South knew that seven hearts would at best depend on the trump finesse, so he settled in six hearts.

As it turned out, even six hearts was in jeopardy. South won the opening spade lead, ruffed dummy's other spade in his hand, and led a trump toward the North hand, inserting the nine when West played low—a safety-play in case West held all three outstanding hearts.

South won East's diamond return in hand and drew the last trump. Now he would make his slam if the diamonds broke 3-3, or if the queen of clubs were singleton or doubleton or lay in the hand that was long in diamonds.

South began running his trumps, reaching this position:

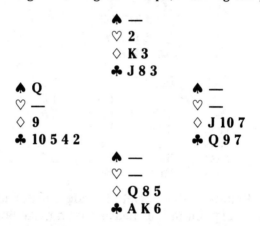

On the lead of dummy's last heart, East was squeezed. Whatever he discarded, South would throw a club, cash the ace and king of clubs and, if the queen had not dropped, try to run the diamonds.

To be honest, though, South was a little lucky. A better play is to cash the ace of hearts at trick two, taking the slight risk that West would hold all three trumps. When the suit does break, he ruffs dummy's losing spade, cashes the ace of clubs, in case the queen is singleton, and then plays on diamonds. If the suit divides 3-3, dummy's club loser can be discarded. However, if they are 4-2, declarer needs to find the defender holding the trump winner with either a singleton club or the queen. Here, the contract goes down. Some would say that one should not argue with success.

SPLINTER BIDS

As with the Jacoby two-notrump response, splinter bids reflect the fact that one key to good slam bidding is the ability to check for wasted strength. Splinter bids provide somewhat greater flexibility than the Jacoby two-notrump response because that is one-way: the responder unearths the opener's shortage, but the opener learns nothing about the responder's hand. Splinter bids allow the responder to show his side-suit singleton (or void), either immediately or on a subsequent round of the bidding, and allow the opener to show support for the responder's suit while indicating his singleton (or void).

A splinter bid is an *unusual* jump, usually a double jump, into a new suit. It guarantees a good fit for partner's suit and strength equivalent to raising the bidding to that level, and shows a singleton or void in that suit (but *a priori* it is almost ten times as likely that one will have been dealt a singleton rather than a void).

For example, if the opener bids one spade, the responder would jump to four clubs with

♠ K Q 8 5   ♡ Q 7 4 3   ◇ A J 6 2   ♣ 5

The bid shows four-card or longer spade support, a singleton (or void) in clubs, and the values for a raise to game.

A splinter bid was used on the following hand:

Dlr: South   ♠ A K 9 7 3
Vul: N-S   ♡ K 8 5
              ◊ 10
              ♣ K 7 5 2

♠ 10 8   ♠ J
♡ J 9 7 6 3   ♡ Q 10 4 2
◊ Q 7 2   ◊ 9 5 4 3
♣ Q 10 4   ♣ A 9 8 6

              ♠ Q 6 5 4 2
              ♡ A
              ◊ A K J 8 6
              ♣ J 3

West	North	East	South
			1♠
Pass	4◊	Pass	4♡
Pass	4NT	Pass	5♡
Pass	6♠	Pass	Pass
Pass			

South knew from North's four-diamond splinter bid that the partnership had some duplication of values; however, South's distribution was good enough to warrant a slam-try. North now took control, using Blackwood and bidding the slam.

Six spades would have been much safer if played from the North position, but there was no way this could be arranged. As it was, if West led a club, South would have to guess whether West was leading from the ace or from the queen in order to make his contract. With any other lead South could discard a club from his hand on dummy's king of hearts. If trumps broke 2-1, he could simply cross-ruff for twelve tricks. If trumps broke 3-0, the contract would be made if the diamonds were 4-3, or if the queen fell singleton or doubleton, or if the ace of clubs were in the West hand.

Until clarified, the unusual jump shows a singleton. But if on the next round the splinter bidder rebids the suit in which he has jumped, he promises a void. For example:

North	South
1♠	4♣
4♡	5♣

South's five-club bid shows a void. Perhaps he holds

♠ K Q 6 5   ♡ K 7 6 5   ◇ A 6 5 4 3   ♣ —

It is just possible that this sequence would be used when holding a singleton ace, but it is advisable to avoid making splinter bids when holding a singleton ace. Partner, with say K-Q-x, will think there is bad duplication when in fact there are three sure tricks in the suit.

Splinter bids may be used by both the opener and responder at a later round of the bidding. Again, the splinter bid is an *unusual* jump guaranteeing a fit for partner's last-bid suit and showing a singleton (or void) in the suit in which the jump is made. For example:

North	South
1♠	2◇
4♣	

A three-club rebid by North would be natural and forcing. Therefore, opener's four-club bid is an unusual jump, showing support for diamonds, extra values, and a singleton (or void) in clubs. Perhaps a hand such as

♠ A J 8 7 4   ♡ A K 3   ◇ K Q 10 8   ♣ 6

In the following auction, responder's jump shows support for hearts, partner's last-bid suit, rather than for spades:

North	South
1♠	2◇
2♡	4♣

If you and your partner are considering adopting splinter bids, there is one family of auctions that you must discuss. Is South's bid in these sequences a splinter bid or preemptive?

North	South
1♡	3♠
1♠	4♡
1♣	3♡

Employing the splinter interpretation "feels" right.

THE THREE-NOTRUMP RESPONSE

Traditionally, a three-notrump response to an opening bid of one heart or one spade showed a flat hand with 16-18 points. Such hands, however, can be bid in other ways, and the jump to three notrump can be used more profitably as a forcing raise with a balanced hand. This bid is useful in narrowing the definition of the Jacoby two-notrump response, and essential if that convention is not being used.

There are two schools of thought about the differences between the three-notrump and Jacoby two-notrump raises. One uses it to show four-card support and 12-15 points; the Jacoby two notrump is used for stronger hands, and with three trumps the reply is a forcing one notrump followed by a jump to game in the major. The second uses it to distinguish between three- and four-card support in all balanced hands; two notrump is bid with four, three notrump with three. In these partnerships, two notrump followed by a game bid indicates a minimum forcing raise, and cue-bids show extra values and alsm interest; a one-notrump reply followed by a jump to game shows the values for a limit raise, but one that has been improved by opener's second bid.

INVERTED MINOR-SUIT RAISES

The general acceptance by American experts of the limit-raise concept has caused one problem: What do you do when partner opens one of a minor and you, the responder, have the equivalent of a forcing raise? If you have a singleton or void, of course, you can make a splinter bid, but without that possibility, what do you do? You could use two notrump in the same way as over one of a major, but this will give you other, bigger headaches.

The best answer is to adopt inverted minor-suit raises. In this method, which is rapidly gaining popularity, a jump raise of one club to three clubs or one diamond to three diamonds is preemptive, showing length in the trump suit but a weak hand in high cards: usually eight points or less. But a single raise of one club to two clubs or one diamond to two diamonds shows a good fit for partner's minor, denies holding four or more cards in a major, indicates ten or more points, and is forcing.

If partner opens one diamond, you would bid three diamonds holding something like

♠ 8   ♡ Q 8 4   ◇ K J 8 6 2   ♣ J 7 5 4

but bid a quiet two diamonds with

♠ Q 6   ♡ A 10 8   ◇ K 9 5 4 3   ♣ K 8 6

Playing the strong notrump, an inverted minor-suit raise is usually played as forcing to two notrump or three of the agreed minor. Opener's immediate rebid of two notrump shows a balanced minimum, often with only three cards in the bid minor. An immediate raise to three of the agreed suit is similarly limited but suggests a genuine suit.

With interest in game, the prime concern is to try to reach three notrump when all suits are stopped. As a consequence, the opener bids suits in ascending order in which he has a stopper. If an unstopped suit is uncovered, the bidding may stop below game in the agreed minor suit.

Here is a sample auction:

♠ J 10 3	♠ 4 2
♡ K 8 5	♡ A Q 4
◇ Q 6	◇ A K 3
♣ A K 10 7 6	♣ Q 9 8 5 4

West	East
1♣	2♣
3♣	3◇
3♡	5♣
Pass	

East's two-club bid showed a good fit, at least ten points and, if holding extra values, denied a singleton. West's three-club rebid warned of a minimum opener but promised genuine clubs. East indicated a diamond stopper, and West showed his heart card. Now East knew that there was no spade stopper as West would have bid three notrump, not three hearts, with stoppers in both major suits. However, he had too much to stay out of game, knowing that the hands were fitting well.

At the other table in a team-of-four match in New York, justice was done when the East-West pair bid to three notrump and lost the first five tricks in spades.

PASSED-HAND RAISES

When the responder is a passed hand, he must bear in mind that the opener might not have full high-card values, especially if he started the proceedings in the third seat. As a consequence, the late Douglas Drury invented the convention that bears his name.

Drury

This is an artificial bid of two clubs opposite a third- or fourth-position opening bid of one spade or one heart. It shows a maximum pass and at least three-card support for

the opener's suit. It asks the opener to describe his hand
further.

In its original form, the opener rebid two diamonds to
warn of a minimum or subminimum opening bid. However,
the responder could not pass, as the bid could prove to be
natural, showing a sound opening bid, not enough values to
leap directly to game, and a diamond side suit. If the opener
rebid his major, he showed a genuine opening, but nothing
extra. Other bids were natural game-tries showing an interest in game, but not enough to bid four hearts or four spades
immediately.

Most pairs today play Reverse Drury. In this form, two of
the opener's major is the weakest rebid. This has two clear
advantages: it takes up more bidding space, making it harder
for the opponents to compete, and it stops them from being
able to make a double of the conventional two-diamond
rebid. Now, if the opener has a genuine opener but no real
game interest unless a particularly good fit is found, he
rebids two diamonds.

One final refinement that a lot of pairs add to Drury is a
rebid of two notrump by either player. This asks for a singleton, and came up on the following deal:

Dlr: North
Vul: None

         ♠ 9 8 7 6
         ♡ A 4 3 2
         ◇ A Q 2
         ♣ J 2

♠ 5 4   ♠ 3 2
♡ K Q J 10 9   ♡ 8 7 6
◇ 8 7 6   ◇ K J 10 9
♣ Q 6 5   ♣ 10 9 8 7

         ♠ A K Q J 10
         ♡ 5
         ◇ 5 4 3
         ♣ A K 4 3

West	North	East	South
	Pass	Pass	1♠
Pass	2♣	Pass	2NT
Pass	3♠	Pass	4♣
Pass	4◇	Pass	4NT
Pass	5♡	Pass	6♠
Pass	Pass	Pass	

After North used Drury, South asked for a singleton. He learned the responder did not have one, but liked his hand anyway (with a minimum he would have jumped to game). The opener cue-bid with four clubs, received a cue-bid in return, used Blackwood, and bid the ambitious slam.

West led the king of hearts, and the declarer failed to give himself the best chance. He drew trumps in two rounds and took the diamond finesse. When this lost, he had an unavoidable second diamond loser.

A more astute player would have given himself two chances instead of one. After winning the opening lead and playing a trump to hand, he leads a club toward the jack. If West has the queen and rises with it, there are two discards for dummy's losing diamonds. If West plays low, there is one discard, and declarer can try the diamond finesse for an ovetrick. However, if East holds the queen of clubs, declarer needs the diamond finesse to succeed.

Jump Shift by a Passed Hand

What does a jump shift by a passed hand show? In the old days, it indicated a maximum pass, but, apart from the fact that this uses up bidding space unnecessarily, this interpretation has become obsolete since the advent of weak two-bids. It is logical that the jump is inspired by a fit for the opener's suit, and there are two logical meanings: fit-showing or splinter-showing. In other words, the responder has a good fit for the opener's suit and either is showing his own second suit or is indicating a singleton (or void). It is not obvious which is the better approach; it depends on the hand the responder is holding at the time. Assuming a one-spade opening, with something like

♠ K J 7 6   ♡ 4 3   ◇ A Q 10 8 7   ♣ 8 2

he would like to make a fit-showing jump to three diamonds to describe the two-suited maximum pass. However, with a hand like

♠ K Q 5 4   ♡ A 4 3 2   ◇ 2   ♣ J 9 7 6

he would prefer to be able to jump to three diamonds to show the singleton.

If you're playing Drury and its singleton-asking refinement, there seems to be no need to employ the splinter jump over a major-suit opening bid, and so it is preferable to use the fit-showing jumps. And for consistency, thus reducing the memory strain, it is wise to use the same style opposite a minor-suit opening.

The fit-showing jump shows at least nine cards in two suits, the one bid by the opener and the one bid by the responder, and most of the responder's points should be in those two suits. Normally, the responder will have four-card trump support and his own five-card suit, but sometimes it will be the other way round. If the opener bids one heart in the third or fourth position, the responder would jump to three diamonds holding either of these hands:

	1.		2.	
	♠ 3 2		♠ 8 7 6	
	♡ A Q 3 2		♡ K J 5 4 3	
	◇ K J 7 6 5		◇ K Q J 4	
	♣ 3 2		♣ 2	

That seems fine, but what about jumps to two notrump and three clubs? In the latter case, because there is no weak two-bid available in clubs, this jump does indicate a maximum pass with a respectable six-card club suit. Perhaps

♠ 4 3   ♡ K 6   ◇ J 10 7   ♣ A Q 10 8 7 6

That leaves two notrump available as a *fit-showing jump in clubs*. Over a one-spade opening bid, a possible hand for a jump to two notrump is

♠ A J 7 6   ♡ 4   ◇ 8 4 3   ♣ K Q 10 6 2

The following hand features the use of a fit-showing jump; and the correct (and winning) line of play was overlooked by several good players.

Dlr: North
Vul: E-W

	♠ K Q 4 3 2	
	♡ A 4	
	◇ Q 4 3 2	
	♣ 3 2	
♠ 8 7 6		♠ A J 10 9
♡ Q J 10 9 8		♡ K 7 6 5
◇ 5		◇ 8 7 6
♣ Q 10 9 8		♣ 7 6
	♠ 5	
	♡ 3 2	
	◇ A K J 10 9	
	♣ A K J 5 4	

West	North	East	South
	Pass	Pass	1 ◇
Pass	2 ♠	Pass	3 ♣
Pass	3 ◇	Pass	4 ♣
Pass	5 ◇	Pass	Pass
Pass			

Six diamonds is not a bad contract, but if only game has been reached, declarer should try to play as safely as possible to make his contract, not grieve about a potential missed slam (except, perhaps, in a matchpointed pair event).

West leads the queen of hearts, leaving declarer with two top losers and a problem in the club suit, there being a risk that East will overruff the dummy if holding only a doubleton club. The right play represents a blind spot for many players. Declarer should win the first trick with the ace of hearts, cash the ace and king of clubs, and lead a third club, *discarding dummy's heart loser.* This trades one loser for another, and there is no risk dummy will be overruffed in hearts.

Let us assume that West returns a heart. Dummy ruffs, a trump is played to hand, and a club is ruffed with the queen of diamonds. At that point, declarer draws trumps, concedes a trick to the ace of spades, and claims his contract.

♠
♡
9 # The Blackwood Convention
◇
♣

In the 1940s not many top-ranked players had a good word to say for the Blackwood convention.

Today virtually every expert uses Blackwood, and as for the rank and file of bridge players, they have always doted on it. The Blackwood convention has achieved a worldwide following exceeded only by that for the take-out double.

The take-out double dates from 1915 and its authorship, as noted earlier, has been widely disputed. This is not an unusual state of affairs in bidding conventions. Several of the most popular of them have been independently worked out by different players in different parts of the world.

The authorship of the Blackwood convention has never been in doubt. Easley Blackwood, of Indianapolis, Indiana, solely invented it in 1933 and first published it in 1934. He endured several years in which his convention was either ignored or scorned, and then he saw it rapidly capture favor throughout the world. Innumerable variations, some of them quite complicated, have been built on the original Blackwood idea.

The Blackwood principle is simple. When a player wishes to know how many aces his partner has, he bids four notrump. His partner must respond five clubs with no ace, five diamonds with one ace, five hearts with two aces, five spades with three aces. Originally a response of five notrump was used to show all four aces, but later Blackwood adopted the clever device of using the five-club response to show either no ace or all four aces. This is a workable solution, because it should always be clear from the previous bidding whether a player may have an aceless hand. However, before moving on, let it be noted that this is not always the case! In the 1971 World Championship, the French team had already qualified for the final. In the last qualifying round, two players who had never played together before went into action. The bidding of one hand started like this:

North	South
	1 ♣
1 ◇	1 ♡
3 ♡	4NT
5 ♣	

North intended his three-heart bid as a mere invitation, but South thought it was strong and forcing. Therefore, when South, who was looking at an aceless hand, heard his partner's five-club response to Blackwood, he assumed North had four aces when in fact he held none. South jumped to seven hearts, which the opponents rather unsportingly doubled.

Moving on, a later bid of five notrump by the player who first bid four notrump announces that all the aces are held and that a grand slam is a possibility. In pristine style, partner shows the number of kings he holds in identical fashion: six clubs shows no king or all four kings, six diamonds indicates one king, six hearts denotes two kings, and six spades reveals three kings. (Some players use six notrump to guarantee all four kings, not six clubs, and there is a good case for a player who holds all the kings in this auction to jump to seven of the agreed suit; how many more kings can one hold? Similarly, if the responder holds a long solid suit he can jump to a grand slam without showing his kings.)

Nowadays, many pairs play that partner shows *specific* kings, bidding the lowest-ranking suit in which he holds a king. This method works well when the Blackwood bidder needs to know about a particular king.

The popularity of Blackwood's slam method is due largely to its simplicity, but there is nothing very simple about the experts' application of it. "We use Blackwood," they explain, "when the bidding makes it obvious that four notrump means Blackwood and not something else." Unfortunately, what is obvious to an expert may not be obvious to the average player. On occasion it may not even be very obvious to the expert's partner, and the wrong contract is reached.

A slam usually results from the combination of two strong hands, but there are two distinct types of strong hand:

♠ A J 4	♠ 5
♡ A 3	♡ K Q 10 8 7 6 4
◇ A 7 6 3	◇ K Q 8 5
♣ A Q 8 2	♣ 3

West's hand is strong because it has a lot of high-card points and those four aces, but alone it could guarantee no contract whatsoever. Opposite a Yarborough it might conceivably win only four tricks.

East's hand is strong because it will win a lot of tricks with hearts as trumps, but its ability to make a game or slam depends on how many aces West holds.

It is difficult, in the opening bids and responses, to differentiate between a hand that has its strength primarily in high cards and a hand that has little in high cards but much in playing strength. Since the essential requirement for any slam is the ability to win twelve or more tricks, it is better for the hand with the playing strength (such as East's above) to become the master hand in slam bidding. This is the hand whose four notrump must be construed as Blackwood; this is the hand that should make the decision.

With the two hands shown above, it is patently unproductive for West to use a Blackwood four-notrump bid. West, having all four aces, knows what his partner's response will be: five clubs. West still will have no useful information on which to base a slam decision.

Even if West, seeing all four aces in his own hand, could elicit a response telling him that East had all four kings, West still could not confidently bid a slam. East could have such a hand as

♠ K 5   ♡ K J 8 7 4   ◇ K 8 5   ♣ K 4 3

—and there might be little or no play for twelve tricks.

It is entirely different when, on the hand previously shown, East is permitted to bid four notrump and find out about his partner's aces. The bidding might go:

West	East
1♣	1♡
2NT	3◇
4◇	4NT
5♣	

The five-club bid shows all four aces. Holding 1-7-4-1 distribution, East can bid seven hearts (or seven notrump) with this information. A 3-2 diamond break will give him his contract easily, and even against a 4-1 diamond break he has several plays for the grand slam, making the prospect better than the 2-to-1 chance to win that is the rule-of-thumb requirement for grand slam bids.

The best application of the Blackwood convention therefore requires the player whose hand has good high-card strength but lots of "holes" in it to refrain from bidding four notrump himself and also to bid so as to make it easy for his partner to bid four notrump. Then if his partner has an appropriate hand for the Blackwood bid, the way to a slam will be eased.

The bidding usually makes it clear when a hand has a solid, trick-winning pattern and needs only information about high cards. For example:

Dlr: South
Vul: None

	♠ Q J 7 6 2	
	♡ A 6 4 3	
	◇ A 10	
	♣ 7 5	
♠ 10 8 5 4		♠ K 9 3
♡ —		♡ J 10 8 7
◇ 8 6 5 3		◇ 9 2
♣ Q J 9 3 2		♣ K 10 6 4
	♠ A	
	♡ K Q 9 5 2	
	◇ K Q J 7 4	
	♣ A 8	

West	North	East	South
			1♡
Pass	1♠	Pass	3◇
Pass	4♡	Pass	4NT
Pass	5♡	Pass	7♡
Pass	Pass	Pass	

South's four notrump had to be a slam-try; he would have had no other reason to disturb a good game contract. And he could not be trying to give information by bidding four notrump, since he had a two-suiter and the strong trump suit, thus leaving him in the ideal position to make the final decision. Therefore his four notrump had to be Blackwood, and North responded accordingly.

The grand slam was easy to bid. North had shown eight cards, at least, in spades and hearts, by bidding the former and giving a jump raise in the latter. He could have no more than five cards in diamonds and clubs, and South's diamond suit and ace of clubs were more than enough to take care of those. North had shown the other two aces by his five-heart response.

The hand required some judgment in playing. West opened the queen of clubs and South won. Since South's technique was good, he first got the ace of spades out of the way, then led a low heart to dummy's ace.

This is the standard method of handling a suit containing nine combined cards with the king-queen-nine opposite the ace (or the equivalent). The single honor must be played first to retain a finessing position in case the outstanding trumps break 4-0.

The 4-0 break seldom occurs, but this time South was unlucky enough to get it. Now he had to plan so that he could lead hearts twice through East, so as to pick up the jack and ten, and also get rid of the losing club either from his own hand or from dummy.

There were two ways in which South might get a club discard and still have enough entries to finesse trumps twice through East.

South could play for East to have the king of spades, and also to have two diamonds. The queen of spades would be led from dummy, and if East held the king and covered, South would trump. Then South would lead a low diamond to dummy's ace, discard his club on the spade jack, lead a heart, and capture East's ten of hearts with the queen. Another low diamond lead would put dummy in again with the ten of diamonds, and a final heart lead from dummy would give South an indicated finesse and the remaining tricks.

Or South could play for East to have at least three diamonds. In this case, after winning with the ace of hearts South would immediately lead a heart through East, overtaking the ten of hearts with the queen. Three high diamonds would be cashed, dummy's club being discarded on the third. If East followed to this third diamond, South would trump his club in dummy and take a final heart finesse.

The odds were against the success of either plan, but they were the only two available and South had to try one of them. Luckily for South, he chose to play East for the king of spades and that line of play succeeded where the other would have failed. *A priori,* South's 50 percent finesse was wrong, for East will have at least three diamonds about two-thirds of the time. But the known heart distribution greatly increased the chance that West would have diamond length.

But since the 4-0 trump break will not occur once in ten times, the grand slam contract was an excellent one.

WHEN BLACKWOOD IS NOT "OBVIOUS"

Blackwood originally established two principles for his slam convention:

1. Provided either partner has previously bid any suit, a bid of four notrump is always conventional, calling for an ace-showing response.

2. The player who bids four notrump takes complete charge of the bidding. His partner must respond as directed and can make no decision as to the final contract.

Neither principle is wholly accepted by expert players, for reasons that may be rooted in the psychology of the bridge expert, who wishes to make his own interpretation of bids and to retain freedom of action in all circumstances.

When four notrump is bid as a direct raise of partner's notrump bid, nearly all experts treat it as a natural bid and not as Blackwood, even if a suit has been bid previously.

West	North	East	South
	1 ◊	Pass	1 ♠
Pass	2NT	Pass	4NT

South is deemed to have a balanced hand, also of the notrump type, that makes a slam seem possible but that does not permit a spade rebid, a diamond raise, or the showing of a second suit. Such a hand might be:

♠ K Q 9 5　♡ A J 6　◇ J 7　♣ Q 8 7 3

North is not expected to show his aces in response. He may decide to go to a slam if his hand is suitable, perhaps with a good diamond suit plus outside controls. Maybe:

♠ A 8 4　♡ K 4　◇ A K Q 9 8　♣ K 4 2

Consider also this sequence:

West	North	East	South
	1♠	Pass	2♡
Pass	3◇	Pass	3NT
Pass	4◇	Pass	4NT

North has made a slam-try with his bid of four diamonds. However, South's bid of four notrump would not be treated as Blackwood by most experts; it would be expressing no interest in a slam, but warning North that most of his high cards reside in hearts and clubs. A possible hand for South would be:

♠ 4 3　♡ A Q J 6 5　◇ 5 4　♣ K Q J 8

BLACKWOOD AND VOID SUITS

The original Blackwood convention was often criticized because it shut out information about void suits, which can be even more valuable than aces. Blackwood devised a solution to this problem, as shown in the following deal:

Dlr: South   ♠ —
Vul: None   ♡ K J 8 6 3
                      ◇ A 9 4 2
                      ♣ K 10 6 3

♠ Q J 10 9 5 3   ♠ A 6 4 2
♡ 4   ♡ 10
◇ J 8   ◇ 10 7 5 3
♣ Q 9 8 2   ♣ J 7 5 4

                      ♠ K 8 7
                      ♡ A Q 9 7 5 2
                      ◇ K Q 6
                      ♣ A

West	North	East	South
			1♡
1♠	3♠	Dble	4NT
Pass	6◇	Pass	7♡
Pass	Pass	Pass	

North's three spades was a splinter bid showing a singleton or void in spades, heart fit, and the values for at least game. His subsequent response to the Blackwood four notrump bid was his natural response, but one level higher, to show that in addition to his ace or aces, he had a void; since a response of five diamonds would show one ace, six diamonds indicated one ace plus a (spade) void. This made it easy for South to bid seven hearts.

There are other schemes for showing voids. A sensible one is to respond with five notrump to show two aces and a void, jump to six of the void suit if it is below the agreed trump suit to indicate one ace and the void, and to jump to six of the agreed suit to promise one ace and a void in a higher-ranking suit.

The opportunity for use of this convention arose when the following deal was played:

Dlr: South   ♠ —
Vul: E-W   ♡ J 10 9 7 5
              ♦ A J 3 2
              ♣ Q J 10 4

♠ K J 9 5 3		♠ A 10 7 6
♡ 8		♡ 4 3
♦ Q 8 6 5		♦ K 10 7 4
♣ 9 6 3		♣ 7 5 2

          ♠ Q 8 4 2
          ♡ A K Q 6 2
          ♦ 9
          ♣ A K 8

West	North	East	South
			1♡
Pass	3♠	Pass	4NT
Pass	6♡	Pass	7♡
Pass	Pass	Pass	

Over North's three-spade splinter bid showing a raise to four hearts (or more) with a singleton or void in spades, it was automatic for South to use Blackwood. North was then able to guarantee one ace and a higher-ranking void with the jump to six hearts, leaving South with an easy raise to the grand slam.

GERBER

As a raise of a one- or two-notrump opening bid to four notrump is quantitative, an alternative method is needed to ask for aces. The solution was devised in 1937 by the late Johnny Gerber of Houston; the bid that asks for aces is four clubs.

Some players only treat a four-club bid as Gerber when it is a direct response to an opening notrump bid. Others would allow any jump from one or two notrump to four clubs. For example:

West	North	East	South
	1 ◇	Pass	1 ♡
Pass	2NT	Pass	4 ♣

The responses are similar to those over a Blackwood four-notrump bid, but one step higher:

> 4 ◇ : no ace or all four aces
> 4 ♡ : one ace
> 4 ♠ : two aces
> 4NT: three aces

Over the response, a continuation of five clubs guarantees all the aces are held and asks for kings.

Gerber was used on the following deal, from a pair event, with an unusual purpose and with unusual effect.

Dlr: East
Vul: Both

♠ A Q J 10 7 6 3
♡ 7
◇ 6 2
♣ J 7 6

♠ 5
♡ K 8 5 4 3
◇ K Q J 5
♣ 10 8 2

♠ 9 4 2
♡ J 10 9
◇ 9 7 3
♣ A Q 5 4

♠ K 8
♡ A Q 6 2
◇ A 10 8 4
♣ K 9 3

West	North	East	South
		Pass	1NT
Pass	4 ♣	Pass	4 ♠
Pass	Pass	Pass	

The four-club bid was the Gerber convention, and the four-spade response showed two aces; but in this case North's use of Gerber was not the usual slam-try, it was a most unusual attempt to get a good score in a pair tournament in

Europe. The North hand could hardly produce a slam opposite a notrump hand. North intended to pass if South
showed three aces, since four notrump is a more lucrative
contract than four spades; to bid four spades if South
showed one ace; and to pass if South showed two aces.

Of course, if North-South had been using transfer bids
(see page 132), North would have just bid four hearts, transferring the spade declaration into the South hand.

ROMAN KEY CARD BLACKWOOD

This version of Blackwood (usually abbreviated to RKCB) is
played by almost all experts in the United States, and is
slowly gaining popularity in the rest of the world. In theory, it
is an excellent method. The king of the agreed suit is
counted as an ace (or key card), and the responses show
how many of the five "aces" are held. Also, in one situation
the queen of trumps can be shown as well. These are the
responses:

5♣: zero or three of the five key cards
5◇: one or four key cards
5♡: two (or five) key cards but no queen of trumps
5♠: two (or five) key cards and the queen of trumps

Over the five-club and five-diamond responses, the RKCB
bidder may ask for the queen of trumps by bidding the next
suit up (or the one above that if he would be bidding the
agreed suit). In the original method, without the queen of
trumps, the responder bids the next step up, with the queen
of trumps but no side-suit king, he rebids five of the trump
suit (if not the next step) or five notrump. (Some pairs,
though, play that a minimum bid in the trump suit denies the
queen of trumps and other bids promise it. Each partnership
must decide which approach they prefer.) Bidding another
side suit shows the queen of trumps and the king of the bid
suit, at the same time denying the king in a suit skipped.
Finally, bidding six of the agreed suit shows the queen of

trumps and the king of the "one-step" suit that could not be bid as it would have denied the queen of trumps.

West	East
1♣	1♠
3♠	4NT (a)
5◇ (b)	5♡ (c)
5♠ (d), or	
5NT (e), or	
6♣ (f), or	
6◇ (g), or	
6♡ (h)	

(a) Roman Key Card Blackwood
(b) 1 or 4 key cards
(c) Do you have the queen of spades?
(d) No, I do not
(e) Yes, I do, but I have no side-suit king
(f) Yes, and I have the king of clubs, plus, perhaps, a higher-ranking king as well
(g) Yes, and I have the king of diamonds but not the king of clubs
(h) Yes, and I have the king of hearts but not the king of clubs or king of diamonds

Here is an auction that highlights the advantage of being able to show the trump honors and a side-suit king.

♠ K Q 6 5	♠ A 9 8 3 2
♡ 7 2	♡ A K Q J 10
◇ A K	◇ 2
♣ A 7 6 4 3	♣ 9 5

West	East
1♣	1♠
3♠	4NT (a)
5♣ (b)	5◇ (c)
5NT (d)	7NT
Pass	

(a) Roman Key Card Blackwood
(b) 3 key cards (it cannot be zero after the jump raise)
(c) Do you have the queen of spades?
(d) Yes, I do, and I have the king of diamonds (the king in the suit bid by partner when asking for the queen of trumps)

If instead of asking for the queen of trumps, the RKCB bidder continues with five notrump over his partner's response, he announces possession of all five key cards and the queen of trumps, and is expressing an interest in a grand slam. In pristine style, partner is expected to tell how many kings he holds, but, as already discussed, a better method is to cue-bid specific kings. The Blackwood bidder is more likely to want to know where a specific king is located rather than receive quantitative information.

One problem that has always plagued Blackwood concerns the minor suits. Suppose clubs is the agreed suit and you need two aces for a slam. To use Blackwood risks hearing the one-ace five-diamond response, carrying you beyond the level of game. Unless five notrump offers a safe haven, you will be in a slam off two aces. Some pairs use what is called Kickback, jumping to the suit above the agreed suit as RKCB. For example:

West	East
1♣	1◇
3◇	4♡

Four hearts is RKCB in diamonds. This gives the partnership the same amount of space as in normal Blackwood when spades is the agreed suit.

There are other variations on the Key Card theme, sometimes showing key cards in two suits when both have been bid and supported, or excluding one suit from the responses, but they are outside the scope of this book.

A drawback of Key Card Blackwood is that the king of trumps is *not* an ace. Suppose you hold the following hand:

♠ J 10 8 7 5 4   ♡ A K Q J 10   ◇ A   ♣ A

Your partner surprises you by opening with a weak two spades, showing a six-card suit and some 5-10 high-card points. What would you bid?

Using simple Blackwood, you would respond four notrump, proposing to bid seven spades over a one-ace five-diamond reply. Even if the king of spades is missing, it will not matter, as you have a twelve-card fit.

Using RKCB, though, if partner indicates one "ace" it could be only the king of spades (a key card), not the ace, that he holds. It would be embarrassing to bid seven spades off the ace of trumps.

Another, more common problem occurs when there is confusion over the agreed suit. Suppose an auction starts like this:

West	North	East	South
			1♠
Pass	2♣	Pass	3♣
Pass	3♠	Pass	4NT

Which is the agreed suit, spades or clubs? Most pairs would assume spades, the last suit bid; whereas a few pairs make things even more complicated by playing Six Ace RKCB in this position. They count all four aces and both kings of the supported suits as aces. Also, the two key queens can usually be uncovered as well.

Nothing is perfect, but if pairs have discussed these auctions, they should be able to derive considerable benefit from this version of Blackwood.

WHEN THE OPPONENTS INTERFERE

Sometimes when the partnership is trying to find out whether or not to bid a slam the opponents try to muddy the waters by bidding over Blackwood or Gerber. For example:

West	North	East	South
			1♠
3♡ (a)	4NT	5♡	?

(a) Weak

After this intervention by East, how should South show his aces?

Several methods have been devised to deal with this situation, all of them recognizing that the intervention puts at the responder's disposal two additional calls: pass and double. The simplest solution is that if the intervention is *below* five of the agreed suit (as in the above example), double shows no aces, pass indicates one ace, the next step up two aces, and so on "up the line." For obvious reasons, this is known as DOPI. However, if the intervention is five of the agreed suit or *above,* double shows an even number of aces (0, 2, or 4) and pass indicates an odd number (1 or 3). This is known as DEPO.

If RKCB is being employed, it is standard to use DOPI and DEPO key card responses, so that, in the case of DOPI, double says that the responder's bid would have been five clubs without the intervention (showing zero or three key cards), pass indicates he would have bid five diamonds, and so on.

DEPO has the advantages of saving room and allowing the partnership to elect to defend even when the Blackwood responder has two aces. Its drawback is that the responses are somewhat ambiguous, and if expert players of international caliber can err in judging whether a response shows no aces or four, it must be expected that error will often occur in deducing whether partner has no aces or two.

♠

♡

10 The Grand Slam Force

♢

♣

The French bridge magazine *Le Bridgeur,* like nearly all bridge periodicals, conducts regular bidding competitions.

In presenting one set of problems in 1962, *Le Bridgeur* stated that there are only two conventions it assumes everyone uses: the take-out double and the Grand Slam Force.

Le Bridgeur made no mistake, so far as its enlightened readers were concerned. Everyone does use the take-out double. Every expert does use the Grand Slam Force. This makes the Grand Slam Force the Cinderella among bidding conventions.

Ely Culbertson introduced the Grand Slam Force in the first edition of his *Gold Book,* published in 1936, now out of print. At the time, it was greeted with disdain by nearly all experts and it encountered almost universal nonacceptance among the bridge-playing masses. Now the vast majority of experts worldwide use it.

The Grand Slam Force is a free bid of five notrump after a trump suit has been agreed upon. The five-notrump bid requires partner to bid seven if he has two of the three top honors in the agreed trump suit: the A-K, A-Q, or K-Q. Having none of these trump combinations he is supposed to bid six.

The implied accolade given to the Grand Slam Force by *Le Bridgeur* in 1962 was balanced by an error made by that same publication the year before. Then the Grand Slam Force was referred to in the magazine as *le coup Joséphine.* This name attributed invention to Josephine Culbertson (Mrs. Ely Culbertson). Unfortunately, this is not one of the credits due to Mrs. Culbertson.

In preparing his *Gold Book,* Culbertson was assisted by an impressive staff of experts that included (among others) Richard L. Frey, Sam Fry, Theodore Lightner, A. Mitchell Barnes, A. Moyse, Jr., Josephine Culbertson herself, and, incidentally, Albert Morehead.

Every one of these people strongly opposed Culbertson's Grand Slam Force, for which he was solely and obstinately responsible. Mrs. Culbertson was not only among the opponents but also she had the unique advantage of being able to voice her opposition in bed.

However, Culbertson, who was the boss, had seen this deal come up not long before:

Dlr: South
Vul: E-W

        ♠ A K 9 5 3
        ♡ 8 7 3
        ◇ 10 9 8 7 2
        ♣ —

♠ J 10 8   ♠ —
♡ A Q 6 5 2   ♡ K J 10 9 4
◇ 3   ◇ Q 5 4
♣ 10 7 6 2   ♣ J 9 8 4 3

        ♠ Q 7 6 4 2
        ♡ —
        ◇ A K J 6
        ♣ A K Q 5

The bidding had proceeded:

West	North	East	South
			1♠
Pass	4♠	Pass	6♠
Pass	Pass	Pass	

North-South were laydown for a grand slam but South, on the information he had, gambled slightly when he bid the small slam.

With Culbertson's proposed Grand Slam Force the bidding would be:

West	North	East	South
			1♠
Pass	4♠	Pass	5NT
Pass	7♠	Pass	Pass
Pass			

And, of course, if North lacked the ace or king of spades, he would sign off in six spades, which South had been willing to bid anyway without any extra information.

To make seven spades, after West leads the ace of hearts, requires only care, but an unthinking player might go down by trying to trump three hearts in his hand.

The sure winning play is to trump the heart, draw three

rounds of trump, and cash the ace of diamonds. If both opponents follow, three of dummy's diamonds are discarded on the high clubs and a diamond ruff in the dummy establishes South's suit. If either opponent shows out on the ace of diamonds, the other opponent's queen can be trapped either by a straight finesse or a ruffing finesse.

Soon afterward, there was a deal in which a player's suit was ♡ A J 5 4 3 2, and he knew that his partner had only two-card support. However, he used the five-notrump bid, found his partner with king-queen doubleton and so reached a grand slam.

Impressed by these examples, Culbertson put the Grand Slam Force into his book—as an optional convention—in defiance of the counsel of all his advisers.

However, the Grand Slam Force seemed to be a failure, and in Culbertson's marked copy of the 1941 edition of the *Gold Book,* opposite the space allotted to this convention, is his handwritten note: "condense? or omit?"

The resurgence of the Grand Slam Force undoubtedly began in 1941, when Lee Hazen and Richard L. Frey formed a new partnership and had a remarkable series of successes in major tournaments. One of the bidding tools they used was the Grand Slam Force, Frey apparently having withdrawn his earlier objections to it.

The attention of the world's experts was drawn to the bid by a few dramatic cases in which Hazen and Frey reached grand slams that their opponents missed. Adoption of the bid was gradual, but by the time Culbertson died in 1955 there was no doubt that the Grand Slam Force was one of his greatest successes.

EXTENSIONS OF THE GRAND SLAM FORCE

Many extensions of the Grand Slam Force have been proposed, and others are still being suggested. Culbertson proposed that in response to five notrump partner should give greater definition when not holding two top honors. He suggested that if the agreed suit is spades, partner bid six spades to show four spades but no top honor; six hearts to show five spades headed by the ace or king; six diamonds to show four spades headed by the ace or king; six clubs to show any five spades. When hearts is agreed, six hearts denies a top honor, six diamonds shows five hearts headed by the ace or king, and six clubs indicates only four trumps headed by the ace or king. And when diamonds is the agreed suit, six clubs promises five trumps to the ace or king.

This takes care of the cases in which the player who bids five notrump needs only to know that the combined hands have at least ten trumps, including the ace and king, in which case the odds are almost 4-to-1 that no trump trick need be lost.

Such a response was used in the following deal:

Dlr: South
Vul: E-W

```
                    ♠ A J 6 5 4
                    ♡ 6 2
                    ◇ —
                    ♣ A K Q 8 6 5
   ♠ Q 10                              ♠ 9
   ♡ Q 9 7 4                           ♡ J 10 8 5
   ◇ Q 6 4 2                           ◇ A J 10 9 8 5 3
   ♣ J 9 4                             ♣ 3
                    ♠ K 8 7 3 2
                    ♡ A K 3
                    ◇ K 7
                    ♣ 10 7 2
```

West	North	East	South
			1♠
Pass	3♣	3◇	Pass
Pass	3♠	Pass	4♡
Pass	5NT	Pass	6♡
Pass	7♠	Pass	Pass
Pass			

South's six-heart bid showed at least five spades headed by the ace or king. Having been told by the four-heart cue-bid that his partner also had the ace in that suit, North could bid seven spades with assurance.

It is, however, possible to modify those responses to make them a little clearer. Assuming spades is the trump suit, over five notrump partner bids:

6♣: ace or king of trumps
6♢: queen of trumps or *two* trumps more than promised
6♡: no honor, but one extra trump
6♠: no honor and minimum length

When hearts is the agreed suit, the responses are the same except that six hearts and six spades are pushed together. If diamonds is trump, six clubs shows one top honor, six diamonds none, and seven diamonds two. Finally, when clubs is fixed, there is no space at all.

There are two key features here. If a major is agreed, over six clubs, the Grand Slam Force bidder may relay with six diamonds to ask for an extra trump in an effort to reach the ten-card-fit grand slam. Secondly, two trumps more than promised is equivalent to holding the queen. A-K-x-x opposite six low cards is actually slightly preferable to A-K-x-x opposite Q-x-x-x.

There is one other possibility that makes a lot of sense: a jump to five of the suit above the agreed suit is the Grand Slam Force. For example:

West	North	East	South
			1♠
Pass	3♢	Pass	5♡

Five hearts is the GSF in diamonds. This retains the maximum amount of space: use the same responses as when spades is the agreed suit and the five-notrump GSF is used.

GRAND SLAM FORCE AFTER BLACKWOOD

The Grand Slam Force is particularly useful when the five-notrump bidder holds a void. In this case, using Blackwood is of no use, as partner might hold a useless ace in the void suit.

Sometimes the solidity of the trump suit is not the partnership's only concern. For instance, when there is not enough space to cue-bid all the aces, one player may need to use Blackwood. Now, after the ace-showing response, five notrump is no longer the Grand Slam Force but is an inquiry for kings.

When no void is held, the use of Roman Key Card Blackwood has removed this problem as that convention, considered in the previous chapter, uncovers all the trump honors. However, for a pair not using RKCB, there are two possible solutions.

The one most common in England is to bid six of the suit under the agreed suit, asking partner to bid seven with two of the top three trump honors.

The second possibility, which has enjoyed popularity in North America, is to bid six clubs over the ace-showing response (unless, of course, clubs is the agreed trump suit). Such an agreement would take care of the following hands:

♠ K Q 9 6 3	♠ A J 8 2
♡ A Q 3 2	♡ 9 8
◇ A	◇ K Q J 9 4 3
♣ 7 5 4	♣ A

West	East
1 ♠	3 ◇
3 ♡	3 ♠
4 ◇	4NT
5 ♡	6 ♣
7 ♠	Pass

♠
♡
11 Negative and Responsive Doubles
♢
♣

In the summer of 1957, Alvin Roth flew to Europe to play in a high-stakes rubber-bridge game with Tobias Stone against an Italian pair. While he was on the plane, it occurred to Roth that it would be more valuable to double an opponent's overcall for take-out than for penalties. When Roth landed, he told Stone about his idea and they adopted it immediately. Both give it much of the credit for the fact that they won the match by a big margin.

DEFINITION AND REQUIREMENTS

The Roth-Stone negative double—originally called Sputnik after the Russian satellite launched at about the same time—is an immediate double of an opponent's overcall in a bidding situation such as the following:

West	North	East	South
	1 ♣	1 ♠	Dble

or

West	North	East	South
	1 ♠	2 ♣	Dble

According to bidding rules that were universally un-challenged from the first days of contract bridge until 1957, South's double in either case was for penalties and North was expected to pass. Roth and Stone construed South's double for take-out, over which North was expected to bid again. Furthermore, their interpretation of the negative double went all the way up to the four-level. If East's overcall had been three diamonds, or even four hearts, South's double would still have been for take-out. However, many partnerships agree on lower levels: for example, "negative through three diamonds."

The minimum values shown by a negative double depend upon the level of the double. At the one-level, it promises no more than 6 points: enough to have made a one-level response if the opening bid had not been overcalled. At the three-level, though, near-opening-bid values are required.

It used to be that the negative double had a maximum upper limit, and therefore, unlike other take-out doubles, it did not discourage a penalty pass. If the moderate strength it showed seemed insufficient for a game but the opposing contract could probably be defeated, the opener would pass. Now, pairs do not have an upper limit for a negative double, so the opener will pass at a low level only with a particularly strong holding in the overcaller's suit. But as the level increases, converting the negative double into one for penalties is more likely.

The Roth-Stone requirements for a negative double were 7 to 10 high-card points including one or two quick tricks. The double that was effectively made in the following deal was typical.

Dlr: South
Vul: N-S

```
                  ♠ K 10 9 8
                  ♡ 6 4 2
                  ◇ Q J
                  ♣ K J 9 8
  ♠ 6 4                            ♠ Q J 5 3 2
  ♡ A K Q 10 9 8 5                 ♡ J 7
  ◇ 7 5                            ◇ 6 4 3 2
  ♣ 3 2                            ♣ 6 5
                  ♠ A 7
                  ♡ 3
                  ◇ A K 10 9 8
                  ♣ A Q 10 7 4
```

West	North	East	South
			1 ◇
3 ♡	Dble	Pass	6 ♣
Pass	Pass	Pass	

This deal occurred in a tournament, and Tobias Stone, North, was paired with his wife, Janice.

With 10 points in high cards, North had exactly what South could expect for a negative double; and since South knew that these high cards were chiefly in suits other than hearts, they were almost sure to be useful. The six-club contract was laydown, South having twelve tricks after West cashed the king of hearts.

Other pairs were prevented from bidding their slam by West's preemptive overcall. Without a negative double, North was left with an unenviable bid. He could not bid three spades without a five-card suit, he could not bid three notrump without a heart stopper, and he could not support diamonds with only a doubleton. That left a penalty double, which netted only 300 when South passed, expecting his partner to have more of his points in hearts. Perhaps this is poor thinking (North is unlikely to have a lot of points in hearts unless West is an undisciplined preemptor), but a penalty double is a penalty double. (In some cases West bid four hearts instead of three, but using a negative double

North still could have doubled, over which it would be even easier for South to bid the slam contract.)

The most useful negative double occurs when a minor-suit opening bid is overcalled by spades at the one- or two-level. This virtually guarantees at least four cards in hearts. If the doubler follows with a minimum bid in hearts, he suggests a six-card suit with limited high-card strength.

ARGUMENTS PRO AND CON

Originally the argument in favor of the negative double went like this: Bridge players no longer make weak overcalls, so the penalty double of a simple overcall has become a wasted bid. It may as well be applied to a useful purpose.

To this statement the rebuttal is: Yes, but if you remove the only possible deterrent to weak overcalls—the hair-trigger penalty double—your opponents will again go wild with overcalls as they did, years ago, before the mass of bridge players learned that it can be profitable to double low-level bids.

Finally, the counterrebuttal is: The negative double does not materially lessen the possibility of penalizing the opponents if they make weak overcalls; in fact, sometimes you get a penalty that would have been missed. If the responder is strong in the opponent's suit and wishes to make a penalty double, he must pass, relying on his partner to reopen with a double so that he may pass again, converting the double into one for penalties. Secondly, the opener may occasionally pass his partner's negative double, if he is strong in the overcaller's suit. This penalty would be unattainable without negative doubles.

For example, South holds

♠ K 3 2   ♡ 4   ◇ A J 10 7 6   ♣ 7 6 4 3

and the bidding starts

West	North	East	South
	1♡	2◇	?

He must pass, hoping that the auction will continue like this:

West	North	East	South
	1♡	2◇	Pass
Pass	Dble	Pass	?

Now South will pass, and the effect is the same as if he had made a penalty double on the previous round.

This sort of auction is a little dangerous, as North's balancing double used to guarantee extra values. Now, though, if the opener thinks his partner wished to make a penalty double of the overcall and he would have been happy to pass that penalty double, he should double in the balancing seat.

For example, suppose North holds

♠ A 10 7   ♡ A Q 10 7 6   ◇ 3   ♣ A 8 5 2

Normally, this hand would pass out two diamonds, being a minimum opening bid. Now, though, he should double, expecting partner to hold a penalty double of two diamonds. (If partner does not have a penalty double and could not make a negative double, where are all the points and why have the opponents stopped bidding so soon?)

This is fine if the responder does have a penalty double of the overcall, but suppose instead he has a few values but not enough for a negative double. He must be careful to allow for the opener's holding a minimum. Every convention has its price to pay.

THE RESPONSIVE DOUBLE

The responsive double is a double in response to partner's take-out double, partner having doubled the opening bid and the opener's partner having raised:

West	North	East	South
1♠	Dble	2♠	Dble

South's double is not for penalties. It shows the values to make a bid at the three-level, but no obvious bid to make.

A possible hand might be

♠ 5 4 3   ♡ J 7   ◇ K 8 7 6   ♣ K J 5 2

South would prefer his partner select a minor suit for fear that he will pick the wrong one.

This use of the responsive double deserves its popularity. Seldom will one wish to double such a raise for penalties.

RESPONSIVE DOUBLE OVER PARTNER'S OVERCALL

The responsive double can also be used when partner has overcalled and the opening bid has been raised, as in this auction:

West	North	East	South
1◇	2♣	2◇	Dble

Logically, this double suggests length in both major suits. There can seldom be an opportunity to make a profitable penalty double of a low-level contract when one opponent has bid a suit and the other has raised.

A possible hand might be:

♠ Q J 10 6 5   ♡ K J 10 5 3   ◇ 6   ♣ 8 2

A variation on this double that enjoys reasonable popularity in the tournament world is when three suits have been bid. For example:

West	North	East	South
1♡	2♣	2◇	?

Given that two diamonds is forcing, there is little point in making a penalty double, as the opponents are not going to stop in that contract. If South wishes to double for penalties, he must pass and hope to be able to double diamonds at a higher level.

So what does a double show? The normal interpretation is length in the fourth, unbid suit and some tolerance for partner's suit: perhaps honor doubleton or three low cards. Maybe

♠ A K J 8 7   ♡ 4 3 2   ◇ 8 6 4   ♣ Q 3

If instead South bids the fourth suit:

West	North	East	South
1♡	2♣	2◇	2♠

he shows that suit but warns partner of no support for his suit, clubs here. Perhaps South holds

♠ A K Q 8 7 5   ♡ 4 3 2   ◇ 8 6 4   ♣ 3

NEGATIVE FREE BIDS

When an opponent overcalls, moderate hands with a long suit can present a problem. Suppose your partner opens one club and your right-hand opponent overcalls one spade; what would you bid with each of the following hands?

1. ♠ 3 2	2. ♠ 4	3. ♠ 4
♡ K Q J 9 4	♡ K Q 9 6 5 2	♡ Q 7 2
◇ K 8 2	◇ Q 7 2	◇ K Q 9 6 5 2
♣ 7 6 2	♣ 5 4 2	♣ 5 4 2

Most players would make a negative double with hands one and two, and do some head scratching when a raise to two or three spades came back to them. They would pass reluctantly with hand three and be even worse off.

A modern tendency is to bid the long suit immediately with the understanding that the bid is non-forcing. It shows moderate values and a good five- or six-card suit. The opener then should know what to do when the fourth player raises spades.

These "negative free bids" apply only if there is a partnership agreement and are usually restricted to the two- and three-levels. Of course, there is a price to pay: a player who is sure he wishes to reach game has to bid something else. That something may be a jump shift, if the suit is strong, or a negative double.

This has an impact on the negative double, which has to be used on many strong hands. If the negative doubler follows with a new-suit bid, it is forcing. In the sequence described above, the negative double does not guarantee hearts. It promises hearts and/or the values for an opening bid.

WEAK JUMP SHIFTS IN COMPETITION

Weak jump shifts in uncontested auctions were considered earlier (see page 81). These do not enjoy widespread popularity, but weak jump shifts in competition are used by many expert pairs. Because negative free bids do put a strain on negative doubles, many pairs prefer to use weak jump shifts on this type of hand. Hand one above still makes a negative double, but hand two jumps to three hearts and hand three leaps to three diamonds. These bids are equally descriptive and make it more awkward for the fourth player to contest the auction, but carry the bidding a level higher if there is a misfit.

♠
♡

12 Slam Double Conventions

♢
♣

THE LIGHTNER DOUBLE

The Lightner slam double convention is more a principle than a convention. Anyone could have and should have thought of it. However, Theodore Lightner did think of it first, and despite its logical basis, he had to argue its merits for two or three years before it was generally adopted by other experts. Since there are no possible arguments against it, he was bound to be successful eventually; and for the last forty years the slam double convention has been accepted without question by all expert players.

The principle, briefly stated, is this: When competent opponents bid a slam voluntarily (that is, not as a sacrifice) they are pretty sure to be within a trick or two of making it. It cannot often pay to double them for the sole purpose of increasing the score for undertrick penalties. Therefore the double can best be used to guide partner's opening lead.

Consequently, when a defender who is not on lead doubles a slam contract his purpose is to call his partner's attention to the proper opening lead. He would not have to call the leader's attention to a normal opening lead, so a double of a slam contract asks for some unusual opening lead.

There should be no set rules as to what should be led when a slam contract is doubled. The winning lead is not necessarily the declarer's second suit or dummy's first suit. The defender who has the lead is expected to look at his hand, decide what he would have opened normally, and then lead something else.

Lightner figured this out in 1928 or 1929, when contract bridge was in its infancy. He tried to sell the idea to his bridge partner, Ely Culbertson, who was then codifying the bidding system that became the basis of expert bidding. Unfortunately, Lightner's first demonstration was far from successful. The opponents bid a slam and he doubled, because an unusual opening lead from Culbertson was the best hope of defeating the contract. Lightner forgot that it was not his partner's lead, but his own. With the lead in his own hand, there was no hope of defeating the contract. The opponents redoubled and scored several hundred extra points. Culbertson became so prejudiced against the convention that it was four years before he would listen to Lightner's arguments again. However, by 1933 Culbertson succumbed and adopted the Lightner slam double convention, and since then there has not been a dissenting vote.

An illustration of the convention can be found in the bidding:

West	North	East	South
			1♠
Pass	2♣	2♡	3♣
Pass	4♠	Pass	4NT
Pass	5♡	Pass	6♠
Pass	Pass	Dble	Pass
Pass	Pass		

West has the lead, holding the following hand:

♠ **6 3**   ♡ **3**   ♢ **J 10 7 6 5 2**   ♣ **10 7 6 3**

West's "normal" lead would be his singleton heart, since his partner bid the suit. However, his partner's double tells him not to make this lead. Casting about for another lead, he will think first of his long diamond suit, in which East may be void. But can North-South have seven diamonds between them, and East be void? Unlikely. Then he remembers that North has bid clubs and South has raised them freely. West has four of them; East may be void. West opens a club and, sure enough, East is void and ruffs. East proves also to have the ace of diamonds, which defeats the contract. The normal heart lead would have failed because East did not have the ace of hearts. The diamond lead would have failed because then East would never have had the chance to ruff a club. Only an opening club lead could have earned the setting trick.

Some effort has been made to conventionalize the slam double even further and make it call for a lead in the first suit bid by dummy. In the previous example it would have worked. But many cases indicate that this may be carrying matters too far. Almost always the opening leader, if warned that he must make an unusual lead, can figure out what kind of hand his partner has and which suit should be led. West did so in this deal, which occurred in a pair tournament:

Dlr: South   ♠ K Q J
Vul: None   ♡ 7
                 ◊ Q J 7 5
                 ♣ A K Q 5 2

    ♠ 6 4   ♠ 8 3 2
    ♡ K Q 8 4 2   ♡ J 9 6 5 3
    ◊ K 8 6 3   ◊ —
    ♣ 8 3   ♣ J 10 9 7 6

                ♠ A 10 9 7 5
                ♡ A 10
                ◊ A 10 9 4 2
                ♣ 4

West	North	East	South
			1♠
Pass	3♣	Pass	3◊
Pass	3♠	Pass	4◊
Pass	4NT	Pass	5♠
Pass	5NT	Pass	6♣
Pass	6♠	Dble	Pass
Pass	Pass		

When East doubled the slam, West could immediately rule out a heart lead. Hearts, the only unbid suit, would be his natural choice. The slam double never calls for a trump lead; so West had to select between clubs and diamonds.

In the bidding, South's five-spade response to Blackwood showed three aces. By responding six clubs to five notrump, South indicated that he did not have a king.

North's bid of five notrump guaranteed that his side held all the aces, so East could not be sitting with the ace-queen of clubs hovering over North's king—which could be one reason for doubling. Nor could East be void in clubs when West had only two.

West therefore decided that his partner must be void in diamonds. North had cleverly tried to forestall such a conclusion by concealing his good support for his partner's rebid suit; but the message got through despite his best efforts.

When West led the three of diamonds, East ruffed it and that gave the defenders one trick.

East returned the jack of clubs and dummy was in. Declarer ruffed a club with the nine of spades and drew two rounds of trumps with the jack and queen of spades. However, since the clubs were not breaking, South could discard only two of his three low diamonds, and West had to get the setting trick with the king of diamonds.

Without East's double, West would never have opened a diamond away from the king into a rebid suit. He would have led the king of hearts.

THE LIGHTNER DOUBLE APPLIED TO LOWER CONTRACTS

The slam-double principle has come to be applied to lower contracts. A double of three notrump, for example, when neither defender has bid, shows strength in dummy's suit and suggests, even if it does not demand, a lead in that suit.

In most cases an unexpected double tells the doubler's partner not to make what could be expected to be his normal lead.

In the next deal the double by East carried that message against a major-suit game contract.

Dlr: North
Vul: Both

	♠ 10 8 4	
	♡ K J 9	
	◇ A Q 6 3	
	♣ K 8 4	

♠ J 3		♠ A Q 9 7 5 2
♡ 7		♡ A 6 5 2
◇ J 9 8 7 4 2		◇ —
♣ Q 6 5 2		♣ 9 7 3

	♠ K 6	
	♡ Q 10 8 4 3	
	◇ K 10 5	
	♣ A J 10	

West	North	East	South
	1◇	1♠	2♡
Pass	3♡	Pass	4♡
Pass	Pass	Dble	Pass
Pass	Pass		

Without East's double, West would have led the jack of spades, the suit East had bid. Against this opening lead, South would have had no difficulty in making four hearts, and would probably collect an overtrick. East would win the first trick with the ace of spades, hoping West had a singleton. South would win the second trick with the king of spades and lead trumps until East won with the ace.

East would lead the queen of spades, but South would ruff and play any remaining trumps, squeezing West in the minor suits. To hold four diamonds, West would have to reduce his hand to a doubleton club. South would then cash his five minor-suit winners, dropping the queen of clubs and making an overtrick.

However, when East doubled the four-heart contract, West inferred some defensive feature of East's hand not shown by the moderate overcall of one spade. He led the seven of diamonds and East ruffed.

Now East's problem was to get West back on lead so that he could ruff another diamond. To this effect, East led a low spade.

South put up the king of spades and won the trick, knowing from East's overcall that he probably had the ace. But when declarer started the trump suit, East ducked the first round to get some assistance from his partner. On the next heart lead, West discarded the discouraging two of clubs. East won with the ace and led another low spade. This lead put West in with the jack and he led another diamond, which East trumped for the setting trick.

The double of four hearts on East's hand must be treated as a gamble that will sometimes go wrong, giving declarer's side a bigger score for making a doubled or redoubled contract plus even a bonus for an overtrick. East had no assurance that the contract could be defeated or even that the double would guide West to a diamond opening. But the reward when the double succeeds is the saving of game and rubber, a total gain of 820 or more points, and that justifies taking some chances.

THE "UNDOUBLE" SLAM DOUBLE

While there is no doubt that all expert players use the Lightner double in most slam situations, within the past two decades a few have given a different meaning to doubles of slams reached after competitive auctions in which their side may want to sacrifice. For example, with North-South vulnerable:

West	North	East	South
	1♣	2♠ (a)	4♣
4♠	4NT	Pass	5♦
Pass	6♣	?	

(a) Weak

If six clubs can be made, East-West undoubtedly can profit by sacrificing. But if East and West have two defensive tricks, they do not want to sacrifice.

In these situations, where the partnership has bid and supported a suit and the hand "belongs" to the other side, some players use the double of a slam not to suggest a lead but to exchange information on the number of defensive tricks held.

The most logical way to play these cooperative slam doubles is for the partner having the first call (above, East) over the slam bid to double if he has two defensive tricks; with one or no tricks he should pass.

The partner in the pass-out seat (West) passes, of course, if East has doubled to show two tricks. However, if his partner has shown one or no tricks by passing, West will pass if he has two defensive tricks (ending the auction with the opponents in an unmakable slam); sacrifice if he has no defensive trick; or double if he has one defensive trick. In this last case, the ball is back with East, who will pass if he has one defensive trick, and "undouble" (sacrifice) if he has no defensive trick.

Some New York experts used to favor an immediate double to show no defensive trick, but this bizarre idea is obsolete.

Here is an example of the non-penalty slam double.

```
Dlr: South              ♠ 10 7 6 3
Vul: E-W                ♡ —
                        ◇ 9 8 7 4 3 2
                        ♣ A 8 3
        ♠ 4                             ♠ A
        ♡ Q 9 8 7 4 2                   ♡ A 10 6 5 3
        ◇ 10 6 5                        ◇ A K Q
        ♣ J 10 9                        ♣ K Q 7 4
                        ♠ K Q J 9 8 5 2
                        ♡ K J
                        ◇ J
                        ♣ 6 5 2
```

West	North	East	South
			4♠
Pass	Pass	Dble	Pass
5♡	5♠	6♡	Pass (a)
Pass	Dble (b)	Pass	Pass (c)
Pass			

(a) I do not have two defensive tricks, otherwise I would double.

(b) I do not have two defensive tricks either—I would pass. And I do not have any defensive tricks—I would bid six spades. So I have one trick, and you have to decide whether to save or defend, partner.

(c) I have one trick as well—the king of hearts—so we'll defend.

♠
♡
13 Counters to a
♢ One-Notrump
Opening Bid
♣

It is dangerous to overcall a one-notrump opening bid because the notrump bidder's partner can double so easily. He knows his partner has at least two cards in the over-caller's suit, and that the odds favor his partner's having an honor in the suit as well.

If North opens one notrump and East overcalls with two diamonds, South can and should double with a hand like this:

♠ **A 8**   ♡ **K 7 4 3**   ♢ **10 7 6 2**   ♣ **J 7 6**

Assuming that his partner has a standard notrump hand, the combined North-South hands will have some 24 points in high cards and six or more diamonds, and it is unlikely that East will win eight tricks.

East knows all this, of course, and probably has a hand on which he cannot be badly hurt, but it is the readiness of

South to double that requires him to have such a hand. If South stopped doubling freely, East could overcall more audaciously.

There are many cases in which East would be unable to overcall because he has no trump suit strong enough, and would be unable to double because a double of one notrump is primarily for penalties, but East-West could still compete profitably against the notrump bid if they could *safely* find their best-fitting suit.

This is an old problem against all bids of one notrump, whether they are strong or weak, and whether they are opening bids, responses, or rebids. The problem was intensified when the weak one-notrump opening of 12-14 points came into common use in the 1950s, for there are necessarily more hands with which one might compete against a weak notrump than a strong one. It is also more likely that the non-opening side can make a game.

Lessening the requirements for a double of one notrump does not solve the problem. A double of one notrump should remain for penalties; but the equivalent of a take-out double is needed, too.

LANDY

The simplest of the substitutes for the take-out double is the Landy convention, named for Alvin Landy, who from 1951 until his death in 1967 was executive secretary of the American Contract Bridge League, and for many years had been a high-ranking American tournament player.

Landy devised his convention originally as a defense against the weak notrump, bid on such a hand as this:

♠ K Q 8 4   ♡ 10 8 7 6 4   ◇ A Q 3   ♣ J

The Landy convention is a two-club overcall of an opponent's one-notrump opening bid, indicating a major two-suiter. (Partner may pass with long clubs, or bid two diamonds with length in that suit, but he should prefer a major if possible.)

The two-club overcall has been widely adopted, and has been extended for use against a strong notrump opening, as in this example deal when a thin Landy overcall tempted West to try for a penalty.

Dlr: West
Vul: None

```
                    ♠ A Q 5 4
                    ♡ K 8 7 4 3
                    ◇ 2
                    ♣ 9 8 3
      ♠ K J 9 8                      ♠ 7 2
      ♡ A Q 10 5                     ♡ J 9 2
      ◇ K Q J                        ◇ 10 9 8 5 3
      ♣ J 2                          ♣ A K Q
                    ♠ 10 6 3
                    ♡ 6
                    ◇ A 7 6 4
                    ♣ 10 7 6 5 4
```

West	North	East	South
1NT	2♣	Dble	2♠
Dble	Pass	Pass	Pass

West led the obvious-looking king of diamonds, but things backfired badly. Declarer won with the ace and led a heart. West rose with the ace and, wishing he had led the card at trick one, switched to the jack of spades, but declarer was in control. He finessed dummy's queen successfully, cashed the king of hearts, ruffed a heart, ruffed a diamond, overruffed East in hearts, ruffed another diamond, and claimed the ace of spades for his contract-fulfilling trick. Minus 470 was poor compensation for the plus 400 available in three notrump.

After winning the second trick with the ace of hearts, West could have defeated the contract by switching to a club. East cashes three tricks in the suit, and West discards a diamond. Now comes a spade switch, and the defense must take six tricks: two spades, one heart, and three clubs.

If West had led a low trump at trick one, he would beat the contract by one trick. Declarer wins the first trick with the ten of spades and leads a heart, but West goes in with the ace and continues with a second trump. Declarer comes to seven tricks by way of three trump tricks, the king of hearts, the ace of diamonds, and two ruffs.

Even better is the opening lead of a spade honor. That locks declarer in the dummy. He must cross to hand with a diamond in order to lead his heart, but West wins with the ace of hearts and leads his second spade honor. In this way, the contract goes down two; but it is still an unsatisfactory result.

The big drawback of Landy is that it permits the overcall to show one two-suiter (the majors, with a bid of two clubs) and three one-suiters (with bids of two diamonds, two hearts, and two spades). This is obviously inefficient, only one step better than playing all suit overcalls as natural. This has resulted in several other conventional defenses against a one-trump opening.

A simple one plays that two clubs shows a minor two-suiter, two diamonds a major two-suiter, and bids of two hearts and two spades are natural. This seems an improvement, but is not really. Do you wish to compete at a low level with a minor two-suiter? You leave the opponents with a fielder's choice: they can double for penalties or compete in the higher-ranking major suits.

Other methods are more efficient. Here is a summary, taking the conventions in alphabetical order. The reader is invited to play the one he and his partner find most compatible with their style of play.

ASTRO

This is named after Paul *A*llinger, Roger *St*ern, and Lawrence *Ro*sler. A two-club overcall shows hearts and a minor suit (maybe both minors), and a two-diamond overcall indicates spades and another suit (maybe both minors).

Over the artificial minor-suit bid, without a good fit in the "anchor" major, partner bids the next step up (two diamonds over two clubs, or two hearts over two diamonds) asking for the second suit. The Astro bidder does as his partner requests; or bids two notrump when holding length in both minors.

Astro works well, and as with many of the conventions described in this section of the book, it poses only the problem of how far a partnership wishes to go in the use of specialized gadgets.

There are two other variants of Astro. There is *Aspro,* in which the two-club overcall shows hearts and another suit (or both minors), and two diamonds indicates spades and a minor (or both minors). Also, there is *Asptro,* in which two clubs shows hearts and another suit (or both minors) and two diamonds indicates spades and another suit (or both minors). The advantage of this last approach is that the overcaller can tell his partner about unequal length in the majors. When holding a major two-suiter, an Astro, Aspro, or Landy bidder is forced to make one specific bid. The Asptro bidder may call two clubs *or* two diamonds. The usual style is to show one's longer major first.

BROZEL

This convention is designed to compete against the strong notrump, because it uses a double in a non-penalty sense. The double indicates a one-suited hand in any suit. Obviously, partner may pass with a good hand, but with no desire to defend, he bids two clubs, over which the overcaller names his suit.

The other bids in Brozel show two-suiters, with hearts as the "wheel." Thus:

> 2♣: hearts and clubs
> 2◇: hearts and diamonds
> 2♡: hearts and spades
> 2♠: spades and a minor
> 2NT: clubs and diamonds

CAPPELLETTI

This is similar to Brozel, but retains the penalty double. The different bids are:

> 2♣: a one-suiter in any suit
> 2◇: hearts and spades
> 2♡: hearts and a minor
> 2♠: spades and a minor
> 2NT: clubs and diamonds

Over two clubs, partner may pass with long clubs, but usually bids two diamonds to ask for the suit.

CRASH

This approach was originally used as a defense to a strong-club opening bid, but can be applied effectively against one notrump. The three key calls indicate either-or two-suiters.

Dble: red suits or black suits (*C*olor)
2♣: majors or minors (*RA*nk)
2◇: spades and diamonds or hearts and clubs (*SH*ape)

Partner will usually make a bid in the lowest-ranking suit he is happy to play in assuming that is one of the CRASH bidder's suits. If he has some hope of game, he bids two notrump to ask for definition.

RIPSTRA

This was developed by J. G. Ripstra, a former president of the American Contract Bridge League. The two-club or two-diamond overcaller promises length in both majors, and he has bid his longer minor.

LEBENSOHL

And now, the counter to the countermeasures. When your right-hand opponent takes action over your partner's one-notrump opening, you often have a problem. The modern solution is the Lebensohl (or Lebensold) convention.

No one knows who invented Lebensohl. It was first publicized by George Boehm in the November 1970 issue of *The Bridge World.* Boehm had assumed it was a misspelling of Kenneth Lebensold's name, but Lebensold denies any involvement in the development of the convention. The Lebensohl name has stuck.

Suppose the auction begins 1NT-[2♠]. What would you bid with each of these hands?

1. ♠ 6 3
   ♡ Q J 9 8 6
   ◇ K 10 8 7
   ♣ J 8

2. ♠ 6 3
   ♡ A Q 10 5 4
   ◇ A J 8
   ♣ K 7 3

3. ♠ Q 10 3
   ♡ K J 10 8
   ◇ 5 3
   ♣ A J 7 6

4. ♠ 6 3
   ♡ A Q 10 5
   ◇ K Q J 8
   ♣ J 9 3

5. ♠ K J 6
   ♡ 9 8 6
   ◇ A Q 9 8
   ♣ Q J 8

6. ♠ 10 4
   ♡ 9 7 6
   ◇ A Q J 5 3
   ♣ K J 6

On the first hand, you would like to bid a competitive three hearts. On the second, you wish to force to game, show your five-card suit and let partner choose between three notrump and four hearts. Obviously, you cannot bid three hearts with both hands.

The last four hands have game values. But how do you distinguish between those that do or do not have a spade stopper, and do or do not have four hearts?

The answer is to employ Lebensohl. The key aspect of this convention is the use of two notrump as an artificial bid, asking partner to relay with three clubs. This introduces a two-step element to all auctions. Either you make an immediate cue-bid of the opponent's suit, or you make it via two notrump. Similarly, you bid three notrump or a new suit either immediately or via two notrump. This doubles the number of hands you can show.

Given the form of the convention most commonly employed, on hand one you bid two notrump and follow up with three hearts over partner's forced three-club rebid. That shows a *competitive* heart bid. With hand two you bid an immediate three hearts, natural and forcing to game.

With hand three, you bid two notrump and then three spades, showing a spade stopper *and* four hearts. With hand four, you cue-bid three spades immediately to show four hearts but no spade stopper.

Similarly, with hand five you bid two notrump and then three notrump to indicate a spade stopper but fewer than four hearts. And with the last hand, you jump immediately to three notrump to show no spade stopper and fewer than four hearts.

(This version is commonly known as "slow shows"—a bid of two notrump followed by a cue-bid or three notrump *shows* a spade stopper; an immediate cue-bid or jump to three notrump denies a stopper. It is possible to play it the other way around ["fast shows"]. The thinking behind using slow shows is that the overcaller's partner is less likely to bid when the responder has a stopper in the overcaller's suit. Also, when the responder does have a stopper and the overcaller's partner decides to enter the auction, a lucrative penalty double may be available.)

In every case, the opener decides where to play the

hand—usually in three notrump or four of the responder's major. However, he might have a problem. Suppose the opener has this hand:

♠ 8 7 5   ♡ K 4   ◇ A Q J 6   ♣ A Q 10 3

If the responder denies a spade stopper by jumping immediately to three notrump or cue-bidding with three spades, the opener knows that three notrump is impossible. He must continue with four clubs and hope to find a minor-suit fit.

The price to pay in using Lebensohl is the loss of a quantitative raise to two notrump. This is a small sacrifice for the increased accuracy in competitive and game-forcing auctions.

The other main problem to consider in this situation is how to play a double of the overcall. Traditionally, it is for penalties. However, a few experts, especially in Britain, play that it shows a raise to two notrump, thus compensating for the loss of that bid. However, in North America, playing the double as negative is becoming more and more popular among experts. The bidding begins 1NT-[2♡]. What do you bid with this hand:

♠ K 10 8 7   ♡ 4 3   ◇ K 6 4   ♣ Q 8 7 5

You wish to contest the auction, but to bid two spades risks ending in a 4-2 fit. The perfect answer is a negative double.

Naturally, if you do employ the negative double here, if an overcall is passed back to the opener, he should reopen with a double when short and weak in the overcaller's suit.

Lebensohl can be employed in situations other than those following a one-notrump opening. The most common is after partner has made a take-out double over an opponent's weak two-bid.

For example, the auction begins 2♠–Dble–Pass. What would you bid with each of these hands?

1.	♠ 6 3	2.	♠ 6 3
	♡ Q J 9 8 6		♡ A Q 10 5 4
	◇ 8 7 4 3		◇ Q 9 8
	♣ J 8		♣ 8 7 3

On the first, you wish to make a bid of three hearts and have partner pass. But with the second, you would not mind if partner bid on to game with a few extras. You distinguish between the two hands via Lebensohl. With the first hand, you first bid two notrump and then three hearts, showing a weak hand. With the second, you bid an immediate three hearts, showing invitational values. The auctions featuring a cue-bid and three notrump carry the same messages as those given above following the one-notrump opening.

This same idea may be applied in other situations. Suppose the auction begins like this:

West	North (Partner)	East	South (You)
	1♠	2♡	Pass
Pass	Dble	Pass	?

What would you bid with either of these hands?

1.	♠ 6	2.	♠ 7
	♡ 8 6 5 4		♡ 9 8 4
	◇ J 8 7 4 3		◇ K Q 9 8 6 5
	♣ J 8 5		♣ Q 7 3

With hand one, you wish to play in three diamonds. With the second, you wish to invite game; you wished you had been able to bid a non-forcing three diamonds on the previous round (a negative free bid—see page 209).

The answer, not that you need to be told now, is to bid two notrump and then three diamonds over partner's three-club relay on the first hand; but to try an immediate three diamonds on the second, showing values that were not quite sufficient for action on the previous round.

14 Defensive Two-Suited Bids

Two-suited hands can produce more tricks than their point-count would suggest if partner can fit one or both of the suits. As a consequence, bids to indicate two-suiters enjoy considerable popularity.

The original two-suited bid arose around 1950 as part of the Roth-Stone system.

THE UNUSUAL NOTRUMP

This convention caused no stir when first it was publicized, partly because it had no catchy name. It received its present moniker when it was adopted into the Kaplan-Sheinwold system in about 1954.

In its simplest form, the Unusual Notrump is as follows: If a player bids two or three (or, exceptionally, four) notrump when he cannot have a hand strong enough to play in such a contract, he shows great length in both of the minor suits, clubs and diamonds. Usually he will have at least five cards in each suit.

The notrump bidder's partner must then bid his "better" (longer) minor suit, even if he has only two or three cards in it. The bid cannot be passed.

In the first book on the Roth-Stone system, published in 1952, this convention was described via the following bidding sequence:

West	North	East	South
Pass	Pass	1♠	Pass
1NT	Pass	2♠	Pass
Pass	2NT	Pass	?

What should South do now? His hand is powerful, in view of his previous passes:

♠ 7 6 2   ♡ A J 10 8 4   ◇ Q 9   ♣ K 10 3

If North had a genuine two-notrump bid, South would have more than the values required to bid game in notrump or hearts. But North cannot have a genuine two-notrump bid because he passed originally, and there is no such thing as a hand that can make two notrump yet is too weak for an opening bid. Therefore, North is asking to be taken out of his notrump contract.

Opposite a normal take-out bid, such as a double, South would unhesitatingly bid his very good heart suit. In this case he must not. This is the respect in which the Unusual Notrump ceases to be a logical bidding message and becomes a convention, or arbitrary message. Being an Unusual, or non-genuine, notrump overcall, North's bid of two notrump demands a minor-suit response; and Roth's official answer to the question was: "Three clubs. No choice. Partner is requesting a minor suit."

North's hand, to justify his bid of two notrump, would be expected to be the following or its equivalent:

♠ 8 3   ♡ 5   ◊ K J 10 7 6   ♣ A Q 9 5 4

Such a hand would be a minimum, and acceptable only when not vulnerable, except in matchpoint duplicate bridge where an opposing partscore must be contested even at some risk. If the opponents have not already passed the hand out at a low level, the Unusual Notrump bidder should be stronger—perhaps with a 6-5 two-suiter such as

♠ 3   ♡ 4   ◊ K Q 10 8 7 6   ♣ A J 9 8 5

CALLING FOR UNBID SUITS

From its original use to show a two-suiter in the minor suits, the Unusual Notrump has developed in many partnerships as a convention to show a two-suiter in the two unbid suits, when the opponents have shown strength and have bid only two suits. An example is the following deal.

Dlr: West
Vul: E-W

	♠ 5	
	♡ Q 8 6 4 3 2	
	◊ 9	
	♣ K 10 7 4 3	
♠ K Q 7 2		♠ A 10 8 4 3
♡ A 5		♡ J 10 9
◊ A Q J 7 4		◊ K 6 3
♣ 8 5		♣ J 6
	♠ J 9 6	
	♡ K 7	
	◊ 10 8 5 2	
	♣ A Q 9 2	

West	North	East	South
1◊	Pass	1♠	Pass
3♠	3NT	4♠	5♣
Pass	Pass	Dble	Pass
Pass	Pass		

North's Unusual three-notrump bid was used to show a two-suiter in the two suits East-West had not bid. Since South had quite a good hand, the result was excellent for North-South. They lost only one spade, one heart, and one diamond trick, going down one and losing 100 points as they were non-vulnerable. At this small cost they prevented a vulnerable game worth 650 points that their opponents could have made.

The East-West bidding is not exempt from criticism. West's pass of five clubs, which would be meaningless in the average game, carried a distinct message in the expert circles in which it was being made. It was a forcing pass, meaning that West could stand a five-spade contract if East could bid it. Probably East should have bid five spades, but North or South could have bid six clubs, going down two tricks or 300 ponts and still saving 350 points.

A most extreme use of the Unusual Notrump occurred in the following deal.

Dlr: South   ♠ K
Vul: N-S   ♡ K 6
             ◇ A 9 8 5 4 3
             ♣ 10 8 7 4

♠ Q 8 5   ♠ 10 9 7 6 3 2
♡ 10 8 4 3   ♡ Q J 9 7 5 2
◇ Q J 6   ◇ 10
♣ 9 6 2   ♣ —

            ♠ A J 4
            ♡ A
            ◇ K 7 2
            ♣ A K Q J 5 3

West	North	East	South
			2♣
Pass	2◇	Pass	3♣
Pass	4♣	Pass	4NT
Pass	5◇	Pass	5NT
Pass	6♡	6NT	

The opening two-club bid was not the artificial and forcing bid played by experts today but the natural strength-showing bid of yesteryear. The two-diamond response by North was a natural positive bid showing strength; North's "bust response" would have been two notrump. Blackwood followed, and when North had shown one ace and two kings facing an opening two-bid, East could tell that South was fairly sure to bid a grand slam.

It was almost axiomatic in bridge at that time that there was no such thing as a bad sacrifice by a non-vulnerable player against a vulnerable grand slam that his opponents could make. The vulnerable grand slam is worth at least 2140 points, and prior to 1987 a non-vulnerable pair could bid seven and go down eleven tricks, conceding 2100, and still show a profit. The only reason there were not more sacrifices against grand slams is that hope springs eternal and there is always a chance that the grand slam may be beaten. With the scoring change in the Duplicate Laws, making undertricks cost 300 points each after the first three, a sacrifice can only go down by eight tricks before the penalty exceeds the value of the grand slam.

South did bid seven clubs, and West, who was enjoying one of his better days, read East's bid of six notrump as indicating a major two-suiter. He bid seven hearts and played the hand there, doubled, going down five and losing 900 points (which would be 1100 in a duplicate event today).

North-South could have made seven clubs easily. They could have made seven notrump by a squeeze. Note that a grand-slam venture does not need the normal odds if the opponents have found a cheap save (see page 342).

THE UNUSUAL NOTRUMP AS A CONVENTION

The Unusual Notrump described (*sans* name) by Roth and Stone in 1952 was interpreted by logic. Now the take-out message is assigned to it arbitrarily, so that most experts bid as follows:

West	North	East	South
		1♠	2NT

South's two-notrump bid is the Unusual Notrump. It shows that South has a two-suiter in the minor suits and is willing to go to the three-level in the one that best fits North's hand.

The argument used to justify this interpretation is that South could double first, to show strength, and later bid notrump if he had a genuine two-notrump hand.

The advantage of the bid is that South avoids being shut out of the bidding. If South passed on the first round, West might bid two or three spades and East might bid four and South could not safely come in. If South overcalled with two diamonds on the first round and the bidding reached four spades by the time it came around to him again, it might not be safe for him to bid *five* clubs. So North, who might have a fine fit for clubs, could never learn about the two-suited nature of South's hand.

With the Unusual Notrump used as an immediate jump overcall, South can show the nature and approximate strength of his hand with a single bid and without being forced too high.

The strength required varies according to vulnerability, as is the case with all overcalls. The hand shown earlier in this section:

♠ 8 3   ♡ 5   ◇ K J 10 7 6   ♣ A Q 9 5 4

would be good enough only if non-vulnerable or if reopening the bidding against opponents who have already stopped at a low contract and cannot have great strength. A vulnerable player should usually have a 6-5 hand or a very strong 5-5:

♠ 6   ♡ 5   ◇ K Q 10 8 7 5   ♣ A J 10 7 3

or

♠ 6   ♡ 9 4   ◇ A Q 10 7 6   ♣ A K J 5 2

The bid is somewhat safer if the opponents' suit has been raised, for then partner is unlikely to have length in that suit and is more likely to fit one of the minors. In the following situation:

West	North	East	South
		1♠	Pass
2♠	2NT		

some pairs play that this two-notrump bid is natural and strong, but if it is being treated as Unusual, North does not need quite so much as South needed for his immediate jump to two notrump in the preceding bidding diagram. The fact that South has passed is not a consideration. In overcalling one does not rely on finding more in the hand of a partner who had not yet been heard from than in the hand of a partner who has passed. And once the opponents have found a fit it becomes more likely that your side has one as well.

THE PROS AND CONS OF THE UNUSUAL NOTRUMP

The major advantage of the Unusual Notrump is that in a single bid it gives one's partner a choice of suits to support, before the opponents, who have the higher-ranking suit(s), have a chance to raise the level of the bidding so high that both suits cannot be shown.

However, this one bid that gives partner such precise information also alerts the opponents. Therefore, if the side that called on the Unusual Notrump does not buy the contract, the bid has become a liability rather than an asset.

In each of the examples given earlier, the Unusual Notrump bidder had either a good playing hand or a hand so extreme in distribution that a profitable sacrifice was likely if partner fit either of his suits. However, consider what is likely to happen if the notrump bidder has a poor hand and the opponents buy the contract:

Dlr: North
Vul: N-S

	♠ A J 7 2	
	♡ A K	
	◇ A 10 7 5 4	
	♣ 8 5	

♠ Q 9 6		♠ 5
♡ J 10 7		♡ Q 8 6 4 3
◇ Q J 8		◇ 9 2
♣ Q 10 9 2		♣ K J 7 4 3

	♠ K 10 8 4 3	
	♡ 9 5 2	
	◇ K 6 3	
	♣ A 6	

West	North	East	South
	1 ◇	Pass	1 ♠
Pass	3 ♠	3NT	4 ♣
Pass	4 ◇	Pass	4 ♠
Pass	5 ♡	Pass	6 ♠
Pass	Pass	Pass	

West leads the jack of hearts. In the absence of any adverse bidding, declarer's normal play would be to cash the ace and king of trumps rather than to take a finesse. On this deal, however, declarer was forewarned that East had at most three cards in the spade and diamond suits, since his Unusual Notrump bid announced at least ten cards in the other suits.

Declarer therefore cashed the king of spades and, when both opponents followed low, he took the precaution of leading a diamond to the ace and a low diamond back, to get as complete a count as possible of East's hand. When East followed to both diamonds, the spade finesse through West was clearly marked. If East had ruffed the second diamond no harm would have been done since declarer must lose a diamond anyway; if East had discarded on the second diamond, declarer would have been back to guessing whether to finesse or to play for the queen of spades to drop.

This was a case in which the Unusual Notrump side did

not buy the contract, and its use may have cost them 1530 points because it gave the declarer a clear indication of how to play the hand, whereas without adverse bidding he might easily have gone wrong.

RESPONDING TO THE UNUSUAL NOTRUMP

Strict discipline is required in responding. The longer minor suit must be bid, even on a hand like this:

♠ K 10 8 6 2   ♡ A J 5 3   ◇ 7 5 4   ♣ 3

The response must be three diamonds, not three of either major and not pass.

While the Unusual Notrump seldom shows a real powerhouse, it is after all a hand capable of undertaking a three-level contract. If the responder has a good minor-suit fit and a smattering of high-card strength, he must make a jump response:

♠ A 5 4   ♡ 9 7 5 2   ◇ 8   ♣ A 9 7 5 2

This hand calls for a jump to five clubs over an Unusual Notrump. With the king instead of the ace in clubs, five would still be the bid unless the Unusual Notrump were a "balancing" bid (to reopen the bidding).

One cannot count points in responding to the Unusual Notrump. Only an ace is a dependable trick in a major suit. A king may be worthless, because partner may have a singleton; a queen almost surely *is* worthless; and even a king-queen may be worth no more than two low cards. But any strength in either minor is worth a great deal and the queen of the other minor is almost as good as an ace.

EXTENSIONS OF THE UNUSUAL NOTRUMP

What is the meaning of two notrump in this auction?

West	North	East	South
		1 ◇	2NT

A few experts still limit the Unusual Notrump to the minor suits; the majority apply it to the unbid suits. Most pairs play that this shows the two lower unbid suits: clubs and hearts. However, against a pair using five-card majors, some pairs still play the Unusual Notrump to indicate a minor two-suiter. The only observation that has any real bearing on which arrangement is preferable is that even playing five-card majors, an opening bid of one of a minor is nearly always on at least a four-card suit.

If the opening bid is in a major, say, one spade, some pairs play that the bid shows *any two* of the other three suits. Partner responds in his better minor; and a suit rebid by the notrump bidder shows that the two-suiter was composed of hearts and the other minor. However, this has the disadvantage that the notrump bidder's partner cannot jump the bidding with one long minor for fear that his partner does not have support for the suit. Using the Michaels Cue-Bid is a better approach.

It has been stated that the strength of the Unusual Notrump bidder's hand is limited, and normally it is. However, it is possible that the Unusual Notrump bidder will have a powerhouse: a hand so strong that he is planning to make another bid even though his partner just bids his longer minor at the minimum level. For example, holding

$$\spadesuit\ 2 \quad \heartsuit\ 3 \quad \diamondsuit\ A\,Q\,J\,10\,7\,6 \quad \clubsuit\,A\,K\,Q\,10\,9$$

over an opening of one of a major, bidding two notrump, proposing to jump in diamonds on the next round, is not a silly way to bid the hand. Making a take-out double with a singleton in the unbid major is dangerous; and jumping to four notrump (assuming partner would read it as a big minor two-suiter) preempts the bidding on a hand which is so strong that the holder has reason to expect to be able to outbid the opponents on power.

Another possibility occurs on a hand of this type:

$$\spadesuit\ K\,J\,2 \quad \heartsuit\ — \quad \diamondsuit\ A\,Q\,J\,8\,7 \quad \clubsuit\,A\,K\,J\,10\,9$$

Over an opening bid of one heart, the player who held this hand jumped to two notrump. When his partner responded with three clubs, he continued with three spades to describe his distribution and extra strength.

THE MICHAELS CUE-BID

With the Unusual Notrump gaining such popularity, other two-suited bids were devised. The "best-seller" is the Michaels Cue-Bid. The inventor of the convention was the late Michael Michaels of Miami, Florida.

Michaels used the cue-bid much as the Unusual Notrump is employed: to indicate a two-suited hand, but to warn of limited strength. Any bidding above a minimum level done by the cue-bidder's partner is done on his own.

Over an opponent's one-diamond opening, Michaels bid two diamonds on any of the following hands (his examples):

1. ♠ J 7 6 4 3	2. ♠ Q J 9 6 5	3. ♠ K Q 8 7
♡ A K J 4	♡ J 9 7 6 3	♡ A 7 6 3
◇ 2	◇ K 4	◇ 8 2
♣ 7 6 3	♣ 7	♣ 9 5 4

Michaels' range was some 6-11 high-card points. Today, most experts would use the cue-bid with the first two of these examples, especially when non-vulnerable, but not with the third hand.

The argument for this use of the cue-bid is twofold: The ultrapowerful cue-bid is largely wasted because appropriate hands so seldom occur; and a bid is needed for hands on which an overcall would be unsafe but a tentative contract in a suit that fits is usually safe.

The Michaels Cue-Bids were devised chiefly for tournament play in which it is important to sacrifice even when the gain will only be a few points.

The cue-bidder's partner, in the Michaels method, takes charge. If he makes a minimum response in his longest suit, the cue-bidder simply passes. If partner is strong, he responds with a cue-bid of his own:

West	North	East	South
1 ◇	2 ◇	Pass	3 ◇

South holds, for example:

♠ K 7 6 4 3   ♡ A 2   ◇ A Q 6   ♣ 9 8 3

The basic scheme is that the cue-bid of a minor suit shows a major two-suiter, whereas a cue-bid in a major suit shows the other major and either minor. Holding

♠ 6   ♡ K Q 10 9 6   ◇ A J 10 6 5   ♣ 3 2

one would make a cue-bid of two spades over an opposing opening bid of one spade. In this situation, if the partner of the cue-bidder wishes to know which minor suit is held, he bids two notrump.

Some pairs play that the cue-bid is either weak or strong. If weak, the cue-bidder will pass any minimum bid by his partner; if strong, he will bid again. Holding

♠ 2   ♡ A K J 10 6   ◇ K Q J 10 8   ♣ A 4

the player will cue-bid with two spades over an opening one-spade bid, planning to jump to four diamonds over two notrump or three clubs, or to raise a bid in a red suit.

Another style that has a small following is called Colorful Cue-Bids. In this case, a cue-bid over a major-suit opening bid shows the two suits of the other color. This can have the advantage of avoiding an ambiguity when the cue-bidder's partner is not sure which minor suit is held, but stops one from showing a major-minor two-suiter with opposite colors.

As is so often the case in bridge, you need to discuss these bids with your partner and decide which approach you prefer.

PART III

The Process of Card Valuation

♠
♡
1 Approach to
High-Card
◇ Valuation
♣

It is trite but true that hand valuation is "mental play." To estimate the trick-winning value of his hand, the player must foresee the conditions that will obtain when the cards are actually played. The better the player, the more accurate his valuation; for he can foresee only those plays which he can actually execute.

The expert recognizes two kinds of trick-winning strength: high-card and distributional. Basically, the plays that establish distributional trick-winners are more complex than the plays that establish high-card trick-winners. Any beginner can lead out an ace; far greater proficiency is required to establish a two as the thirteenth card of its suit and then win a trick with it. So it is in hand valuation. The average player readily grasps the fact that an ace will win a trick; he cannot so readily grasp the fact that a hand distributed 5-4-3-1 is more promising than a hand distributed

5-3-3-2 because the four-card suit in the former distribution may yield a trick-winner.

In their valiant efforts to educate the average bridge player by substituting rule for reason, bridge writers have made many attempts to formulate hand valuation. Some have sought a mathematical or point-count basis; others have tried to translate the experts' "mental process" into tables of quick tricks or honor tricks.

In a point-count formula, each high card from the ace downward to the jack or ten is given a rating in points. The original schedule of this sort assessed the ace as worth 7 points, the king 5, the queen 3, the jack 2, and the ten as 1. In other counts, the assigned values are 6-4-3-2-1; 4-3-2-1; 3-2-1-½; and so on. Since none of these schedules is entirely accurate and any will yield a rough approximation of relative values, it matters little which is used. The popularity of a point-count formula seems to depend on ease of counting, and perhaps on other, psychological factors; the 4-3-2-1 count has become standard (and is used in this book wherever "points" are mentioned) although it probably is not quite so accurate as the 6-4-3-2-1 and 3-2-1-½ formulas.

Except in making an opening bid, the player can get little competent guidance from a quick-trick table. This is not only because the high-card counts fail to reflect distributional values, which have a decisive influence on bidding; but even more because the high cards themselves do not have constant values. They depend upon the contract, the holdings of all four players at the table, and the line of play that must consequently be adopted—and these conditions vary from deal to deal.

Thus it can seldom suffice to say, "Such-and-such a bid requires four honor tricks." The question would arise, "What kind of honor tricks?"

FIRST PRINCIPLE OF VALUATION

The value of a high card in any one suit depends on the number and nature of the high cards held in the other suits. In different circumstances a queen may be equivalent to an ace; an ace may be worth more or less than a K-Q. Two aces in a given hand may be inadequate; two K-Qs may be inadequate; and yet the combination of *one* ace and *one* K-Q may be ideal.

Beyond all such considerations are the cases—and they play a major role in expert competition—in which no formula can even approximate the trick-winning power of a hand. This is the "mental play" referred to before.

Dlr: South
Vul: Both

	♠ Q 10 2	
	♡ 10 8	
	◇ A Q J 6	
	♣ Q 10 8 2	
♠ A		♠ 8 7 5 3
♡ A 6 5 3		♡ Q J 9 7 2
◇ 9 7 5 3 2		◇ —
♣ K J 6		♣ 9 5 4 3
	♠ K J 9 6 4	
	♡ K 4	
	◇ K 10 8 4	
	♣ A 7	

West	North	East	South
			1 ♠
Pass	2 ◇	Pass	3 ◇
Pass	3 ♠	Pass	4 ♠
Dble	Pass	Pass	Pass

South went for 1100, and what valuation system could rate West's hand highly enough to predict even a one-trick defeat of the contract?

But because of North's diamond bid and South's diamond raise, West expected his partner to have at most a

singleton in diamonds. West could therefore open a diamond; regain the lead on the first round of trumps; lead a
second diamond for his partner to trump; and get in once
again with the ace of hearts to give his partner a second ruff.

West's double was based upon mental play of a most
elaborate sort, tantamount to a play-by-play forecast. But
such a forecast is largely an unconscious and automatic one,
for West did not repeat the series of plays to himself. He knew
that a trump stopper and a quick entry outside, combined
with a singleton in his partner's hand, add up to four tricks,
and four tricks are enough to warrant doubling.

West opened the nine of diamonds, a suit preference
signal indicating that he preferred a heart to a club return.
His hopes were more than realized when East was able to
trump on the first round, not the second.

East read the suit preference signal and led back the
queen of hearts. South played low; there was not the re-
motest chance that East had the ace of hearts and South did
not wish to create two heart entries for West in case West
had A-J. So the queen of hearts won the trick.

East continued with the jack of hearts and West won
with the ace. Then he led the two of diamonds for East to
ruff.

The next lead by East was a club, and South had a
problem because he could not see his opponents' hands and
could not know that his play would make no difference. If
East had started with only three spades, and if West had the
king of clubs (as indicated by his leading the two of diamonds, another suit preference signal), South could save a
trick by putting up his ace of clubs and leading trumps. If
East had the king of clubs, South might save two tricks by
playing his low club.

South decided to play the ace of clubs and lead a spade.
West won with his ace of spades, gave East a third diamond
ruff, and won the next trick with the king of clubs for the
defenders' seventh trick.

The process of valuation by "mental play" permitted not only the diamond lead that gave the defenders a four-trick set but also West's double, which gained at least 700 points for the defenders.

♠
♡
2
♢
♣

Timing Value of High Cards

Any high card may have a dual function: as a trick-winner and as a stopper. Usually it performs both of these functions. Occasionally its sole value will be as one or the other.

When a high card serves primarily as a stopper, its value is solely one of timing. Depending upon the contract, it may be required to win a trick on the first round, or on the second round, or on a later round, *or not at all*. A card may serve its purpose by preventing the opponents from making a damaging lead. It would win a trick if they made that lead; therefore they do not make that lead; therefore the card never wins a trick. But it may have been worth more than an ace.

Any bridge player understands the essential nature of timed stoppers at slam contracts:

♠ A K Q 8 5 4   ♠ J 9 6 3 2
♡ 7 3   ♡ A K Q J 8 5
◇ K 4 3   ◇ 8
♣ K 7   ♣ 2

The East-West cards will readily produce twelve or more tricks, but cannot make a slam because the opponents have two aces. Here it would be ridiculous to insist that two kings are worth 6 points and an ace only 4. One more ace in West's hand, instead of the kings of diamonds and clubs, would permit the slam to be made but the hand's count would be 2 points less.

The average player recognizes the timing function of high cards in slams; the expert extends the same recognition to lower contracts.

♠ A 8   ♠ 10 9 4 3
♡ A 6   ♡ J 10 5 2
◇ A K Q J 6 5 2   ◇ 8 7
♣ Q 5   ♣ J 4 3

To West, playing in a three-notrump contract, the Q-5 of clubs are worth virtually as much as the ace of clubs would be. West requires no additional trick-winners to make his contract; he has nine tricks in spades, hearts, and diamonds. All he needs is to stop the club suit, and the queen combined with the guarded jack in dummy is sufficient for that task.

It is the nature of West's entire hand that determines the value of that queen. If West did not have nine tricks in the other suits, the queen would not assume so exaggerated an importance.

By the 4-3-2-1 count, the queen of clubs counts 2 points in West's hand, while the king of spades or hearts would count 3 points, but the queen of clubs limits the opponents to two club tricks and probably is worth three tricks in all, while a major-suit king might be worthless if North-South could start off by running five club tricks against a notrump contract.

Translating the value of the queen of clubs into total points, in the notrump game contract it is probably worth 500 + 30 points (the value of the game plus 30 points for a notrump trick), but only because West can win nine tricks in the outside suits. If West lacked the ace of spades or hearts, the queen of clubs would be worth at most 30 points. If diamonds were trumps, the queen of clubs would be worth *nothing;* West's holding the Q-5 of clubs would be worth no more than a holding of the 6-5 doubleton, for the opponents would win exactly two club tricks in either case.

In nearly every valuation method, including the 4-3-2-1, a K-Q combination is rated higher than an ace—5 points against 4—because the K-Q may win two tricks, while an ace can win only one. But there are many cases in which the holder does not need to win two tricks; all he wants is one trick, but he wants to win that trick immediately.

1.	♠ 6 3	2.	♠ 6 3
	♡ J 10 6 5		♡ J 10 6 5
	◇ 9 6 5		◇ 9 6 5
	♣ J 10 4 3		♣ J 10 4 3
	♠ A K		♠ A K
	♡ K Q 4		♡ A 8 4
	◇ K Q J 10 4 3		◇ K Q J 10 4 3
	♣ A 5		♣ A 5

With the first hand, declarer cannot make three notrump. The opponents will lead spades, continue spades when they get in with the ace of diamonds, and defeat the contract when they regain the lead with the ace of hearts. With hand two, though, declarer can make three notrump, for he will win the opening spade lead, establish his diamonds, and run out his nine tricks when he wins the second spade lead. Here an ace is worth some 450 or 700 points more than the K-Q-x.

In actual bidding, this distinction should be recognized and utilized by the expert. For example:

West	North	East	South
		1 ♠	Dble
2 ♠	Pass	Pass	?

South, holding the first hand, should not bid three notrump; knowing from North's pass that he can hardly have an ace, South should anticipate that the opponents will knock out his two spade stoppers before he can establish and win nine tricks. He should double again, or bid diamonds. But if he holds the second hand, South should jump to three notrump, knowing that against the anticipated spade lead he can take nine tricks before his opponents can defeat him.

The expert is not so painstaking as to forecast a play-by-play result for each deal. He has learned, however, that *every contract requires a certain balance of trick-winning cards and timing cards.*

1.	2.
♠ 6 3 2	♠ 6 3 2
♡ J 6 2	♡ J 6 2
◇ 9 6 5	◇ 9 6 5
♣ J 10 4 3	♣ J 10 4 3
♠ A K 8	♠ A K 8
♡ K Q 4	♡ A 8 4
◇ K Q J 10 4	◇ K Q J 10 4
♣ A 5	♣ A 5

Now the ♡ K-Q-4 appears far more valuable than the ace. With the first hand, declarer will probably make a game in notrump since he can establish two hearts, four diamonds, two spades, and one club: nine tricks in all. With the second hand, though, the declarer will probably go down in three notrump, for he can establish no heart trick besides his ace, and can consequently muster only eight tricks.

NUMBER OF STOPPERS NEEDED—THE "WEAK SUIT"

For the successful fulfillment of any contract, declarer's side needs a certain number of stoppers in the suit or suits the defenders choose to lead. The exact number of stoppers depends in any given instance upon how many tricks declarer needs, and how many times he must lose the lead in establishing them.

The defenders have the opening lead and usually can get the lead two or three times again (in game contracts, once or twice again) while declarer is establishing his tricks. Therefore:

In trump contracts, declarer must usually be prepared to draw the opposing trumps and have two extra trumps to act as stoppers-at-large. Against normal distributions this requirement is met by a combined trump length of eight or more cards. Hence bidding is designed to discover at least an eight-card trump suit.

In notrump contracts, declarer's side must usually have at least two stoppers in the shortest combined suit. Notrump bidding can seldom be so arranged as to reveal the exact location of miscellaneous high cards in short, and therefore unbiddable, suits. Experience proves, however, that it is unsafe to initiate a game-going notrump contract with more than one "weak" suit.

A weak suit may be defined as a short suit containing no more than one possible stopper. The holding A-10-x, K-J-x, or better *may* become two stoppers; but A-6-2 or K-6-2 will not, and these are therefore weak suits.

One weak suit is acceptable; partner is likely to provide a second stopper in it. Two weak suits are dangerous; partner is unlikely to have protection in both, unless, of course, he has already promised such protection by his bids.

When assessing a weak suit for notrump purposes, a factor to consider is the ability to hold up a winner. If the combined suit has four cards, notrump is usually unsatisfactory. However, A-x opposite a small doubleton is worse than

A-x-x opposite a singleton because holding up the ace twice may be effective if the opposing cards are split 6-3. Similarly, A-K doubleton opposite a small doubleton is worse than A-K-x opposite a singleton.

In the more common, and more acceptable, case in which your weak suit has five cards, A-x-x opposite a small doubleton is better than the converse, and A-K-x opposite a small doubleton is better than the converse.

We may now return to the valuation and consequent bidding of the hands previously shown:

1. ♠ A K 8   2. ♠ A K 8
   ♡ K Q 4   ♡ A 8 4
   ◇ K Q J 10 4   ◇ K Q J 10 4
   ♣ A 5   ♣ A 5

A player may choose the first hand to make an opening bid of two notrump. He has only one "weak suit"—clubs. With the second, he should prefer an opening bid of one diamond. He has two weak suits and will postpone suggesting a notrump game unless his partner has indicated ability to stop at least one of them.

Thus in some cases K-10-9 or Q-J-x-x may appear more valuable, and may better justify a bid, than an ace, though both of the former combinations rank below the ace in all formulas.

West	North	East	South
	1♠	Pass	2◇
Pass	2♡	Pass	2NT
Pass	3◇	Pass	?

South should not bid three notrump with this hand:

♠ 9 6   ♡ A 7   ◇ K J 10 6 5   ♣ A 8 3 2

North's bidding has shown strength in the other three suits, and consequently weakness—probably a small singleton—in clubs. South has only one club stopper and cannot reasonably expect to run nine tricks before letting his opponents get the lead. If South is loath to give up hope of game, he must bid four clubs or four diamonds. But suppose South has this:

♠ 9 6   ♡ A 7   ◇ K J 10 6 5   ♣ K J 8 2

Now South's best bid, and best hope of game, is three notrump. South would as readily bid three notrump when holding ♣ Q J 10 2 or even ♣ Q J 7 2. The club suit promises to produce two stoppers, giving South time to establish his diamond suit and, with the tricks he expects in North's heart and spade suits, to amass nine tricks before the opponents get in again to run clubs.

UNIQUE VALUE OF THE ACE

Nevertheless the value of the ace is unique, because no other card fully satisfies the requirement of time and delivers a sure trick as well.

Among all the high-card holdings, only aces are essential to game contracts. While it is far from impossible, rarely can a game be made when the opponents hold a majority of the aces.

Consider this hand:

♠ A K Q J 10   ♡ 6   ◇ K Q   ♣ K Q J 10 5

This hand failed to make a four-spade contract, though the dummy held three spades and the opposing spades were divided 3–2. The opponents had three aces; and with the opening lead and with each of the aces they led hearts, forcing declarer to trump. Eventually he ran out of trumps, before he had established a trick with the K-Q of diamonds. If he had held the A-x of diamonds instead, he would have made his contract. The full deal was:

Dlr: South   ♠ 9 6 3
Vul: None   ♡ 10 7 4 2
       ♢ 10 5 4
       ♣ 8 4 3

♠ 8 2   ♠ 7 5 4
♡ A K 8 3   ♡ Q J 9 5
♢ J 9 7 6   ♢ A 8 3 2
♣ A 7 2   ♣ 9 6

       ♠ A K Q J 10
       ♡ 6
       ♢ K Q
       ♣ K Q J 10 5

West	North	East	South
			2♣
Pass	2♢	Pass	2♠
Pass	2NT	Pass	3♣
Pass	3♠	Pass	4♠
Pass	Pass	Pass	

South's two-club opening bid was artificial and forcing. North made the negative two-diamond response; and followed with a second negative bid of two notrump. After that, South drove to game.

West led the king of hearts and East played the queen, asking for a low heart lead next. West obliged, leading the three of hearts at trick two. Dummy played low and South trumped East's nine with the ten of spades.

South drew trumps in three rounds, but this left him with only one spade. When South next led the king of clubs, West took the ace and forced out South's last trump with the ace of hearts.

Now South ran his four good clubs, leaving only the K-Q of diamonds in his hand. East discarded down to the ace of diamonds and jack of hearts, and took the last two tricks to defeat the game contract.

South could have played much more cleverly, although in this case it would not have helped him to do so. After trumping the second round of hearts and leading only two rounds of spades, South should have shifted to the king of clubs, which would have lost to the ace. After trumping a third round of hearts, South should have continued to lead clubs, leaving one opposing trump outstanding.

If West had held not only three clubs but also three trumps, this would have made the contract. On the fourth club lead, South could overtrump in dummy if West trumped or discard dummy's last heart if West did not trump; either way, South could no longer be forced to trump a fourth heart lead and would have time to establish the one diamond trick he needed.

But West did not have the three-card trump holding. East had it, so even if South had perceived and pursued this plan it would not have worked. East would have trumped the third round of clubs and cashed the ace of diamonds for the setting trick.

THE TWO-ACE REQUIREMENT

Declarer's side need not have a majority of the aces, but it should have at least two of them in the combined hands before undertaking a game contract on the "book" requirement of 26 points.

That is why experts hesitate to make opening bids on strong hands that lack aces, and hesitate to pass relatively weak hands containing two or more aces.

	1.		2.	
	♠	A Q 6 4 2	♠	K Q 10 9 5
	♡	A 6 5	♡	K J 7
	◇	9 7 4 3	◇	Q J 9 7
	♣	7	♣	6

In days gone by, many experts would open with the first hand but pass on the second. Yet the latter counts two points more and in trick-winning power is at least one trick better, if not two or more.

A CLASSIC FREAK . . .

There was a classic hand in which a player held 150 aces (well, not literally 150 aces: all four aces, counting 150 points at rubber bridge!) but could not defeat an opposing three-notrump contract.

Dlr: North
Vul: N-S

		♠ K 10 2	
		♡ Q J 9 5	
		◇ K J 10 6	
		♣ K 8	
♠ A 6			♠ 9 7 4 3
♡ A 8 7 4 2			♡ 10 3
◇ A 8 3			◇ 7 5 2
♣ A 5 4			♣ 9 7 6 2
		♠ Q J 8 5	
		♡ K 6	
		◇ Q 9 4	
		♣ Q J 10 3	

West	North	East	South
	1 ◇	Pass	2NT
Pass	3NT	Pass	Pass
Dble	Pass	Pass	Pass

South's two-notrump response showed a balanced 11 or 12 points, a common expert practice today (though a one-spade response is preferred).

West led the four of hearts and South took East's ten with his king and led spades until West took his ace on the second round. West cashed the ace of hearts and led another heart, which dummy won, South discarding a diamond.

South led clubs until West took his ace, and at this point South had nine tricks with three spades, three clubs, and three hearts. West could take his ace of diamonds now or later. The four aces were the only tricks he could get.

. . . AND ITS PRACTICAL COUNTERPART

The deal just shown was a freak, but occasionally players can recognize and exploit a similar pattern:

```
Dlr: North              ♠ Q 9 6 4
Vul: None               ♡ A 7
                        ◇ Q J 10 2
                        ♣ K Q J
         ♠ A J 10                    ♠ 8 5
         ♡ 10 8 6 3 2                ♡ Q 5 4
         ◇ A 5 3                     ◇ 9 8 6 4
         ♣ 8 6                       ♣ A 5 4 2
                        ♠ K 7 3 2
                        ♡ K J 9
                        ◇ K 7
                        ♣ 10 9 7 3
```

West	North	East	South
	1 ◇	Pass	1 ♠
Pass	2 ♠	Pass	2NT
Pass	3NT	Pass	Pass
Pass			

Rarely would an expert pair relinquish an opportunity to play in a major suit divided 4-4 (of which more later), but North could recognize this as a case in which South's spades were weak and the other suits were solid. North was right, because in four spades South would have had to lose two trump tricks and two aces and could not have made game. South made three notrump, though it was not without its pitfalls.

West opened the three of hearts and South won East's queen with his king. South led the king of diamonds, which held, and another diamond, taken by West's ace. A second heart lead took out dummy's ace.

After cashing two more diamonds and discarding two spades, South led a spade to his king. West won with the ace and now had no quick entry to his hearts, so he continued with the jack of spades. This was won with the queen in the dummy.

The king of clubs lost to East's ace, and dummy was thrown back in with a club. A spade lead from dummy gave the defenders their fourth and last trick, for South still had the high heart.

Solid as the North-South hands were, the power of the three aces was so great that if South had slipped even slightly he would have failed to make game. For example, if South had led a club instead of a spade from dummy after cashing his diamonds, he would have gone down. East would have taken his ace of clubs, a heart lead would have knocked out South's last stopper, and West would have had two good hearts and the ace of spades for three more tricks.

Making three notrump, or a major-suit game, tends to be difficult when three aces are missing. So if you suspect that this is the case, and your values are borderline, you should consider putting on the brakes below game.

♠
♡
3 Valuation of High-Card Combinations
◇
♣

The trick-winning power of a high-card combination is measured by four different standards:

1. Trick-winning potential
2. Ease of establishment
3. Combining quality
4. Security

The *potential* of a high-card combination is the maximum number of tricks it may produce. It is in trick-winning potential that K-Q-x is superior to A-x-x. Opposite partner's strong one-notrump opening bid, the first hand below is a sound raise, and the second is a quick pass, though each counts 8 points:

1.	♠ A 6 3	2.	♠ A 6 3
	♡ Q 8 5 4		♡ 8 5 4 2
	◇ J 9 5		◇ 9 5 3
	♣ J 4 2		♣ A 4 2

The second hand can produce only two tricks; the first hand may produce three or four tricks.

This fine distinction is a debatable one. Some modern experts would make it, but the majority, including the authors of this book, in 1989, would not.

Trick-winning potential also makes honors in combination more valuable than scattered honors.

1. ♠ 4 3 2	2. ♠ 4 3 2
♠ K 6 5	♠ K J 5

The first holding will produce one trick 50 percent of the time, with no legitimate chance for two tricks. But bring in a jack from another suit (which might have been useless there) and suddenly declarer will get one trick 76 percent of the time and two tricks 24 percent of the time.

It is *ease of establishment* to which the expert refers when he speaks of his ability to "handle" a combination of cards. Though it would appear that K-Q-x is as good as K-Q-J if the ace is known to be at the holder's right, K-Q-J is patently superior. To establish K-Q-J as two tricks, the holder need only lead them out. To establish K-Q-x he must lead toward them twice; if entries are lacking, K-Q-x cannot be "handled" for two tricks.

The expert gauges the trick-winning power of any combination by his knowledge of suit-establishment technique. Unless he can "handle" the suit, he assigns little value to it. A poll of experts once revealed that the majority favored opening on the first hand below but passing on the second.

1. ♠ A J 5	2. ♠ A J 5
♡ K Q 8 4	♡ K Q 8 4
◇ Q 10 4 3	◇ Q 8 4 3
♣ 8 7	♣ 8 7

Obviously the distinction must be explained by the presence of the ten of diamonds in the first hand, since all the other cards are identical. But the expert is not thinking of individual cards. He is considering how he will play the combination if he becomes the declarer.

1.	◊ 5 2	**2.**	◊ 5 2
	◊ Q 10 4 3		◊ Q 8 4 3

In the second situation, there is no standard suit-establishment play by which South can plausibly hope to develop a trick-winner. The chance that East will hold both the ace and king is 3-to-1 against, a hope too remote to be leaned upon.

In the first diagram, however, South can finesse East for the jack, with an eventual trick in sight if East holds the A-J or K-J in the suit. Because he can foresee a way of playing the suit, South considers it valuable.

The *combining quality* of high cards is measured by the chance that they may be improved by unbid and unbiddable cards in partner's hand. This is another point in favor of Q-10-4-3 over Q-8-4-3. If partner should hold the jack of the suit, the Q-8 combination gains little in value, while the Q-10 combination becomes a sure trick.

Similarly, A-10-2 is considered by the expert to be worth, in trick-winning value, almost twice as much as A-3-2; for the former will produce an extra stopper opposite Q-x, J-x, or 9-x-x-x, while the latter will gain nothing in value if partner holds the jack or nine and will gain but a dubious possibility of an extra trick if partner holds the queen.

The suit K-Q-x-x is doubly superior to the suit A-x-x-x, first in trick-winning potential, as has been shown, and also in combining quality; for A-x-x-x does not gain in value if partner holds J-x, while opposite K-Q-x-x the J-x may be worth a trick.

The *security* value of a high card is found in the degree of the probability that it will win a trick. As an assurance of one trick, Q-J-10 is better than K-J-x though it counts one point less; Q-J-x, never rated higher than K-x-x, is superior to it as a stopper and is on occasion so acknowledged in expert bidding—or should be.

Dlr: North
Vul: Both

	♠ Q 8 5	
	♡ 8	
	◇ A 4	
	♣ A K J 10 7 5 3	

♠ K 7 2		♠ A 10 9
♡ A Q J 9 7 2		♡ 10 6 5
◇ Q 7 3		◇ J 10 9 5
♣ 8		♣ 9 6 4

	♠ J 6 4 3	
	♡ K 4 3	
	◇ K 8 6 2	
	♣ Q 2	

West	North	East	South
	1♣	Pass	1◇
1♡	3♣	Pass	3NT
Pass	Pass	Pass	

From the bidding, West could read the nature of the North-South hands. North had to have a very long, strong club suit, and South had to hold the king of hearts, without which he could not have bid three notrump after the heart overcall. West wished to put his partner on lead for a heart return through South's king. Diamonds seemed like a poor choice in view of South's earlier bid in the suit, so West opened the two of spades.

East won with his ace of spades and led the ten of hearts. It made no difference whether or not South covered. West ran six heart tricks before cashing the king of spades, and South was down four.

In this case, Q-J-x would have been a much safer heart stopper than the king for South. Unless West had the A-K-10 of hearts and East had the A-K of spades with which to gain the lead twice—an unlikely chance—the Q-J-x would be a stopper. East needed only one entry to destroy the value of the king of hearts.

South did not need a heart trick. He had nine tricks—seven clubs and two diamonds—as soon as he got the lead, and he had only to prevent the opponents from running five tricks before he could get in. With Q-J-x as his heart holding, South would have made his game, for the defenders could have taken only two spade and two heart tricks.

Also, Q-J-x is superior to the king in combining quality, since the presence of the ten in partner's hand will make the assurance complete.

♠
♡
4 **Effect of the Rank of Low Cards**
♢
♣

Every card has, theoretically, a greater value than any lower-ranking card. A position can be arranged in which a three is of greater value than a two:

	♡ 8 7 6	
♡ 5 4		♡ J 10 9 2
	♡ A K Q 3	

West leads the five of hearts, and East must cover dummy's card. Upon North's gaining the lead twice more, the process is repeated until South holds and leads the three of hearts, which wins the trick from East's two.

   Usually any distinction in value between two low cards is owing to the vagaries of distribution and cannot be foreseen:

```
                      ♠ Q 4 3
                      ♡ 10 8 7
        ♠ 7 2                          ♠ J 10 9
        ♡ 9 5                          ♡ A K Q J 4 3
                      ♠ A K 8 6 5
                      ♡ 6 2
```

Spades are trumps. West leads hearts and East plays three rounds. On the third round South can win the trick by ruffing with the eight of spades. He could not have done so had he held, instead, ♠ A K 7 6 5.

Rarely can such fine shadings in the relative values of spot-cards control a choice between bidding and passing. There are, nevertheless, many cases in which the superior timing value of an eight or nine over a lower card may be recognized in the bidding. The holding A-Q-9 is frequently one full trick better than the holding A-Q-8. The former may permit a double finesse if partner has 10-3-2. A throw-in play may be possible with A-Q-9 that would not be possible with A-Q-8 or lower. Here is another case:

```
                      ♠ 6 3 2
        ♠ K 7 5                        ♠ J 10 8 4
                      ♠ A Q 9
```

The two of spades is led from the North hand. If East plays low, South may finesse the nine, forcing out West's king and giving South two tricks in the suit. If East puts up the ten or jack, South covers with the queen. West can win with the king, but now South has a tenace over East and will get two tricks in the suit.

Obviously, if South had only A-Q-8 in the suit, he could win only one trick, his ace. His queen would be killed by the king in any event, and East would still have the suit stopped.

In that case the nine is demonstrably superior to the eight. Similarly, having an eight, instead of a lower card, is not without its value in many cases.

♣ 7

♣ Q 9 8 6 2   ♣ A 10 4

♣ K J 5 3

In notrump, West leads the six of clubs. East wins with the
ace and returns the ten. If South covers with the jack, West
can force out his only club stopper immediately. If South
puts up the king, and East has one entry, West's entire club
suit will be realized.

Consider the difference if South held the eight of clubs:

♣ 7

♣ Q 9 6 5 2   ♣ A 10 4

♣ K J 8 3

West leads the five of clubs; East wins with the ace and
returns the ten. *South covers with the jack.* Now West cannot
lead the suit again because it would give South an extra club
trick. East may have an entry, but he must use it to get the
lead again, and now when he leads the four of clubs South
still has the suit stopped by putting up his king.

This is the exact principle which, at times, makes the
famous Bath Coup such an effective timing play.

Dlr: South
Vul: None

```
                    ♠ 8
                    ♡ 7 4 2
                    ◇ Q 10 7 5 3
                    ♣ K 9 5 2
♠ K 10 7 5 2                         ♠ Q J 9 4 3
♡ K Q 10 9                           ♡ 8 6 5
◇ 9 4                                ◇ A 6 2
♣ 10 3                               ♣ 8 7
                    ♠ A 6
                    ♡ A J 3
                    ◇ K J 8
                    ♣ A Q J 6 4
```

West	North	East	South
			1♣
1♠	2♣	2♠	3♠
Pass	4♣	Pass	5♣
Pass	Pass	Pass	

The Bath Coup was originally used to trick the opponent into leading into a tenace, but it has its straightforward uses too, as this example shows.

West leads the king of hearts. If South wins it, he will go down; because when East gets in with the ace of diamonds he can lead a heart to give West two tricks in the suit. If South ducks the first heart, he cannot be defeated. West cannot continue the suit, and when East gets in for the first and last time it will be too late, for the second heart trick will not be established for the defenders.

It is no doubt possible to compute the relative values of all cards—Dr. Emanuel Lasker attempted it and perhaps succeeded—but the respective values so established are useless in hand valuation. They are too indefinite, for they are subject to some degree of modification on every hand. Authorities seldom attempt to rate the ten and lower cards, having to fall back on "body" to describe the relative advantage of holding nines, eights, sevens, and sixes instead of an equal number of two, threes, fours, and fives.

A single ten or lower card in the hand seldom controls a player's bid. The presence in his hand of several such cards may be decisive. Suppose North opens one heart, East overcalls one spade, and South holds one of these two hands:

1.	♠ K 6 4 3	2.	♠ K 10 9 4
	♡ 5 3		♡ 10 7
	◇ A 10 6		◇ A 10 6
	♣ 6 5 3 2		♣ 9 8 7 2

In the modern game, in which the word "pass" is dying out, most players will bid one notrump with both hands, but feel much happier if holding number two. In fact, the wise players will pass with the first hand.

The second hand is stronger by two tens, two nines, and an eight. South may expect at least one of these five cards to win a trick, or to furnish an extra stopper, or to facilitate the handling of an establishable suit. *A hand that has "body" is therefore one in which high spot-cards are the rule rather than the exception.* Such a hand may often be rated about three points higher than its high-card point-count.

Jacks and lower cards are third- and fourth-round stoppers and are useful only when such stoppers are needed. With surplus trumps to act as stoppers-at-large in all side suits, a player does not need "fillers."

♠ A K Q J 8 4 3   ♡ J 10   ◇ J 10   ♣ J 10

With spades as trumps, the J-10 doubletons are hardly worth more than 3-2 doubletons. But this is not so unless the trump suit is very strong.

Dlr: South
Vul: N-S

```
                    ♠ 10 8 4
                    ♡ K 6
                    ◇ A 10 8 3
                    ♣ Q J 7 3
    ♠ 6                            ♠ J 9 7 2
    ♡ A 8 7 3                      ♡ 10 9 5
    ◇ 9 7 5 2                      ◇ K Q 6 4
    ♣ 9 8 6 2                      ♣ A 5
                    ♠ A K Q 5 3
                    ♡ Q J 4 2
                    ◇ J
                    ♣ K 10 4
```

West	North	East	South
			1♠
Pass	1NT	Pass	2♡
Pass	3♠	Pass	4♠
Pass	Pass	Pass	

North's one-notrump response was forcing (see page 122), and his subsequent jump to three spades showed a limit raise with three-card trump support.

West leads the two of diamonds, and dummy's ace wins the trick. If North's diamonds were any weaker—if even they were A-10-7-3—South could not make his contract. With two aces and a trump trick, the defenders could force South to ruff two diamonds, after which he would have insufficient trumps to prevent a final diamond trick from being cashed. With North's diamonds as strong as they are, the defenders cannot lead the suit three times without establishing dummy's ten, whereupon their setting trick is gone.

In actual play, the ten of diamonds will never win a trick and the importance of the eight of diamonds will be a potential one only, for the defenders will shift suits rather than establish the ten. This need not blind the bidder to the true value of such cards.

♠
♥
5 Long-Suit Tricks
♦
♣

Distributional values are, in the expert mind, no different from high-card values. Both are means of winning tricks and of stopping the opponents from winning tricks. In trick-winning power South's cards in the following examples are of identical value:

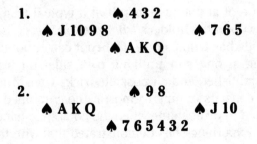

1.   ♠ 4 3 2
   ♠ J 10 9 8   ♠ 7 6 5
          ♠ A K Q

2.   ♠ 9 8
   ♠ A K Q   ♠ J 10
        ♠ 7 6 5 4 3 2

Either combination will produce three tricks for South. Number one, however, will produce three tricks without establishment; number two requires for establishment three losing leads, and these must be compensated by three stoppers in other suits. Distributional values must therefore be appraised in accordance with the number of stoppers in other suits. These stoppers may be high cards; they may equally well be trumps, which are equivalent, in timing value, to aces. In number two above, South has three sure tricks if spades are trumps, for then the suit supplies its own stoppers. Again:

1. ♠ A K Q J 10	2. ♠ A K Q J 10	3. ♠ A K Q J 10 2
♡ 6	♡ 6	♡ 6
◇ K Q	◇ A 2	◇ K Q
♣ K Q J 10 5	♣ K Q J 10 5	♣ K Q J 10

Hand one was previously shown as having failed to make four spades. It was noted that if declarer had held hand number two he could have made four spades. The same is true of number three. The potential winners in the three hands are precisely the same, but either the ace in hand two or the extra spade in hand three gives declarer trump control, which with number one he lacks. Here the extra trump is exactly equivalent to an ace.

TRUMP CONTROL

The value of any long side suit at a typical trump contract depends upon the holder's *trump control.*

A side has trump control when it can continue to ruff an opposing strong suit until its own side-suit strength has been established and all possible tricks won. Trump control usually consists of nine trumps in the combined hands and is deemed to be absolute when the combined hands have ten trumps. Experience has demonstrated that with these trump holdings a partnership can establish the maximum value of its side suits without running out of trumps. A combined holding of eight cards, though it is the standard minimum for a satisfactory trump suit, cannot be relied upon for establishment of a long, weak side suit in which two or more tricks must be lost.

A long suit of freakish length in one hand may supply trump control all by itself:

1. ♠ A K Q 8 7 5 3	2. ♠ A K Q 8 7
♡ 9	♡ 9 8 2
◇ 8 6 4 3	◇ 8 6 4 3
♣ 2	♣ 2

With hand number one, the player counts his diamond length as one full trick because he has trump control. He will bid on the absolute assumption that his hand will win eight tricks. With hand two he counts the diamond suit as being of little value because he will have used up all his trumps before he can establish and win a trick with the fourth diamond. But at any time that partner raises spades, the diamond suit in number two assumes the same one-trick rating that it has in number one.

Thus, to the expert, distributional values are sometimes equivalent to high-card values, sometimes worth less, sometimes worth more, depending upon how many stoppers—whether furnished by aces or by trump control—he has.

1. ♠ A K Q 6 5	2. ♠ A K Q 6 5
♡ A 8 4	♡ A 8 4
◇ 9 6 5 3	◇ 9 6 5
♣ 7	♣ K 7

Suppose either of the above hands to be South's in the following bidding sequence, with East-West vulnerable:

West	North	East	South
			1♠
Pass	Pass	Dble	Pass
2♡	2♠	3♡	Pass
4♡	Pass	Pass	?

South should now consider a four-spade sacrifice bid on hand number one; he should pass on number two. He does not expect to defeat the contract with either hand, for North's first pass has warned him of a total absence of defensive assistance. He does fear, with hand two, that he will lose seven tricks and go down 700 points (800 in duplicate); the king of clubs may not win a trick. He has no such fear on hand one, for with a four-card spade holding in North's hand he has trump control and can confidently expect to win a low-card trick in diamonds, either by establishing his last diamond or by ruffing it in dummy after the opponents' trumps are drawn.

EFFECT OF ENTRIES ON LONG-SUIT VALUATION

In notrump contracts both stoppers and entries affect distributional values. A long suit is more valuable if it contains its own entry.

1.	$\diamond$ 10 8 6 4 2		2.	$\diamond$ A 8 6 4 2	
$\diamond$ K J 3		$\diamond$ Q 9	$\diamond$ K J 3		$\diamond$ Q 9
	$\diamond$ A 7 5			$\diamond$ 10 7 5	

The combined North-South holdings in the two diagrams are apparently identical, but the diamond suit in number two is far more valuable in notrump. In either case, the suit may be established after losing two rounds and winning one (with the ace). In number one, after this process, North must have a side entry or the two remaining cards cannot be cashed. If North has no side entry, or if he has an entry that the opponents can knock out before the diamond suit is established, the suit is worthless. In number two, by ducking the first two leads and winning the third with the ace, it is possible to provide entry to the established cards regardless of the defense.

    Of the following hands, number one was shown as a proper pass of a strong one-notrump bid. Number two would be a proper raise; number three would be a doubtful raise.

1. ♠ A 6 3   2. ♠ A 6 3   3. ♠ A 6 3
   ♡ 8 5 4 2   ♡ 9 5 3   ♡ 9 5 3
   ◇ 9 5 3   ◇ A 8 5 4 2   ◇ 8 5 4 3 2
   ♣ A 4 2   ♣ 4 2   ♣ A 4

Number two contains, besides the two aces, two possible distributional tricks—the long cards in diamonds—and in a suit that provides its own entry. Number three has the same two possible distributional tricks and most players would raise on it, but they should recognize the danger that both aces may be gone before the long diamonds can be made good.

Except in freak cases, distributional strength cannot exist in one hand alone, but is made up of a combination of the two partnership hands.

1. ♠ A K 4 3   2. ♠ A K 4 3 2
   ♡ A Q 7 5   ♡ A Q 7 5 4
   ◇ A 6 3   ◇ A 6
   ♣ 4 2   ♣ 4

To the expert, number one is a dangerous hand, despite its high-card strength; the second is a powerful hand. The reason is that number two will probably produce four or five distributional tricks in addition to its high cards, while number one is unlikely to produce more than one. But this original appraisal is based upon the mathematical likelihood that partner will have at least three cards in either spades or hearts. If the bidding proves this assumption to be false, and if partner reveals that he has a two-suited hand composed of diamonds and clubs, then number one, which will support partner's suits better, becomes by far the superior of the two hands.

HOW SCORING AFFECTS LONG-SUIT VALUATION

In deciding how many tricks a long suit will win, the expert visualizes the various possible distributions of the other players' hands and the suit-establishment methods he may employ. A trump suit of A-Q-x-x-x may win four tricks (if partner holds three cards in the suit and the finesse for the king wins); it may win only three tricks (if in the same circumstances the finesse loses); it may win only two tricks (if partner is short in the suit and an opponent holds K-J-x-x). It is not true, however, that the expert values such suits "optimistically" if he is non-vulnerable and "pessimistically" if he is vulnerable. He notes all contingencies at all times. His bids do depend, of course, on how great and how likely his possible loss is, and on how much he stands to gain by risking such a loss.

Let us say South holds:

♠ 7   ♡ A K J 8 6 4   ◇ Q J 7 3   ♣ A 3

South may win six tricks in hearts; he may win only four. He may win two tricks, or one trick, or no trick in diamonds (depending on whether or not his partner holds a diamond honor, on finding entries to his partner's hand, and on how long his trump control will last if he must repeatedly ruff spade leads). South's trick-winning power, then, may vary from five to nine tricks. He gambles on winning the maximum if he stands to profit greatly; he refuses to gamble if he stands to gain little. Suppose the bidding to be, with neither side vulnerable:

West	North	East	South
			1 ♡
Pass	Pass	Dble	Redble
1 ♠	Pass	2 ♠	Pass!

If South bids three hearts he may make it, but he may as easily go down 500 points. He will not risk 500 points to make a partscore or to prevent his opponents' making a partscore. But suppose other bidding:

West	North	East	South
			1♡
Pass	1NT	3♠	4♡!

Since North's one-notrump response did not necessarily promise more than one trick, South's four-heart bid risks almost as much as a three-heart bid would have risked in the previous bidding situation. But, while South's risk is still at least 500 points, his possible profit is now a game worth about 500 points.

The expert does not—or at least should not—risk when there is little or nothing to gain. In the following deal there was a "fielder's choice" situation, in the experts' vernacular. But somehow the casual player finds a suit such as South's irresistible.

Dlr: South
Vul: Both

```
                    ♠ J 10 9 2
                    ♡ 5 3
                    ◇ 6 4 3
                    ♣ Q 10 9 2
    ♠ K 8 5 4                       ♠ A Q 6 3
    ♡ K 9 8 2                       ♡ 7
    ◇ K 5                           ◇ A 9 8 2
    ♣ 7 6 4                         ♣ K J 8 5
                    ♠ 7
                    ♡ A Q J 10 6 4
                    ◇ Q J 10 7
                    ♣ A 3
```

West	North	East	South
			1♡
Pass	Pass	Dble	Pass
1♠	Pass	2♠	3♡
Dble	Pass	Pass	Pass

West led the four of spades and East won with the ace. Since West's spade bid marked him with four and South with a singleton, East shifted to the two of diamonds. South played the ten and West won with the king. A diamond return to the ace and a diamond continuation gave West a ruff.

West switched to the seven of clubs, covered by the ten, jack, and ace. Next came the ace and queen of hearts, West winning the latter.

A club lead put East in again, and West ruffed the last diamond. South was down three, for 800 points, and East-West could not even make a game.

South's three-heart bid gave his opponents a fielder's choice. If they wished to go on to three or more spades, South's bid could not stop them. If they found it more profitable to double, they could double—as they did.

If South felt a compulsion to rebid his hand, he might far better have bid two hearts over the take-out double. West might have been too weak to make a free bid (he wasn't—he would have bid two spades anyway—but he might have been) and if so the two-heart bid might have prevented East-West from finding their spade fit. And if South were doomed to be doubled, at least it would have been one level lower and would have saved him (and poor North) 300 points. But the important thing is that the two-heart bid might have accomplished something. The three-heart bid could not.

♠
♡
6 Considerations
in Selecting a
◇ Trump Suit
♣

It is almost axiomatic that a partnership should have numerical superiority in any trump suit it selects, and whenever possible this should be clear-cut superiority. A combined holding of seven cards is considered hardly adequate. Eight cards are generally accepted as the minimum for a satisfactory trump suit.

A combined holding of fewer than eight cards may nevertheless be playable, *depending upon the manner in which the trump cards are divided between the partnership hands.* Consider the six trump cards A, K, Q, J, 6, 2. If the division is A-K-Q in one hand, J-6-2 in the other, it is no trump suit at all. If the division is A-K-Q-J in one hand, 6-2 in the other, the suit will prove satisfactory only in freak cases, of which the following is the only representative type:

♠ A K Q J	♠ 6 2
♡ 6 3	♡ 8 5
◇ Q 8 5 4	◇ K 7 6 3
♣ K J 6	♣ A Q 10 7 2

With normal breaks in all suits, these hands will produce game in spades and in no other contract. But such contracts can be made so rarely that bidding methods are not designed to reach them. West's spade holding is at best sufficient to draw the opponents' trumps, and leaves nothing over to stop their strong suit. If the combined hands happen to have high-card stoppers in all the other suits, a notrump contract may be played with equal profit and greater safety. In fact, the spade contract in the above example is always dangerous, for a 5-2 division of the opposing trumps will slaughter it.

Expert players can sometimes recognize an opportunity to play with six combined trumps divided 4-2. The following deal, played by Bill Root (South) and the late Harold Harkavy in a game in Florida, produced one of those rare cases.

Dlr: North
Vul: None

		♠ A Q	
		♡ Q 8 4	
		◇ 7 5 3	
		♣ A Q J 9 6	

♠ 8 7 5			♠ 6 4 3 2
♡ K 3 2			♡ J 10 9 6
◇ A K Q 10 8 4			◇ J
♣ 7			♣ 10 8 5 3

		♠ K J 10 9	
		♡ A 7 5	
		◇ 9 6 2	
		♣ K 4 2	

West	North	East	South
	1♣	Pass	1♠
2◇	Pass	Pass	3♣
Pass	3♠	Pass	4♠
Pass	Pass	Pass	

North bid three spades on a two-card trump holding because his two trumps were both high cards and because he had not raised to two spades over two diamonds; therefore South could not expect to find a great deal of trump support in North's hand.

South bid four spades, gambling on finding no more than four trumps in either opponent's hand. The odds are about 2-to-1 against an opponent's having five trumps when there are seven trumps outstanding.

The contract was made with ease. West won the first three tricks by cashing his high diamonds, but then West could not lead another diamond because dummy could trump it while South discarded. So West led his seven of clubs.

This club lead was won with dummy's jack. Dummy's ace of spades was cashed, then the queen was overtaken by South's king and South continued with his jack and ten of spades, drawing the last of East's trumps. Four more clubs and the ace of hearts made ten tricks.

The essential requirements when one wishes to play for a game with only six trumps, divided four and two, are: First, if either partner can be forced to trump, it must be the dummy, with the two-card trump holding; and, second, the six-card combined holding must include at least the ace, king, and queen.

In such cases, a major-suit game with a six-card combined trump holding is often the only game contract that can be made. In the hand above, North-South could not have made three notrump because West could have run six diamond tricks, and they could not have made five clubs with three quick diamond tricks to lose.

5-1 AND 6-0 DIVISIONS

Divide the given six trumps A-K-Q-J-6 in one hand, the two in the other, and the trump position is somewhat better, but not much. There will be only one extra trump for use as a stopper, and this is seldom sufficient. On partscore hands, such a suit may be the best available; and on very strong hands—when the side suits are solid or are quickly establishable—it may be preferable to a notrump contract. It must be noted, however, that declarer must not lose the lead more than once in establishing his tricks:

♠ A K Q J 6	♠ 2
♡ 8	♡ A 5 3
◇ K 10 9 5	◇ J 8 7 2
♣ 9 8 4	♣ A K 10 5 2

With a 4-3 spade break and a 3-2 club break, West can make four spades; his one extra trump is sufficient to establish his ten tricks, for he need lose the lead only once. A notrump game would hardly be possible with the single heart stopper. But here again the spade contract, while it is the best hope of game, will be costly if the trumps break badly.

When the six trumps A-K-Q-J-6-2 are all in one hand, it is usually a satisfactory trump suit. The top cards will draw the opposing trumps and leave declarer two additional trumps to act as stoppers-at-large, and in most cases two stoppers are enough. Nevertheless, a six-card length opposite a void can be depended upon only when the suit is very strong in high cards—almost never weaker than A-K-Q-x-x-x or K-Q-J-10-x-x.

What has been said of a six-card combined holding may almost be said of a seven-card combined holding, so far as bidding purposes are concerned. Seven trumps in almost any division *may* be adequate, but they cannot be depended upon. Unless the partners together have all the top cards, or one partner has a strong six-card suit, a search should be made in the bidding for a longer trump suit.

In fact, if safety were the only consideration, the longest combined holding would always be most desirable, for there is then less to fear from a bad break. But conditions do not always make caution profitable.

SUPERIORITY OF THE EVENLY DIVIDED TRUMP SUIT

Often, and at some risk, a major suit may be selected in preference to a minor, a seven- or eight-card combined length in preference to a nine- or ten-card. The longest available trump suit is not necessarily the most favorable.

```
Dlr: South          ♠ J 7 4 3
Vul: Both           ♡ K J 6 5
                    ◇ 9 5 3
                    ♣ Q 7
    ♠ 10 9 5                        ♠ 8 2
    ♡ 9 2                           ♡ 3
    ◇ J 10 6 2                      ◇ A Q 8 7 4
    ♣ K 10 6 5                      ♣ J 9 8 4 2
                    ♠ A K Q 6
                    ♡ A Q 10 8 7 4
                    ◇ K
                    ♣ A 3
```

With the ten-card heart suit as trumps, the North-South hands produce only eleven tricks. With the eight-card spade suit as trumps, they produce twelve tricks and make a small slam; for three rounds of spades draw trumps, after which the heart suit provides a discard for North's losing club and permits dummy to ruff a club that would otherwise be lost.

The fact was not recognized in the bidding, which was:

West	North	East	South
			2♡
Pass	3♡	Pass	4NT
Pass	5♣	Pass	6♡
Pass	Pass	Pass	

Having received assurance of heart support, as well as a positive response to his two-bid, South was so well satisfied with his trump suit that he saw no reason to look for another. He made a mistake.

It would not have cost South anything to bid three spades before bidding four notrump, nor North anything to raise three spades to four, confirming four-card support for that suit too. South could then have made his Blackwood bid, intending to bid seven hearts if North showed an ace and six otherwise—but six spades, not hearts.

In such a case, and in nearly all cases in which one cannot count thirteen top tricks, it is not the number of trumps but the division of trumps that determines the choice of suits. Of alternative trump suits, when one suit is evenly divided between the partnership hands and the other is unevenly divided, *the evenly divided suit is usually more productive of tricks.*

Thus, the preceding example did not illustrate the advantage of an eight-card suit over a ten-card suit; it illustrated the advantage of an even division of trumps over an uneven division. As between an eight-card length divided 4-4 and a ten-card length divided 5-5, the ten-card length is almost invariably superior. But as between a 6-4 or 5-4 or 5-3 trump suit and a 4-4 trump suit, the 4-4 suit will often produce at least one extra trick.

CASES IN WHICH A 4-4 TRUMP SUIT IS BEST

There are various hand types on which the superiority of the 4-4 trump suit may be recognized in the bidding.

First type of hand on which the 4-4 trump suit is superior

Any hand that requires one or more ruffing tricks to fulfill its contract.

A suit divided 4-4 can win no more than four tricks if it is not trumps. If trumps, it can win those same four tricks in one hand and add one or more tricks by ruffing in the other hand.

Of course, a 5-3 trump division can produce more than five tricks *if ruffs may be taken with the three-card holding.* This, however, is possible less than half the time. When both a 5-3 and a 4-4 trump suit are available, one partner must *ipso facto* hold 5-4 in those two suits. This is the partner who will be short in the other two suits, and who must most often ruff. If his five-card suit is made trumps, he gains nothing by ruffing unless he can ruff *three times,* which is unusual. He can win a maximum of five trump tricks in the 5-3 suit and four tricks in the 4-4 suit. If his 4-4 suit is made trumps, he can still get five tricks from his 5-3 side suit and he will usually get five or more tricks from his 4-4 trump suit.

Against a 5-3 trump suit, the defenders can often lead trumps until the shorter hand has no more, and thereby destroy ruffing power. Against a 4-4 trump suit they cannot do so; there is no "shorter" hand:

```
Dlr: South          ♠ Q 8 7
Vul: N-S            ♡ K 7 5 4
                    ◇ 10 9 4 2
                    ♣ 10 8
    ♠ 5 3                           ♠ J 10 2
    ♡ 10 8 2                        ♡ J 9
    ◇ K J 6 3                       ◇ A Q 7 5
    ♣ A Q 9 2                       ♣ K J 6 5
                    ♠ A K 9 6 4
                    ♡ A Q 6 3
                    ◇ 8
                    ♣ 7 4 3
```

Given a 3-2 break in both hearts and spades, the North-South hands cannot make four spades if West opens a trump and if the defenders continue to lead trumps at every opportunity. The declarer (South, undoubtedly) can win five spade tricks and four heart tricks for a total of nine; but he cannot get a tenth trick by ruffing a club in dummy, for by the time he has rid dummy of clubs dummy's trumps also will be gone.

No lead and no defense can beat four hearts. After South has drawn trumps in three rounds and has run five spades, South's remaining heart will trump a diamond and North's remaining heart will trump a club.

Second type of hand on which the 4-4 trump suit is superior

Any hand that has ample trick-winning power but a possible shortage of controls. This is sometimes the case at game contracts; it is so often the case at slam contracts that the evenly divided suit should almost always be preferred.

♠ K Q J 6	♠ 5
♡ A 8	♡ K Q J 7 3 2
◇ K Q 6 3	◇ A 9 5 4
♣ 8 5 2	♣ A 7

Against any opening but a club, six hearts would be easy; but assuming a club opening, the only possible slam is six diamonds, which can be made if the diamonds break 3-2. Declarer can win the club lead, draw trumps in three rounds, and discard West's two clubs on the long hearts. East-West do not need an extra trick; they have a superfluity of tricks. But East-West do need *time,* and this time is supplied by the unevenly divided side suit, which furnishes discards and restores control to declarer's side.

East, having heard a diamond bid plus some indication of heart support from West, should bid the slam in diamonds, not in hearts.

Such obvious examples as the foregoing have not failed to make their impression on expert players. Most experts, however, have construed the examples to indicate a specific advantage for the 4-4 suit. This is false, of course. Whatever is said of the 4-4 suit applies with even greater force to the 5-5 trump suit as against any less evenly divided suit:

♠ —	♠ 4 3
♡ 6 3	♡ A 7
◇ A K Q 5 4	◇ J 8 6 3 2
♣ A 10 8 7 5 3	♣ K Q 9 4

West	North	East	South
1♣	1♠	2♣	2♠
3◇	Pass	4◇	Pass
4♠	Pass	5♡	Pass
?			

As between bidding seven clubs and bidding seven diamonds, West should choose the diamonds. Even if East proves to have the same number of supporting cards in clubs and diamonds, the diamond suit will be the more evenly divided and should make the superior trump suit.

The evenly divided diamond suit produces a grand slam, whereas the unevenly divided club suit would not. After drawing trumps, West can discard dummy's low heart on the fifth round of clubs. If East had only four diamonds, and three hearts, the diamond suit would still make the grand slam, for both of East's small hearts could be discarded. The 5-4 trump suit would still be superior to the less evenly divided 6-4 trump suit.

Third type of hand on which the 4-4 trump suit is superior

Any hand on which declarer and dummy each has a weak suit that can be stopped only by ruffing.

♠ A Q J 6 3	♠ 9 7 2
♡ A 10 7 4	♡ K 6 5 3
◇ 9 5 2	◇ 10
♣ 8	♣ 9 7 6 5 3

The East-West hands were played, in a duplicate game, in spades at some tables, in hearts at others. A spade contract developed only eight tricks; a heart contract nine tricks. The opponents had a choice of suits with which to force declarer.

At spades, they properly forced the long trump hand. West was able to establish a third trick in hearts, but he did not have enough trumps, after ruffing repeated club leads, to draw the opponents' trumps and cash his last heart. At hearts, West was able to establish his spades, take two rounds of trumps, and then run the spades.

The point here is: With the 4-4 trump suit it does not matter to declarer which hand the opponents choose to force. With the 5-3 trump suit it does matter.

The expert players of Boston were incredulous when the following deal occurred in a tournament there some fifty-five years ago.

Dlr: South
Vul: Both

```
                    ♠ K 10 3
                    ♡ 9 8 4 2
                    ◇ 10
                    ♣ A J 10 8 2
   ♠ J 4                              ♠ Q 7 2
   ♡ A K J                            ♡ Q 5
   ◇ J 6 5 4 3 2                      ◇ K Q 8 7
   ♣ 7 4                              ♣ 9 6 5 3
                    ♠ A 9 8 6 5
                    ♡ 10 7 6 3
                    ◇ A 9
                    ♣ K Q
```

West	North	East	South
			1 ♠
Pass	2 ♣	Pass	2 ♡
Pass	3 ♡	Pass	3NT
Pass	4 ♡	Pass	Pass
Pass			

No one in conservative Boston had ever heard of bidding as weak a suit as South's hearts, and if a Bostonian had even thought of such a bid he would have expected some God of Bridge to emanate in a flare of lightning and strike him dead.

It was even worse when the Bostonians learned that the crass New Yorker who bid the hearts had made his four-heart game.

They could not believe their ears when they heard that everyone who had tried for four spades or three notrump had gone down. And they were downright indignant when they laid out the four hands and discovered that four hearts could not be beaten and that it was the only makable game contract. In spades, South had to lose three hearts and a trump trick. In notrump, with a diamond lead, North-South could take only eight tricks, then East-West would get in and take the rest with diamonds and hearts.

Against four hearts, West opened the four of diamonds. South took his ace and led a trump. The best available lead for the defense was another diamond. Dummy trumped and played another heart.

West could take both his remaining trumps and lead a third round of diamonds to force out South's last trump, but then South would have the rest with five good clubs and two top spades.

From this and other sensational examples, extremists in all countries soon developed the Cult of the Four-Card Major, and they began to bid four-card spade and heart suits regardless of their weakness. Many of them still do. The answers to a questionnaire circulated in 1961 among bridge experts internationally revealed that many experts will respond or rebid in any four-card major, however weak. Some will open the bidding in such a suit.

Alas, both the doctrine and the ritual of the 4-4 Major Cult went a bit too far.

WHEN A 5-3 TRUMP SUIT SHOULD BE PREFERRED

The frequent and obvious superiority of the 4-4 trump suit has become too well known. Into the expert dogma has crept the tenet that the 4-4 suit should *always* be preferred. The use of the word "always" is just as dangerous in this case as it is elsewhere in bridge analysis. The cases in which a 5-3 or 6-2 suit is superior may not occur frequently but when they do they can normally be recognized during the bidding.

The 5-3 trump suit is usually superior to the 4-4 trump suit when the combined hands have an abundance of winners in the other two suits.

Cases that fit this description are rare. For one thing, both of the available trump suits must be majors; as between a major and a minor, the major will usually be preferred whether it is 5-3 or 4-4. Also, the presence of superfluous stoppers can seldom be recognized except when one partner has made a strong notrump bid. But there are times when the bidders may realize that the 4-4 suit can hardly be superior, while the 5-3 suit *may* be.

```
Dlr: North          ♠ A J 4 3
Vul: N-S            ♡ A J 6
                    ◇ Q J 10
                    ♣ K J 5
   ♠ 10 7                              ♠ Q 8 2
   ♡ K 8 4                             ♡ 9 5
   ◇ K 8 4                             ◇ A 9 7 5 3
   ♣ 9 8 7 3 2                         ♣ A 10 6
                    ♠ K 9 6 5
                    ♡ Q 10 7 3 2
                    ◇ 6 2
                    ♣ Q 4
```

North deals and bids one notrump; South responds two clubs (Stayman) and North rebids two spades. South should now bid three hearts, and if North raises to four hearts (showing three-card support) South should pass.

By one line of bidding or another, most expert pairs will reach and play in four spades on the North-South cards. Yet a four-spade contract requires successful finesses in both spades and hearts (and, as the cards lie, would undoubtedly go down). A four-heart contract requires the success only of the heart finesse, since two of South's low spades can be discarded on North's third diamond and third club. Three notrump cannot be made because East will open diamonds and eventually win four diamonds and the ace of clubs. The only game is in hearts, the 5-3 suit, not in spades, the 4-4 suit, *and South should expect this and bid for it.*

The point is that here it is unnecessary either to ruff or to discard the two side suits, and it is in facilitating additional ruffs and discards that a 4-4 division of trumps is principally valuable.

The 5-3 trump suit should be preferred when it is very strong, the 4-4 suit is or may be weak, and the combined hands contain so many high cards in all suits that trump losers are the greatest danger.

In the following deal, played in a tournament in England, both members of the bidding side might have applied this principle but neither did.

Dlr: South
Vul: None

```
                    ♠ K 8 5 2
                    ♡ K Q J 7
                    ◇ A 5
                    ♣ J 10 7
   ♠ Q 10 9 4                      ♠ J
   ♡ 10 6 5 2                      ♡ A 9 4 3
   ◇ J 8 6                        ◇ Q 9 7 4 2
   ♣ 8 3                          ♣ 6 4 2
                    ♠ A 7 6 3
                    ♡ 8
                    ◇ K 10 3
                    ♣ A K Q 9 5
```

West	North	East	South
			1♣
Pass	1♡	Pass	1♠
Pass	4♠	Pass	4NT
Pass	5◇	Pass	5♠
Pass	Pass	Pass	

Seven expert pairs bid the North-South hands, and one bid as above. Since South must lose two spade tricks and the ace of hearts, he cannot make five spades. No possible bidding result is better calculated to give a bridge player nightmares than to bid five in a major suit and go down one. Yet three of the expert pairs bid, and failed to make, five spades; three others bid six spades and were down two.

And all the time North-South were laydown for six clubs.

South wins the first trick unless West leads a heart, in which case South wins the second trick. The jack of clubs is taken, then the ace and king of diamonds cashed, and a diamond ruffed with the ten of clubs. Trumps are drawn and two spades from South's hand will go off on two hearts in dummy. The ace of hearts is the defenders' only possible trick.

The pairs that bid the North-South cards to five spades in the bidding shown above went back over their bids and found every one of them defensible. If called upon to bid the same hands again, they might reach the same contract.

It is probable that most good American pairs would play the North-South hands in some spade contract, because of the general predilection for major suits and also because "it is well known" that a 4-4 trump suit is better than a 5-3 trump suit.

Given the first three rounds of bidding shown above, South had no reason to fear bidding a slam, with one ace located in North's hand. South had second-round control in the fourth suit, whichever suit it might be. But South did have reason to fear the spade suit because his spades were so weak. Therefore South should have bid six clubs (instead of five spades), showing that his clubs had the tops though his spades did not.

And North, who also had reason to fear the spade suit but who had support for a strong club suit, should have passed for that very reason.

Not even the best breaks would have permitted a slam in the 4-4 spade suit. The slam could have been made in clubs even against a 5-0 trump break if the dangerous opponent's hand had comprised five clubs, three hearts, three diamonds, and two spades—the most likely division of cards, in the circumstances.

The 5-3 trump suit may be superior for a game contract, because it is safer, when the 4-4 suit would have to be selected for a slam contract because it is the only chance.

♠ A K 6 5	♠ 10 7 4 3
♡ A 6	♡ K Q J 10 2
◇ K Q J 5	◇ 6
♣ A 9 8	♣ 8 7 4

West opens two notrump; how should East respond? Here, he should not try for a slam; and expecting three hearts in the opener's hand, and superfluous stoppers in the other suits (because of the two-notrump opening bid), the responder should prefer to play the hand in four hearts even if a 4-4 spade fit exists.

It will be observed that a 4-1 spade break (a 28.26 percent chance) and a club lead will probably defeat four spades; nothing is likely to defeat four hearts.

Now strengthen the East hand slightly:

♠ A K 6 5	♠ Q 7 4 3
♡ A 6	♡ K Q J 10 2
◇ K Q J 5	◇ 6
♣ A 9 8	♣ 8 7 4

Here, the situation is different. There is some chance of a slam, and East would investigate both majors. He responds three hearts, and West bids three spades, showing his four-card suit. East should raise to five spades. If West can bid again, a slam will probably be made; but it can be made only in the 4-4 suit. After a club lead, West will need to draw trumps and discard his losing clubs before conceding a diamond trick. Controls are vital in slam bidding and it can rarely pay to surrender the chance of discarding on the unevenly divided long suit.

Regardless of the nature of the hand, a 4-4 trump suit must be regarded with suspicion if its high-card strength is concentrated in one hand. If the hand with the high trumps must stand repeated forces, a trick may be surrendered. *When such a situation can be foreseen, the 5-3 suit should be preferred.*

Dlr: South   ♠ A 8 2
Vul: Both   ♡ 10 7 4 3
                   ◇ Q 10 6 4
                   ♣ 10 3

♠ J 6		♠ Q 7 4
♡ J 9 5		♡ 8 2
◇ K 8 7 5		◇ A J 9 2
♣ A 7 6 5		♣ J 9 4 2

                 ♠ K 10 9 5 3
                 ♡ A K Q 6
                 ◇ 3
                 ♣ K Q 8

West	North	East	South
			1♠
Pass	2♠	Pass	3♡
Pass	4♡	Pass	Pass
Pass			

West led the five of diamonds, East winning dummy's ten with his jack and returning his low diamond, which South had to ruff. Now declarer had to give up a trick in either spades or clubs, whereupon a diamond continuation would force out one of his high trumps and establish West's jack of hearts as the setting trick.

Four spades would have been easy, of course, because South could stand two forces, or even three, without sacrificing a high trump. And accurate trump valuation would have placed South in four spades. It was obvious from this hand that if anyone would have to trump diamonds, he would; and he could not afford to use his high hearts for that purpose.

It is only when *essential* high trumps must be wasted in ruffing that the 4-4 suit should be avoided. If one partner holds A-K-Q-x and the other holds J-10-9-x, it does not matter which partner must ruff—the other partner can supply equivalent top strength. Also, when there will be no apparent need to ruff with the high trumps it would be pointless to avoid the suit on the grounds that it is "too strong."

♠ A K Q 6   ♠ 8 7 4 3
♡ J 8 7 5 3   ♡ A 9 4
◇ Q J 4   ◇ K 6
♣ 2   ♣ K Q J 5

West	East
	1♣
1♡	2♡
2♠	3♠
?	

West should bid four spades. He will hardly be forced to ruff clubs, the suit East has bid. There is a better play in spades, as there usually is in the 4-4 fit, for one of East's hearts may be discarded on the third round of diamonds.

WHEN 6-2 IS SUPERIOR TO 5-3 OR 4-4

There is finally the choice between alternative eight-card trump holdings of which one is divided 4-4 or 5-3 and the other 6-2.

On two-suited hands that require all or most of the winning tricks to come from the two long suits, *the trump suit that is more unevenly divided should be selected.* That is, 6-2 is better than 5-3 and 5-3 is better than 4-4.

When the combined hands are strong—game-going—the two prospective trump suits may play equally well and the object is not to select the better trump suit so much as to select the higher-scoring trump suit. A 5-3 major-suit fit would take preference over a 6-2 minor-suit fit, and a 4-4 major-suit fit over a 5-3 minor-suit fit. When the hands are very strong—slam-going—a 4-4 fit may produce more tricks even than a 6-2 fit, as has been shown.

But this assumes good suit breaks, or so many high-card controls that good suit breaks are not needed. Few of the 4-4 trump fits shown in previous examples would have played better than the alternative 5-3, 5-4, or 6-2 fits if the opposing trumps had not been divided evenly (3-2), and against bad trump breaks the 4-4 fits could have been hurt much worse. When breaks are bad or the opponents have the preponderance of the high-card strength, the longer suit in a two-suited hand may or may not produce more tricks but *it is always safer.*

A two-suited hand in which the long suits are 5-4 or 6-5 must be short in one or both of the other two suits. When the opponents are strong in these other suits they will lead them, and declarer's only stoppers will be his trumps. The greater length he has in trumps, the more stoppers he will have; that is, his trumps will last longer. One extra stopper may make a difference of several tricks in the play of the hand.

This fact has a profound influence on sacrifice bidding.

Dlr: West	♠ A 6 2	
Vul: E-W	♡ 8 6 4 3	
	◊ 10 6	
	♣ J 10 7 5	

♠ 10 5		♠ 9 7 3
♡ Q J 10 7 2		♡ A K 5
◊ A Q 4		◊ 8 2
♣ A 6 4		♣ K Q 9 3 2

	♠ K Q J 8 4	
	♡ 9	
	◊ K J 9 7 5 3	
	♣ 8	

Because of the prevailing vulnerability, North-South chose to sacrifice rather than permit East-West to play in and make four hearts. In both spades and diamonds North-South held eight cards, and a four-spade sacrifice was one trick lower than a five-diamond sacrifice. Nevertheless, five diamonds was the only safe choice.

The fact is well demonstrated in this deal in which both spades and diamonds "broke"—were 3-2 in the opponents' hands.

In four spades, North-South would probably win only five tricks, going down five—a most unprofitable sacrifice. With a heart opening and continuation South would have to ruff; after going over to the ace of spades and losing a finesse for the queen of diamonds, he would have to ruff again; after giving up his second losing diamond he would have to ruff a third time. Now he could not draw trumps. By other play South might get six tricks, but the loss of 700 points (800 at duplicate) would still be unprofitable.

There is also the matter of entries to be considered. Assuming that the long side suit can be established, it cannot be run unless there is entry to it. With a two-suited hand, declarer's cards in his side suit or suits are usually gone immediately, and his only means of reentry is often a trump. If his trumps have all been dissipated by repeated ruffing, he cannot gain entry to his side suit after he establishes it. In this deal, even if dummy had held ♠ A 10 6 and South could have drawn trumps, he could not then have gained reentry to the four established diamonds.

In five diamonds, North-South would probably win nine tricks, going down only two in a contract one level higher, and effecting a very profitable sacrifice. South would ruff the second heart lead and give up a trump trick; ruff the third heart lead and give up another trump trick; and still have enough trumps to ruff again, draw the last opposing trump, and run his spades without contest. A spade opening and continuation by West, the only defense that would cost South an extra trick, would be difficult in actual play, and against that defense South would be down three, a still-profitable sacrifice of 500 points.

The decision is easy for the player who holds the 6-5 two-suiter (South, in the foregoing deal) if he knows his partner to have at least two diamonds and probably not more than three spades; and sometimes the bidding does reveal such information. If this is the case, the six-card suit is the automatic choice. But usually the decision rests on the bidder's partner, in this case North.

A good North will recognize the situation and will place the contract in diamonds, going one trick higher in a suit in which he has conspicuously weaker support. The bidding might be, with West dealer:

West	North	East	South
1♡	Pass	2♣	2♢
Pass	Pass	2♡	2♠
4♡	Pass	Pass	4♠
Dble	5♢!	Dble	Pass
Pass	Pass		

From South's rebid of his second suit at the four-level, North may assume South's 6-5 distribution. Though longer in spades, North must take the contract to five diamonds.

North should not do this on a strong hand. On weak hands, a desire for safety compels selection of the 6-2 suit.

Readers should not too hastily condemn East-West for failure to bid five hearts and score the vulnerable game they could make. Neither East nor West could be confident of making five hearts. Both knew they could beat four spades or five diamonds, even if they did not know by how much. The biggest winners, in both rubber and tournament bridge, take the sure plus score.

COMPARISON OF 5-4 AND 4-4

The case for the 5-4 fit, as against the 4-4 fit, is the same as the case for the 5-3 fit but just a little bit better. The extra trump in the 5-4 fit provides better control and reduces the danger of a bad break.

If declarer will need one discard (it is the most he can get) for control or trick-winning, he must willy-nilly play in the 4-4 fit. If he has ample controls and tricks in the side suits, the 4-4 fit cannot be superior and may be inferior, as it would have been in the following deal.

Dlr: South
Vul: Both

         ♠ K 8 6 3
         ♡ A K Q 6
         ◇ K Q J 2
         ♣ 8

♠ Q J 2   ♠ 9
♡ 7   ♡ J 10 4 2
◇ 10 7 5 4   ◇ 9 6 3
♣ Q J 10 4 3   ♣ K 7 6 5 2

         ♠ A 10 7 5 4
         ♡ 9 8 5 3
         ◇ A 8
         ♣ A 9

West	North	East	South
			1♠
Pass	3♡	Pass	4♡
Pass	5♠	Pass	6♠
Pass	Pass	Pass	

Since both members of the North-South pair knew the facts about trump suits, North made his slam invitation in spades and South accepted it in spades.

The play in six spades was easy enough. West led the queen of clubs. South won the first trick with his ace, led a low spade to dummy's king, and led a spade back. A spade trick then had to be given up to West's queen but that was all. One of South's low hearts went off on one of dummy's high diamonds, South's losing club was ruffed in dummy, and South had the rest.

Six hearts would have been a losing contract for North-South, because of the coincidence of a 3-1 spade break and a 4-1 heart break. There were not enough high diamonds in the North hand to provide discards for all three of South's losing spades, so eventually North-South would have had to lose a spade trick in addition to the inescapable trump trick. Result, down one for a loss of 100 points instead of a vulnerable slam bid and made for a profit of 1430 points.

Consider this case:

♠ A Q 8 6 4	♠ K 10 7 2
♡ K Q J 6	♡ 10 9 5 4
◇ —	◇ 8 5 3
♣ A 10 7 5	♣ 6 2

The 5-4 spade fit is superior because East has three diamonds for his partner to trump and the four-card suit may not stretch far enough. *A player should not willingly play with a four-card trump holding if he has a void.* His partner should keep this principle in mind when showing preference.

WHEN A 4-3 TRUMP SUIT IS PREFERRED

Even the best players, bound to the dogma that a sound trump suit must have a combined length of at least eight cards, overlook many cases in which a combined seven-card holding divided 4-3 would be their best trump suit and provide their best contract.

The 4-3 trump suit is usually selected only when it is a major, when notrump is out of the question because some suit is unstopped, and when there seems little chance of getting eleven tricks in a longer combined minor suit. In other words, it is a less dangerous version of the 4-2 fit shown earlier.

In the case most often neglected, the 4-3 trump fit is superior because one or two ruffs with the short (three-card) trump holding add essentially to declarer's trick-taking power.

The 4-3 spade fit was correctly selected in the following deal, and while there were collateral reasons for preferring it, the suit would in any event have been the best choice.

Dlr: East
Vul: E-W

       ♠ K 6 5
       ♡ J 6 5 4
       ◇ A K 7 5 4
       ♣ 3

♠ 10 9   ♠ 8 7 4 2
♡ A Q 8   ♡ 10 9 7 3
◇ J 9 8 2   ◇ 10
♣ J 9 6 4   ♣ 10 8 7 2

       ♠ A Q J 3
       ♡ K 2
       ◇ Q 6 3
       ♣ A K Q 5

West	North	East	South
		Pass	2NT
Pass	3♣	Pass	3♠
Pass	4◇	Pass	4♠
Pass	5♠	Pass	6♠
Pass	Pass	Pass	

North wisely preferred to have South the declarer, but if this had been his only reason he would have made six notrump the contract. The principal thought in North's mind was that his low spades might add one or two tricks by ruffing clubs. North did not know South's club suit was so strong, but the one club ruff that North did get proved decisive. No such advantage could attach to the diamond suit, for any ruffs would have to be made with the long diamonds and add no tricks to the total.

    The result proved North right in every respect. Six notrump could not be made because there simply were not twelve tricks. Six diamonds would have been beaten speedily by a heart opening, but even if the ace of hearts had been in East's hand, a six-diamond contract would have been doomed by the 4-1 break. The ace of hearts plus a trump trick would have had to be lost.

The six-spade contract weathered both storms.

West led the ten of spades and dummy's king was put up. South took his ace of clubs and trumped his low club; then he led dummy's last spade and drew trumps. West discarded a heart and a club, dummy two hearts.

South cashed his last two clubs. West could follow to the first, while a diamond was thrown from dummy. (South did not know diamonds would not break, but by relinquishing his chance for an overtrick he maintained his best play for the contract.) On the last club West had to part with the queen of hearts to keep his diamond stopper.

Now the contract was safe. The six of hearts was discarded from dummy and South led his low heart, dropping West's ace and making his remaining cards good.

The squeeze helped, but at worst South would have had a play to find the ace of hearts onside.

A 5-1 spade break would have defeated the contract, but it must be remembered that the odds are 5-to-1 against anything worse than a 4-2 break when you have seven trumps. The odds are only 2-to-1 against a bad break when you have eight trumps.

THE CONSPIRACY AGAINST MINOR SUITS

The scoring laws of contract bridge arbitrarily make diamonds and clubs the "minor" suits, in which eleven tricks are needed for game.

There being no rational reason why one suit should count more than another, innumerable reformers have proposed equalizing the count of the four suits.

Yet the scoring differential between major and minor suits, illogical though it may seem, is one of the primary reasons why contract bridge became and has remained the most popular card game. To equalize the suits would be, practically, to legislate the notrump game contract out of the game. Nearly always a partnership has a good fit in one of the four suits, but when the fit is in a minor suit the tendency is to play in three notrump rather than in five of the better minor.

The reformers have a sound argument, nevertheless, when they say that bidding systems so emphasize the major suits and notrump that good players seldom know how to reach a game-going bid of five in a minor suit when that is the best contract.

In the following deal several good North-South pairs actually bid to four spades, stopped there, and went down two. It never occurred to them to play in five of a minor.

Dlr: South
Vul: N-S

	♠ 10 7 6 2	
	♡ K 3 2	
	◇ 7 4 3	
	♣ A K 5	

♠ 8 4		♠ J 9 5 3
♡ A Q 10 9 4		♡ J 8 6 5
◇ A 6		◇ Q 9 2
♣ 10 8 7 3		♣ 9 2

	♠ A K Q	
	♡ 7	
	◇ K J 10 8 5	
	♣ Q J 6 4	

West	North	East	South
			1 ◇
1 ♡	1NT	2 ♡	3 ♣
Pass	3 ◇	Pass	4 ◇
Pass	5 ♣	Pass	5 ◇
Pass	Pass	Pass	

Few players bid so aggressively as did North and South with only a minor suit to land in, while customarily experts bid their cards in this way when their suit is spades or hearts. But South's contract was a good gambling one, requiring only a successful finesse for fulfillment.

The finesse worked but better defense would have put South to a guess and he might have guessed wrong.

The ace of hearts was opened and won the first trick. West then led the three of clubs and dummy's king won.

South led a diamond from dummy, finessing the jack.

If West had not won this trick with the ace of diamonds, he might have beaten the contract.

When West took his ace, South had no problem. He won a club continuation, finessed again through East's queen of diamonds, and had the required cards to draw trumps and claim the remainder with high spades and clubs.

Suppose West had played low on the first diamond trick. Now South would have known only who held the queen of diamonds. He would not have known which opponent held two diamonds nor which opponent had the ace of diamonds.

South could have overcome this defense only by a perfect guess, whereby he would have led a low diamond after winning with his jack, dropping West's ace. But probably South would have led his other low club to dummy's ace, to take another diamond finesse. This time West would have had to take his ace—but then West could lead a third round of clubs, which East would ruff for the setting trick.

If the choice is between three notrump and five of a minor, the minor should be preferred if the player considering notrump has a doubleton ace or king in an unbid suit and has reason to believe his partner has nothing of value in the suit. This is especially true if there is a long minor that is not ready to run. Consider these cards:

♠ A 5	♠ 4 3
♡ 8 3	♡ A K 7 6 2
◇ K J 9 5 2	◇ Q 8 4 3
♣ A Q J 3	♣ K 4

West	East
1 ◇	1 ♡
2 ♣	3 ◇
?	

The temptation to bid three notrump must be resisted. That contract has virtually no chance after a spade lead, and six diamonds is about even money. The correct bid at this point is three spades, allowing for East to bid three notrump with a spade stopper. Here, five or six diamonds will be reached.

♠
♡
7 Valuation Based
♢ on Partner's
♣ Hand

In appraising any card, or his hand as a whole, the expert leans heavily upon the hand he expects his partner to hold. His picture of partner's hand may come from the bidding, or lack of bidding, or the natural expectation that partner will have one-third of whatever high-card strength is held by the other three players.

When partner is known to be weak, the trick-taking power of most high-card combinations drops sharply.

West	North	East	South
2NT	Pass	Pass	

East's pass in this situation, is made only on a worthless hand, and West may find his own hand two tricks weaker than he thought it was.

♠ A K J 6	♠ 8 2
♡ K Q 10	♡ 8 7 5 4
◇ Q 10 6 5	◇ 9 8 4
♣ A K	♣ J 8 4 3

West may quite reasonably have hoped to win three spade tricks, two heart tricks, two club tricks, and one diamond. This appraisal was, however, based upon two expectations.

The primary expectation in valuation is that declarer can gain entry to his partner's hand, to finesse if he so chooses. An entryless dummy may reduce the power of such a tenace as A-Q-10 from two or three tricks to one trick. In the case of the example above, lack of an entry prevents West's finessing for the queen of spades or for the jack of diamonds, or leading up to his heart holding.

The second expectation in valuation, and often the far more important one, is that declarer and dummy will have at least one suit they can lead without unnecessarily establishing tricks for their opponents. Suppose in this case East held ◇ J 4 3 2. By leading diamonds West could throw his opponents into the lead and they would probably then lead one of the other suits. Except in unusual cases, he would gain a trick by their leads.

Forced to lead from his own hand, West may find his trick-taking power reduced from the original eight-trick estimate to an ultimate five or six tricks.

Such a bidding situation often opens to a defender (South in the bidding sequence above) an opportunity for a lucrative double. South, knowing that West would probably have bid more than two notrump if he had held eight *sure* tricks, may double on the assumption that West held no more than eight *probable* tricks, some of which by reason of East's pass have become improbable. With a smattering of strength, as in the following hand, it may pay South to double:

♠ 10 9 3   ♡ J 6 3   ◇ A J 7   ♣ Q 10 9 2

Every now and then the double will give East-West an un-earned game, but far more often it will pick up an extra 200 or 300 points.

When partner is known to be strong, there is automatic appreciation of values in the appraisal both of high cards and of long suits.

	1.	♠ K 6 3	2.	♠ 8
		♡ Q 8 5 2		♡ 10 8 7 6 3 2
		◇ K 7		◇ 9 7 5 4 3
		♣ 9 6 5 3		♣ 10

Hand one is worth a trick if partner passes; it is worth at least three tricks if partner opens with a two-notrump bid; it justifies a slam-try if partner opens with a game-forcing bid. When the opponents are known to have their share of the high cards, kings and queens lose part of their combining value, since partner may have nothing with which they can combine; they lose part of their trick-winning power, since they may be captured by the opponents' higher honors. When the opponents are known to be weak and partner to be strong, these circumstances are reversed.

Hand two is worthless and dangerous if partner passes, and should not be bid; it is promising and should be bid at least twice if partner makes a moderately strong bid such as a take-out double; it warrants insistence on a game contract if partner makes a very strong bid such as two notrump. In the last case, when partner is known to be strong and to have some strength in hearts, trump control should be expected, permitting the diamond suit to be established. If partner happens not to have the tops in diamonds, then he will be able to stop the spade and club suits, so that the trump control will not be weakened by repeatedly having to ruff the opponents' strong suits.

REAPPRAISAL OF HIGH CARDS

Partner's distribution has an effect on the valuation of high-card holdings both defensively and offensively.

A player should not double his opponent's contract in the expectation of winning two tricks from A-K-x-x-x if his partner has raised the suit; partner probably has length and one opponent probably has a singleton.

If partner makes a preemptive opening bid of four hearts, Q-J-x-x-x-x in a side suit is virtually worthless, and might as well be six low cards, for partner probably has no more than a doubleton and would lose two tricks in either case. But K-x-x-x-x-x has some value, for if partner has a doubleton and the ace is onside, he may save a trick.

When a player has shown that his strength is in one very long suit (as by a preemptive bid) or that he has a two-suiter, the timing function of high cards in side suits becomes paramount. If one partner opens or overcalls and then bids up to three spades, single-handedly, the other partner should raise with two aces but not with two side-suit K-Q holdings. The bidder will probably have a singleton in at least one of the K-Q suits. In this case, a K-Q will be of no value, since partner would lose one trick, and no more than one trick, in the suit anyway.

There is little value to a J-x in diamonds if partner bids spades and hearts, but some value to it if partner bids clubs and the opponents bid spades and hearts, for then partner probably has side strength in diamonds and the jack has combining power.

Before partner is heard from, Q-J-10-x-x-x is a far better suit than K-x-x-x-x-x, for it can be "handled." The former suit sometimes justifies a bid when the latter would be passed.

1. ♠ 6
   ♡ Q J 10 8 7 5
   ◊ A 7
   ♣ J 10 7 3

2. ♠ 6
   ♡ K 8 7 5 3 2
   ◊ A 7
   ♣ J 10 7 3

Over an opponent's one-spade bid, hand one warrants a weak jump overcall of three hearts except at unfavorable vulnerability; hand two suggests a pass, though one might risk a weak jump overcall of three hearts at favorable vulnerability. The apparent superiority of Q-J-10-x-x-x may end, however, when partner's distribution and high-card holding become known.

If partner raises hearts, the suit headed by the king becomes superior. Suppose partner holds four small hearts; then Q-J-10-x-x-x will still lose two tricks, but K-x-x-x-x-x may lose only one.

If partner gives a double raise in hearts, the superiority of K-x-x-x-x-x may be reckoned at half a trick. Suppose partner holds A-x-x-x; then a finesse will be required to clear the Q-J-10-x-x-x suit without loss, but no finesse will be needed with K-x-x-x-x-x.

DUPLICATION OF VALUES

Duplication of values can destroy the effect of any system of valuation.

Values are said to be duplicated when one partner has high-card control in a suit in which the other partner has distributional control, or when the two partners have distributional values in the same suit.

A bidding system should be designed to reveal duplication of values quickly, whenever it is possible to do so.

The following is a case of high-card duplication:

♠ A K Q	♠ —
♡ 9 3	♡ J 6
◇ Q J 4	◇ A K 10 9 6
♣ Q 10 4 3 2	♣ A K J 9 6 5

If East-West play in a club or diamond contract, West might as well have three low spades as the A-K-Q, assuming that the opponents will lead hearts and win the first two tricks. If

West held the ace of hearts instead of the three top spades (five points less) or if East had the J-6 of spades and a void in hearts, the East-West hands would produce a grand slam. With the spade duplication they cannot even make a small slam.

When these hands were bid, with East-West vulnerable, one pair found it possible to detect the duplication and avoid the losing slam. The bidding was:

West	North	East	South
1♣	Pass	2♦	2♠
Pass	Pass	3♣	Pass
3♦	Pass	3♠	Pass
3NT	Pass	4♣	Pass
5♣	Pass	Pass	Pass

West's bid of three notrump was a warning of duplication. On the next round, West would have bid four hearts if he held the ace of hearts. Also, if West had king doubleton of hearts, he probably would have bid two notrump over two spades. His pass suggested no clear action, yet he was later known to have sufficient spade values to undertake three notrump. West's failure to make either of these bids constituted sufficient warning to East that there might be two heart tricks to lose, so East passed five clubs.

Obviously West's three spade honors were not worthless. If he had actually held three low spades instead of the A-K-Q, North-South would have had ten solid spades plus nine solid hearts and probably could have made eleven tricks in one of the majors (or defeated a sacrifice six-club contract).

Duplication of distribution is far more insidious than high-card-plus-distribution duplication. It is not so easy to detect, except when clues are provided by the opponents' bids, but it can be similarly damaging.

For such a case as the following no one has proposed a remedy.

♠ A Q 10 6 3	♠ K J 7 5 4
♡ K J	♡ A 8
◇ A 6 3	◇ J 7 5
♣ 7 4 3	♣ A 10 6

West opened one spade, East raised to three spades, and West bid four—routine (old-fashioned) bidding.

There was virtually no play for the contract. West had to lose two diamond and two club tricks.

If either partner had held his doubleton in any suit but hearts, the game would have been laydown.

Three notrump is laydown and is the safest game contract, but no bidding system provides for a notrump game with a 5-5 major-suit fit.

Experts perforce treat such cases as unlucky breaks, shrug their shoulders, bear the loss, and go on to the next deal. A system designed to detect such cases of duplication would be self-defeating. It would consume bids that can be put to better purposes.

But warnings from the opponents' bidding are not overlooked.

West	North	East	South
			1♡
1♠	2♡	4♠	?

South holds:

♠ 9   ♡ K Q J 10 6 3   ◇ A Q 4   ♣ 9 7 3

The singleton spade is far more dangerous in South's hand than three small spades would be. Perhaps North is also short in spades. If East-West have winning cards in clubs or diamonds they will get them; if North has a long minor suit South may be powerless to prevent a ruff.

♠
♡
8 # Reconciliation of Offensive and Defensive Values
♢
♣

The expert first sees his hand as an offensive weapon and unconsciously labels it a "strong hand" or a "weak hand."

In this first appraisal a strong hand is one with which the holder can do some bidding and expect, or hope, to secure the contract and make it.

There is no strong hand that does not have some high-card strength but there are hands that have much in high cards and still are "weak."

1. *Strong Hand*	2. *Weak Hand*
♠ A 9 7 6 4 2	♠ A 9 7 6 4
♡ A 10 6 5 3	♡ A 6 2
♢ 8	♢ A 8 5
♣ 6	♣ 6 2

Hand one will probably win eight or nine tricks in whichever of its long suits partner can better support, even if partner has no high-card strength. This hand, given a trump fit, has both timing value (aces and trumps to stop the opponents' suits) and trick-winning value (long cards that can be established). Unless partner has shown a misfit, as by bidding the minor suits, hand one should be bid up to the three-level.

Hand two is a doubtful bid at anything above the one-level and a dangerous hand even there. In high cards it is at least 50 percent better than the first, but what does it matter that there is ample time to develop its trick-winners? There are almost no trick-winners to develop.

Valuation systems rely upon the expectation that a hand with 16-18 points will be strong. Usually this expectation will be justified, but not always.

In the previous examples, the superior distribution of hand number one made it a strong hand, but distribution need not be the determining factor. In the following examples, one 15-point hand is strong and another 15-point hand of the same distribution is weak.

	3. *Strong Hand*	4. *Weak Hand*
♠	K Q 9 8	A K 5 3
♡	A 10 9 6	A K 7 2
◇	K J 3	7 6 5
♣	Q 8	J 4

Hand three is superior because of the presence of intermediates; because it has no hopelessly weak suits; because its offensive prospects do not depend on finding a good fit with any specific suit or suits in partner's hand. The holder of hand three knows that an opponent cannot hold a hand like this:

♠ 6   ♡ 5   ◇ A K Q J 4   ♣ A K Q 9 7 2

on which he could bid and make five of a minor redoubled. Against hand number four an opponent might do just that.

Nor can hand four, any more than the previous hand number two, safely enter the auction against opponents' bidding at any level higher than a one-bid or a double of a one-bid. Hand three can, if need be, but it is unlikely that against hand three the opponents will do much bidding.

Yet point-count valuation would rate hands three and four the same and quick-trick valuation would make number four one full trick stronger.

THE MEASURE OF A STRONG HAND

Such anomalies in the popular valuation methods can be avoided if the player always applies dual valuation to his hand, offensive and defensive.

By such dual valuation, hand number one is not strong, despite the expert's desire to consider it so.

The decisive measure of a strong hand is this: *It must be able to penalize the opponents if they outbid it.*

The following declarer's hands are close to being equivalent only offensively (and number six is superior offensively because it is less often subject to a bad trump break).

Dummy
♠ 8 6 4 3
♡ A 4
♢ J 10 7 5 4
♣ 7 6

5.	♠ A K 10 5	6.	♠ K Q 9 7 5 2
	♡ K Q 6		♡ 6
	♢ A 2		♢ A 2
	♣ A 8 5 4		♣ A 8 5 4

Either five or six appears likely, opposite the dummy shown, to produce a game in spades. Number five has nevertheless a vast margin of superiority, for it promises six or more defensive tricks, as compared with two or at most three such tricks for number six. Against six, the opponents can often find a profitable sacrifice bid; against number five, they cannot. The holder of hand five will probably score 450 to 650 points, the holder of number six may score only 100 or 200 points.

The formulas prescribe dependence on quick tricks—that is, on high-card strength alone—for defensive purposes. It is true that at the start of the auction a player has no basis for assigning defensive value to anything but a high card. But as the bidding reveals the hand types that have been dealt, defensive valuation becomes a process no different from offensive valuation. The value of any card is exactly the same to one side as to the other. The card declarer most needs to make his contract, the defenders most need to defeat it.

West	North	East	South
			1 ♦
Pass	1 ♠	Pass	2 ♣
Pass	3 ♣	Pass	5 ♣
Pass	Pass	Pass	

East holds:

♠ K Q 6 2   ♡ A K 6 4   ♦ 9 7 5   ♣ 7 4

He cannot double despite his three quick tricks, for South, having displayed length in two suits, must be short in at least one of the other suits. East may get no spade trick; he may get only one heart trick.

In another case, despite absence of high cards, a player may judge his hand to be defensively powerful:

West	North	East	South
	1 ♦	1 ♡	2 ♣
Pass	2 ♦	Pass	2NT
Pass	3NT	Pass	Pass
Dble			

West holds:

♠ J 6   ♡ J 9 5   ♦ Q J 10 9   ♣ K 10 9 4

He has, by any count, no more than 1½ quick tricks. But South has contracted to win nine tricks, and where are those tricks coming from? Not from spades; neither North nor South was strong enough in spades to bid the suit. Not from hearts; East bid them. Not from diamonds or clubs, since South cannot establish either suit without giving West two tricks in it.

Because it is so clearly understood that no hand can be described unqualifiedly as strong unless it satisfies both offensive and defensive requirements, players hesitate to make bids that are conventionally strength-showing unless they have considerable defensive strength. In consequence, experts have come to depend upon their partners' strength-showing bids to guarantee defensive strength, and lean heavily upon this inferred guarantee in future doubling and slam bidding. Two famous players reached a losing slam through the bidding of the following hand:

♠ A Q 10 9 7 5 3   ♡ K Q 7 4   ◇ 3   ♣ 8

The holder of the hand opened with one spade; his partner responded two diamonds and he jumped to three spades. No lesser bid would properly have portrayed the offensive power of his hand, yet his limited defensive power should have warned against the bid. His partner expected about four tricks in top cards and went to six notrump, which was down four. If the opponents had been bidding and had reached five clubs his partner might have doubled them with equally poor results.

THE RANK OF THE SUITS AS A FACTOR IN BIDDING

There is still another standard for defensive valuation: the rank of the suits. The profit potential of any hand is largely dependent upon the rank of its longest suit.

If one's long suit is spades, the defensive strength can be reckoned one trick higher than if one's long suit is diamonds or clubs. In some cases the superiority of the spade suit can be stated in an exact number of points. The following deal is an example:

```
Dlr: South            ♠ 8 6 4 3
Vul: Both             ♡ A 4
                      ◇ J 10 7 5 4
                      ♣ 10 7
   ♠ J 10                              ♠ A
   ♡ K J 9 7 3                         ♡ Q 10 8 5 2
   ◇ K 8 6 3                           ◇ Q 9
   ♣ K 6                               ♣ Q J 8 5 4
                      ♠ K Q 9 7 5 2
                      ♡ 6
                      ◇ A 2
                      ♣ A 9 3 2
```

West	North	East	South
			1 ♠
Pass	2 ♠	Pass	4 ♠
Pass	Pass	Pass	

West chose to open the seven of hearts, but it made no difference what he led. South could easily make four spades, losing the ace of trumps, plus a diamond trick and one club trick. After trumps were drawn, there were two trumps left in the dummy to take care of South's other two clubs.

Probably East-West should not have let themselves be shut out of the bidding, but it is easier said than done. It would be dangerous for West to make an overcall at the two-level, though many players would enter the bidding over two spades with the East hand. Some might choose to double, and some might be able to bid two notrump if using the Unusual Notrump to show any two-suiter rather than the minors or two lower unbid suits.

There are expert pairs who use a bid of two notrump in this position as natural, indicating a balanced hand with the strength for a one-notrump opening bid and at least one spade stopper. However, those pairs who prefer to treat the

bid as a two-suited action might like to consider its showing
any two suits rather than specifically the minors. In the
above example, West would bid four notrump over four
spades, using his own Unusual Notrump, to say that he has
support for two of the unbid suits. East bids five clubs, West
continues with five diamonds and East corrects to five
hearts.

Pairs who use two notrump as natural in this position
must choose between a pass and a take-out double. Both
have their disadvantages, but experience has shown that it
pays to enter the bidding if short in the opponents' suit.
Here, East doubles and West will bid five hearts over four
spades.

Whatever decision is taken by East, the fact remains that
East-West had a game. In four hearts they would have lost
only three tricks, to the three North-South aces, yet they
never got into the bidding.

Even if East-West had entered the auction, they would
have lost points because they could not outbid the opponents' spades. By making four spades, South scored 620
points, but at best East-West would have had to sacrifice in
five hearts, go down one doubled and lose 200.

EFFECT OF A SHIFT OF SUITS

The following layout of the cards is exactly the same as the deal shown before except that this time East-West have the spades and North-South have the hearts.

Dlr: South
Vul: Both

```
                    ♠ A 4
                    ♡ 8 6 4 3
                    ◇ J 10 7 5 4
                    ♣ 10 7
   ♠ K J 9 7 3                      ♠ Q 10 8 5 2
   ♡ J 10                           ♡ A
   ◇ K 8 6 3                        ◇ Q 9
   ♣ K 6                            ♣ Q J 8 5 4
                    ♠ 6
                    ♡ K Q 9 7 5 2
                    ◇ A 2
                    ♣ A 9 3 2
```

This time the bidding must be different. South opens with one heart. West, who was not strong enough to bid two hearts over one spade, is strong enough to bid one spade over one heart. Once West enters the bidding, East will carry him to four spades. Even if West did not overcall with one spade, East with his spade strength would consider it safe to double when North raised to two hearts, at the same time hoping his partner did not have only diamonds. Because of this risk, an aggressive East might make a Michaels Cue-Bid with three hearts to show his 5-5. However, that hand is not strong enough to drive the bidding to that level.

The bidding would probably be like this:

West	North	East	South
			1♡
1♠	2♡	4♠	5♡
Dble	Pass	Pass	Pass

In the modern game, East would probably bid differently, his jump to four spades being treated as preemptive. He might make a splinter bid of four hearts (which is usually best avoided holding a singleton ace) or cue-bid three hearts to indicate a high-card spade raise.

South would make the same ten tricks as before, but this time he would be down one, doubled and vulnerable, and would lose 200 points.

The value of the spade suit in such a case is therefore at least 400 points, for the side that has the spades will be plus 200 points instead of minus 200 points. The value can go still higher, for in the first deal South was permitted to play in four spades and score 620, and in the second deal East-West might possibly be permitted to play in four spades and score 620. North might consider his hand too weak to give a free raise in hearts, and in that case South probably would not risk a sacrifice five-heart bid; but today there are few players who would not raise freely on the North hand.

The value of the higher-ranking suits is a practical consideration in many bids. One example is when a player decides whether or not to open the bidding in fourth position on a borderline hand. With such a hand as this, it is customary to pass:

♠ 7 3   ♡ 6 4   ◇ A Q 8 3   ♣ A J 9 6 2

The remaining high cards can be assumed to be more or less evenly divided among the other three hands. The opponents probably have a satisfactory spade or heart suit and can outbid the diamond and club suits, making it more likely that they will make a partscore. If fourth hand had his strength in the majors instead of the minors, he would open the bidding. If one of his suits were spades, he would bid, as in this hand:

♠ A Q 8 3   ♡ 7 3   ◇ 6 4   ♣ A J 9 6 2

Here the spade suit will probably outbid the opponents if the strength is evenly divided; the hand with the spades is worth one more trick defensively than the hand without spades.

EFFECT OF THE RANK OF THE SUITS AT LOWER LEVELS

Not only in competitive bidding does the rank of the suits exert its influence. At every stage the thinking player must consider the likelihood that his opponents can enter the bidding cheaply, or outbid him in a contested auction, with a higher-ranking suit. Pervading his thoughts at all times must be the question "Who has the spades?"

As one example only, bridge books uniformly tell what is required to give a single raise when partner makes an opening suit-bid.

It is as absurd to generalize on single raises as it is to say there are five vowels in the English language. Just as the vowel *a* differs in *father, cat, ball,* the expert's single raise varies according to the suit his partner has bid and what he has in other suits.

A raise of one spade to two spades has a powerful preemptive effect. The opponents must go to three to overcall. Among all the single raises, this one may show the least trump support. Experts have been known to bid it on hands like this:

1.	♠ Q 3	2.	♠ 10 8 6 5
	♡ 10 8 6		♡ 7
	◇ 9 7 6 3		◇ 8 3
	♣ Q 8 5 2		♣ Q 9 7 6 5 3

The essential requirement is that the responder be able to pass the opener's new-suit rebid with relative safety, even if the suit is short or weak, or to go safely back to the first suit.

A raise of one heart to two hearts may have a similar preemptive effect, but only if the responder has the spade suit protected. On the following hand, which ideally meets the book requirements for a single raise in hearts, an expert did not raise partner's one heart to two:

♠ 6   ♡ J 8 5 4   ◇ K 7 6   ♣ Q 8 6 4 3

He bid four hearts. Two hearts might not have shut out the opponents' spade suit. But he would have bid two hearts on the following hand.

♠ Q J 3   ♡ J 8 5 4   ◇ Q 8 6 4 3   ♣ 6

This time the opponents probably would have no spade suit.

If a pair is not using Inverted Minor-Suit Raises, a response of two diamonds to one diamond can have only one of three purposes: to show distributional trump support in case five diamonds is the only game; to prepare for a sacrifice; or to promise solidity for a long suit in partner's hand in case partner may wish to run a string of diamonds at notrump. Here again the advisability of the bid depends on how much one must fear the opponents' major suits. With

♠ 10 7 6 3   ♡ Q 8 5 2   ◇ Q 10 8 6   ♣ 5

one would respond one heart and never two diamonds. With

♠ 5   ♡ Q 8 5 2   ◇ Q 10 8 6   ♣ 10 7 6 3

many experts would bid one heart because they are bound to systems in which failure to bid a four-card major denies having one, but two diamonds is a better bid.

A raise of one club to two should never be as weak as a single raise in spades may be, because there is little preemptive value. Nor can the trump length be less than four cards when one raises a club bid, because despite all disclaimers in bridge books (including this one) one is permitted to remember that his partner may have opened on a short club suit. The raise to two clubs does have some preemptive value and any other response should be preferred only when there remains some hope of finding a major-suit fit. With

♠ 7 2   ♡ 8 6 3   ◇ A 10 8 4   ♣ J 10 8 3

a raise of partner's club bid to two clubs is better than a one-diamond response, which can lead nowhere if not to two clubs (response one diamond, rebid one spade, responder's rebid two clubs). But with

♠ 8 6 5 3   ♡ 7   ◇ A 10 8 4   ♣ J 10 8 3

the response is one diamond, because it is better to hope for a spade rebid by partner than to rely on a two-club bid to shut out an opposing heart suit.

TWO MAJORS AND TWO SIGNALS

The rank of the suits, plus two basic card-playing conventions, affected the results of this deal:

Dlr: North
Vul: E-W

	♠ A 8 3	
	♡ 7 5	
	◇ K 10 9 8	
	♣ J 10 4 2	
♠ 6 5 4		♠ 7 2
♡ A J 10 9 4 2		♡ 8 6 3
◇ 2		◇ A J 6 4
♣ 8 7 5		♣ A K Q 3
	♠ K Q J 10 9	
	♡ K Q	
	◇ Q 7 5 3	
	♣ 9 6	

West	North	East	South
	Pass	1 ◇	1 ♠
3 ♡	3 ♠	4 ♡	4 ♠
Dble	Pass	Pass	Pass

East-West were using the modern style in which the three-heart bid was weak, showing just about the kind of hand held by West. This is logical, since a two-heart response would be forcing; there is no need for two strong heart bids; it is unlikely West will have a hand powerful enough for a classical strong jump shift after two players have bid; the weak jump gives the opener an accurate description of the responder's hand; and the extra space taken up makes life more difficult for the opponents.

West could have made four hearts, losing two spades and one heart, so South did not miscalculate greatly when he decided to sacrifice in four spades. But West was on top of the situation when he doubled despite his paucity of high cards. By doubling he warned East not to bid five hearts, which could not be made; and the singleton diamond promised several tricks because on the bidding East was due to have the ace of diamonds.

The two of diamonds was duly opened, and East won and returned the four of diamonds for West to trump.

The four of diamonds was the suit preference signal, invented by Hy Lavinthal in 1934, which has influenced the card-playing habits of expert bridge players throughout the world more than any other development in this century. By leading his lowest diamond, East instructed his partner to return the lower of the two available suits other than trumps—in this case, clubs rather than hearts.

West trumped with the five of spades, starting a trump echo. The trump echo, a high-low play with two low trumps, informs partner that one has an additional trump and wishes to ruff with it.

Obedient to East's suit preference lead, West led the eight of clubs. East took the trick with his queen and led the six of diamonds. West trumped with the four of spades completing the trump echo.

Another club lead and East was in again, with the king. The trump echo having told East that West had another spade, he led his fourth diamond and West got a third diamond ruff. He cashed the ace of hearts to put South down four. The 700-point penalty (800 at duplicate) gave East-West a good profit: 80 points more than they would have received for making their vulnerable four-heart contract.

Without the trump echo by West, East might not have led that fourth diamond. On the bidding, South could easily have had a six-card spade suit. If West could not trump another diamond, it would be important for East to lead a heart and cash West's ace while there was still time. Otherwise South could establish the jack of clubs in dummy and discard a heart on it.

PART IV

The Theory and Strategy of Bidding

1 Mathematics and Bridge

The science of contract bridge may have a root in mathematics, but if so the root is a slender one at best. Both in bidding and in play, the only mathematics required to justify correct technique is simple arithmetic.

The bridge expert does proceed on certain assumptions that have a mathematical basis. He knows that the odds favor certain contingencies and oppose others. He knows that winning the first game of a rubber has a total value of approximately 450 points, but only 100 or 120 of these points (the trick score) are immediately set down on the score sheet. His knowledge of the odds and of the existence of unscored values must have come from mathematical calculations.

Yet it is an error to suppose, as many do, that the bridge expert must be an accomplished mathematician. Not five percent are deserving of this designation, and that any bridge expert knows mathematics is purely coincidental. Every expert leans far more heavily upon experience and observation than upon any probabilities he may know or assume. Whatever mathematical information applies to bridge, science must be constantly modified by other knowledge: the relative degrees of skill of the players, the bids and plays they make, and the way they make them.

Since bridge mathematics is so crude in form and so rough a guide, the term itself becomes misleading when applied to bridge, and it is better to use a term from the vernacular: *figuring*. Any pertinent figuring in bridge may be done on the spur of the moment and in the head of one trained to think in bridge terms.

All the figures that govern bidding science arise from the contract bridge scoring table. Every bid puts at stake a certain number of points, in accordance with the existing schedule. The declarer's possible gain is determined by the values established for tricks and bonuses awarded for winning the rubber or making a slam. The declarer's possible loss is stated in the table of undertrick penalties.

WHEN TO BID GAME

1. Rubber Bridge

First, consider traditional rubber bridge, which has dwindled in popularity in North America but is still common in England and some other parts of the world.

Winning the first game takes a partnership half the distance to a 700-point rubber bonus, and is therefore logically worth 350 in unwritten value. The second game matches that, either by equalizing the situation or by going the further distance to score the rubber. (The lawmakers, however, consider a single game in an unfinished rubber worth 300. This is based on the slender argument that the state of being vulnerable carries more risks in terms of penalties than opportunities in terms of slam bonuses.)

The third game, clearly, has a value of 500.

The value of a partscore is a more subjective matter. The lawmakers allow 50, but this is certainly too low. The late John Crawford thought it was worth 200, which is much too high. On the majority of deals the partscore will be irrelevant because one side or the other will have an obvious game or slam. And the partscore can even be a handicap when the partnership has a slam, for many actions change slightly in subjective ways.

The size of the partscore is also a factor, 60 or more is desirable, and 20 is almost useless. Here we assume that the partscore is at least 40.

A good partscore of 40 or more is certainly worth more when both sides are vulnerable, for you are now part of the way to a bigger bonus.

For the purposes of this discussion we will assume that the partscore in rubber bridge is worth about 30 percent of the available game bonus in the particular circumstance: thus, 100 if somebody is non-vulnerable, but 150 if both are vulnerable.

Take this common situation with nobody vulnerable: You have reached three spades, and are considering whether to continue to game. You feel sure that you can make nine tricks, and perhaps ten. There is no prospect that the opponents will double.

If your prospects are fifty-fifty, then your expectation from bidding on is:

(350 [value of game] + 120 [trick score] − 50 [penalty]) /2 = 210

Your expectation from passing is:

(100 [value of partscore] + 120 [trick score] + 100 [value of partscore] + 90 [trick score])/2 = 205

This would suggest that a game hinging on a finesse should be bid, but since the initial assumption, a one-trick defeat and no penalty double, is optimistic, the profit and loss expectations are effectively equal.

This calculation is equally valid if the opponents are vulnerable. But matters change if you are vulnerable.

At unfavorable vulnerability (you are, they are not) the corresponding numbers are 185 and 205. Add in something for the danger of a two-trick defeat and/or a penalty double, and a game depending on a finesse becomes unattractive. A 55 percent chance is on the borderline.

With both vulnerable the numbers are 260 and 255. With a similar adjustment for a bigger penalty, we are again on the borderline with 50 percent. This contradicts the conventional wisdom, which underestimates the value of a partscore when both are vulnerable.

The rubber bridge bottom line is therefore: A 50 percent game is a borderline proposition except when you are vulnerable and the opponents are not. Then it is slightly undesirable.

Psychological factors are often significant. If your partner is the worst player at the table, push slightly in the hope of getting rid of him. If he is the best player, be slightly cautious and improve your chances of keeping him.

2. Chicago or Four Deal Bridge

The calculations are simpler, although the value of a partscore on the first three deals is still a matter of guesswork. Again, we will surmise 100, the amount awarded by the Laws for making a partscore in the fourth deal.

It is true, of course, that all partscores are not quite equal. On Deal One and Deal Two, the dealer's partscore is worth a shade less than one for the opponents, who will be trying for a vulnerable game on the next deal. A Deal Three partscore offers prospects of a vulnerable game next time, but may expire worthless. But we shall assume, nevertheless, a constant value of 100. Readers who disagree with this assessment can adjust the calculations accordingly.

Assume the same scenario: Should we continue from three spades to four spades?

Non-vulnerable, your average result in two deals when the game is a fifty-fifty proposition is: $(300 + 120 - 50)/2 = 185$ for bidding on; and $(120 + 100 + 90 + 100)/2 = 205$ for passing. Make the usual adjustment for the chance that a game bid will attract a penalty double and a 55 percent game is on the borderline.

Vulnerable, the basic numbers 260 and 205. With the usual adjustment, 45 percent is the break-even point and a game on a finesse should be bid.

The bottom line in Chicago is therefore simple: An even-money game is undesirable non-vulnerable but desirable vulnerable.

3. Matchpoints

In duplicate games circumstances count for more than mathematics. Vulnerability is not important: a 50 percent game is borderline in all situations. One factor that may affect a decision is the state of your game, which may induce you to do the obvious and "play with the field" if you are winning, or do the less obvious if you need to strain for good results. Another is the ability of your current opponents. If you do not know them, look at their convention card. There is some correlation between the amount of writing and ability, so be aggressive if the card has a lot of blank space.

4. International Match Points, or IMPs

Virtually all team play around the world is scored in this fashion nowadays, with the net score at two tables converted on a scale that ranges from one IMP (20–40 total points) to 24 IMPs (4000-plus total points).

A growing tendency, with the use of computers, is to play IMP pairs: each North-South receives an IMP comparison with each East-West pair, and vice versa. The final score can be determined in two ways. One is to add all the

IMP scores so obtained. Another (the Butler method) is to average all the scores on the deal (sometimes ignoring two or four extreme scores) and calculate an IMP score for each pair based on this average, or datum.

Two other forms of team scoring are now living fossils. Board-a-Match Teams, which was normal in American tournaments before the advent of the Swiss Team format, is now virtually limited to the Reisinger Teams and three other national events. Total-point scoring, also called aggregate, was the predecessor of IMP scoring. Perhaps it is still in use somewhere.

For the purposes of bidding a game that you expect to make, the opposing vulnerability is not significant. With the usual scenario, passing three spades or continuing to game, we can calculate:

Non-vulnerable. If you bid game and the opposing pair does not, you will gain six IMPs if you succeed and lose five IMPs if you fail. This does not allow for the slight chance of a penalty double, but nevertheless a fifty-fifty game should be bid.

Vulnerable. If you bid game and the opposing pair does not, you will gain ten IMPs if you succeed and lose six IMPs if you fail. With the usual allowance for the penalty double, you should bid the vulnerable game with a 40 percent chance.

We can now tabulate all this. With fifty-fifty game prospects your decision should be:

Vulnerability:	Neither	You	They	Both
Scoring				
Rubber	Doubtful	No	Doubtful	Doubtful
Chicago	No	Yes	No	Yes
Matchpoints	Doubtful	Doubtful	Doubtful	Doubtful
IMPs	Yes?	Yes!	Yes?	Yes!

The bottom line if game prospects are 50 percent: Bid at IMPs or Chicago when vulnerable. Stop short at Chicago non-vulnerable, or at rubber bridge at unfavorable vulnerability. All other situations are borderline.

WHEN TO BID A SMALL SLAM

1. Rubber Bridge

Assume that your choice is between a safe four-spade contract or a six-spade contract with a fifty-fifty chance.

Non-vulnerable, caution will get you $(350 + 180 + 350 + 150)/2 = 515$. Boldness will score $(350 + 500 + 180 - 50)/2 = 490$. It is close, but if you factor in the possibility that a bad break will produce a penalty double it is wrong to bid the slam (unless you are playing with the best player, a partner you wish to keep). The break-even percentage is about 53. The opposing vulnerability has no bearing.

Vulnerable against non-vulnerable, boldness produces $(350 + 750 + 180 - 100)/2 = 590$. Caution scores $(350 + 350 + 180 + 150)/2 = 515$. Again it is close, but even with the usual allowance, the slam should be bid. The break-even percentage is about 47.

Both vulnerable, boldness gets you $(500 + 750 + 180 - 100)/2 = 665$. Caution earns $(500 + 500 + 180 + 150)/2 = 665$. Right on the borderline, without considering the penalty double.

2. Chicago

The same assumption: a fifty-fifty six-spade contract. The opposing vulnerability is irrelevant.

Non-vulnerable, boldness earns $(500 + 300 + 180 - 50)/2 = 465$. Caution is worth $(300 + 300 + 180 + 150)/2 = 465$. On the borderline with the usual proviso.

Vulnerable, the slam bidder collects $(750 + 500 + 180 - 100)/2 = 665$ against $(500 + 500 + 180 + 150)/2 = 665$. Again on the borderline.

3. Matchpoints

In all cases, fifty-fifty is on the borderline and circumstances must guide, as indicated for game bids.

4. International Match Points

We make the usual six-spade assumption. Again, the opposing vulnerability is not relevant.

Non-vulnerable, the slam bidder collects eleven IMPs or loses the same number if he fails. Vulnerable, boldness earns thirteen or loses thirteen. In both cases we are on the borderline.

A cautionary note: A small slam in a suit that hinges on a finesse is rarely exactly 50 percent. There is always the risk that the opposition will have an unforeseen quick ruff.

WHEN TO BID A GRAND SLAM

The calculations for small slams were slightly affected by the remote chance of a penalty double when the trumps are split badly. In grand slam calculations this is rather more than cancelled out by the five-or-seven or four-or-seven hands. The loss from bidding a grand slam is trivial if a small slam was due to fail anyway. Here is an example of what's meant by a "five-or-seven" hand:

```
Dlr: South        ♠ K J 6 3
Vul: Both         ♡ 5
                  ◇ A Q J 10 6 5
                  ♣ 7 2
    ♠ 5                           ♠ 9 8
    ♡ Q 10 8 3                    ♡ K J 9 7 6 2
    ◇ K 8 2                       ◇ 9 4
    ♣ K Q J 8 3                   ♣ 10 9 4
                  ♠ A Q 10 7 4 2
                  ♡ A 4
                  ◇ 7 3
                  ♣ A 6 5
```

South plays in a spade contract. West opens the king of clubs. If the diamond finesse wins, South can make seven spades. If the diamond finesse loses, South cannot make six spades. Obviously North-South should stop at four or bid seven, but any intermediate bid is unintelligent because it accepts the maximal risk in exchange for less than the maximal gain.

1. Rubber Bridge

Assume the choice is between six spades and seven spades.

If you are non-vulnerable, the opponents' vulnerability is irrelevant.

Bidding the grand slam earns $(1000 + 350 + 210 - 50)/2 = 755$. Stopping in a small slam collects $(500 + 500 + 350 + 350 + 210 + 180)/2 = 1045$. Even allowing for five-or-seven, the grand slam is clearly a bad risk and a 65 percent chance is borderline.

A successful vulnerable grand slam against non-vulnerable opponents is worth $(1500 + 350 + 210 - 100)/2 = 980$. Resting in six spades is worth $(750 + 750 + 350 + 350 + 210 + 180)/2 = 1295$.

With both sides vulnerable the numbers are similar: grand-slam bidder collects $(1500 + 500 + 210 - 100)/2 = 1055$; small-slam bidder collects $(750 + 750 + 500 + 500 + 210 + 180)/2 = 1445$.

In all these situations the grand slam is a borderline proposition if it depends on a 3-2 split, roughly a two-thirds chance.

2. Chicago

With the same assumptions we get: Non-vulnerable, the grand slam is worth $(1000 + 300 + 210 - 50)/2 = 730$. Stopping short is worth $(500 + 500 + 300 + 300 + 210 + 180)/2 = 995$.

Vulnerable, the grand slam is worth $(1500 + 500 + 210 - 100)/2 = 1055$. Stopping short earns $(750 + 750 + 500 + 500 + 210 + 180)/2 = 1445$.

Again, a grand slam needs about a 67 percent chance, reduced somewhat by the five-or-seven situation.

3. Matchpoints

Some authorities think that matchpoint grand slams are subject to the same rules. They are not. If the field is highly expert, 50 percent is the break-even point, since it is the frequency of gain and loss that matters, not the amount. But that percentage climbs gradually if the field becomes weaker, and in an average field 60 percent is probably right. Resting in a small slam can gain because some pairs have not reached a slam at all, or by contriving an overtrick that others miss. If the slam prospects are due to a perfect fit, rather than weight of high cards, the small slam will produce plenty of matchpoints and straining for seven is unwise.

4. International Match Points

Here there is another factor, which is indeterminable: might the opponents stop in game?

Bidding a non-vulnerable grand slam that succeeds gains eleven, an unsuccessful effort loses fourteen. A correction for the five-or-seven possibility means that the break-even point is about 55 percent.

Bidding a vulnerable grand slam that succeeds gains thirteen, an unsuccessful effort loses seventeen. The break-even point is about 56 percent.

In conclusion, you should be reasonably aggressive in contracting for small slams, but extremely cautious in bidding grands. It is aggravating to go down one in a grand slam and find that the opponents at the other table (or most of the field, in a pair event) have stopped in game (or, even worse, in a partscore!).

WHEN TO SAVE

The Duplicate Laws as revised in 1987 have complicated this area considerably. In duplicate, but not in other forms of the game, saves (or sacrifices) are less attractive than they used to be if the saver is non-vulnerable. Every undertrick beyond three now costs 300 instead of 200, so the bottom-line numbers are 100, 300, 500, 800, 1100, 1400, and so on. (After the first two undertricks, this sequence follows the vulnerable track, but is one trick cheaper.)

If both sides have a fit, the advice offered by the great British player-writer S. J. Simon more than forty years ago is still valid: When in doubt, bid one more for luck. The big disasters come from allowing the opponents to make a game, or even a slam, when you could have made one yourself. And substantial profits are to be made by pushing the opponents to a point, usually the five-level, at which they are in jeopardy.

Saving involves psychology as well as mathematics. Are the opponents aggressive bidders who will allow themselves to be pushed to a higher level? And if that level is six or seven, are you sure you can beat them?

The type of scoring is much more significant than in non-competitive auctions. Consider first a common situation. The opponents have bid four hearts, and you are considering four spades. You will gain if the save is cheap, or if you push them to the five-level and they go down. You will lose if the save costs too much, or if the opponents would have failed, the dreaded "phantom." And there is always the chance of a delightful surprise: your save is doubled and you make the contract.

If you are sure the opponents will succeed, the number of tricks you need to make in four spades doubled is shown in the following table. A question mark indicates that the save is mathematically on the borderline.

Vulnerability:	Neither	You	They	Both
Scoring				
Rubber	7?	8?	7?	8
Chicago	8	9	7	8
Matchpoints	8	9	7	8
IMPs	8	9	7?	8

The IMP save at favorable vulnerability is less attractive than it used to be. The likely profit is three IMPS, and a four-trick defeat, which used to cost two points, now costs five.

The legal change has its main impact at the slam level. The same calculation for a small slam, when considering six spades over six hearts, gives the following table of tricks needed for a profitable save. (It is assumed that the opposing slam will succeed.)

Vulnerability:	Neither	You	They	Both
Scoring				
Rubber	7	9	6	7?
Chicago	7	9	5	7?
Matchpoints	8	9	6	7
IMPs	8	9	6?	7?

The change in the law was prompted primarily by the possibility of the extravagant save against a grand slam. It was possible to make a profit, at favorable vulnerability, by taking just two tricks, for a penalty of 2100. This was a major consideration at matchpoints, and even at IMPs the save was very attractive.

Now, with the new law, the trick target for a player who is considering a seven-spade save against a making seven hearts is this:

Vulnerability:	Neither	You	They	Both
Scoring				
Rubber	5?	8	3	6
Chicago	5?	8	2	6
Matchpoints	7	8	5	6
IMPs	7	8	5	7

Most of this is well understood, but the situations that arise when your opponents save are not.

If the opponents have found a good save at the six-level, a grand-slam effort becomes much more attractive than it would be in a non-competitive auction.

Suppose that you have bid six hearts, vulnerable, and the opponents bid six spades, non-vulnerable. You estimate that this will fail by two tricks, giving you 300 instead of the 1430 you expected in six hearts.

If you think you have some shot at seven hearts you should probably take the gamble at any scoring except matchpoints. Apart from the possibility that the opponents will play safe by saving in seven spades, your expectation is good if you estimate that your chance of success in seven hearts is 25 percent.

In four deals you will score 2210 once and minus 100 or 200 three times: an expectation of about 440, instead of 300 by taking the easy penalty. The break-even point of 67 percent for a grand slam drops to 20 percent.

Of course, if the expected penalty is greater or the vulnerability is different, the drop in the percentage is less, but still significant.

The same applies at the game level. If you are about to score 620 or 650 in four hearts, and you estimate that an opposing four-spade save would give you a 100-point penalty, five hearts is worth bidding (perhaps except at matchpoints, unless you do not think other pairs will find the sacrifice) if it has a one-in-three chance of success.

Which brings us back to Simon's advice: When in doubt, bid one more for luck. Here is an example:

Dlr: West
Vul: E-W

```
                        ♠ 8 5 3
                        ♡ 8 5 4
                        ◊ J 8 5
                        ♣ K 6 4 2
        ♠ A Q 7 6 4 2                    ♠ K J 10 9
        ♡ A Q 10 9 6 2                   ♡ J 3
        ◊ —                              ◊ Q 10 7 6 2
        ♣ 7                              ♣ 9 3
                        ♠ —
                        ♡ K 7
                        ◊ A K 9 4 3
                        ♣ A Q J 10 8 5
```

West	North	East	South
1♠	Pass	2♠	2NT
6♠	Pass	Pass	7♣
Dble	Pass	Pass	Pass

South trusted to the assumption, usually dependable, that West would not have bid six spades if he had not expected to make it, for West might have bought the contract at a lower and surer level.

If West could make six spades, South would lose about 1400 points (in rubber bridge depending on whether West had honors, in duplicate bridge exactly 1430 points). South accepted a probable loss of 100 to 700 points (800 at duplicate) less 100 honors (at rubber only) to avoid this risk.

West might have achieved the maximum of down two, 300 points, if he had made a different opening lead, but West selected his safest lead, the ace of hearts, which won the first trick and defeated the contract immediately. Then West led the ace of spades.

South ruffed with the eight of clubs, saving the five in case he needed an extra entry to the dummy. The queen of clubs was cashed and the ten of clubs led to dummy's king.

On the lead of the five of diamonds from dummy, East played the two. South followed through on his previous assumption that West could make six spades, and since West

had revealed one club loser, West had to be void in diamonds. So South played low. The five of diamonds won the
trick, and the remaining tricks were safely South's, with two
trumps left in the dummy to take care of South's two other
low diamonds.

Putting up the ten of diamonds on dummy's lead of the
five would not have gained a trick for East. Having saved the
five of clubs, South could get back to dummy to lead the jack
and catch East's queen.

The net score was zero—down 100 offset by 100 honors.
It was cheap insurance.

How about West's refusal to take out insurance, when he
doubled seven clubs instead of bidding seven spades (or
letting East do it)?

West risked a loss of more than 1500 points if South's
distribution were 7-6-0-0—an unlikely contingency but one
that has been known to occur. West surrendered a chance to
score more than 2200 points, for if North led any suit but
clubs West could have made seven spades.

The insurance premium, if West had bid seven spades,
would have been only 100 or 200 points, the amount he
would have lost by going down one.

In the long run West would profit by bidding seven
spades.

♠
♡
2
◇
♣

Basis of Partnership Bidding

Of all factors that influence bidding theory, the partnership factor is least appreciated, though it should be the most easily understood. It is the partnership factor that produces this basic tenet of bidding theory: *Each partner can speak for himself; therefore each partner must be permitted to speak for himself.* There must be no attempt to usurp each partner's prerogative of bidding his own cards.

Any bid entails some risk. To compensate for this risk, the bidder must have some strength. The least extent of his strength is determined by logic but is so well established that it has become conventional. Every bid—except certain responses to forcing bids—guarantees some conventional "minimum." *Each player is supposed to bid only on the values in his own hand plus the minimum he may assume—on the basis of previous bids—in his partner's hand.*

If the partner has more than the minimum previously guaranteed, it is assumed he will bid again. This principle may be evoked in the bidding of the following hand:

♠ **A Q 4**   ♡ **K 6**   ◇ **K Q 6**   ♣ **A J 7 5 3**

On this hand the expert of any class bids one club. Suppose his partner responds one diamond.

The player who is weak on bidding theory might jump to three notrump. His partner need have only ◇ A x x x x and a queen, or perhaps even a J-10 outside to produce an acceptable play for the game. It is reasonable to assume this much strength in partner's hand, and the game will usually be made.

Nevertheless, the theoretically correct rebid is two notrump. If partner does hold ◇ A x x x x and an outside queen or J-10, he will raise to three notrump. If his holding is any less, the three-notrump contract probably cannot be made.

On this reasoning the rebid of three notrump is indefensible. It stands to accomplish nothing the two-notrump rebid would not equally well have accomplished. It stands to lose in those cases in which it results in a penalty that would not have been suffered in two notrump.

Because of this, the jump rebid to three notrump has been defined as denoting a near-solid minor suit and stoppers in the unbid suits: a hand with which the opener is planning to run nine tricks. Something like:

♠ **K 7 6**   ♡ **A 8 3**   ◇ **4**   ♣ **A K Q J 9 8**

This principle does not mean that one should never bid on the hope of finding unrevealed values in partner's hand. Sometimes a keen realization of probabilities will dictate a sheer gamble on finding partner with specific strength that his previous bidding has by no means revealed. For example:

♠ **K Q J 8 6 5 3**   ♡ **Q 3**   ◇ **A K 5 3**   ♣ **—**

The holder of this hand bids one spade; this is overcalled with two clubs, his partner passes, and his right-hand opponent raises to three clubs. The hand shown justifies a rebid of four spades, vulnerable or not.

For the four-spade contract some assistance is required, and it is true that no assistance is ever guaranteed by a partner who does nothing but pass. But the required assistance may take many forms that are not biddable by partner—the queen of diamonds; or a doubleton diamond and 10-x in spades; or the J-10 of diamonds and the king of hearts; or miscellaneous cards that happen to "fit." Holding such cards would not have warranted a bid over the two-club overcall, so there is still a chance that partner may hold them. Surely half the time partner will have something to assist the four-spade contract, and this expectancy justifies a try for game.

South's decision was made in this deal:

```
Dlr: South          ♠ 10 9
Vul: None           ♡ 10 9 8 5 2
                    ◇ Q 8
                    ♣ Q 10 7 6
    ♠ A 4                           ♠ 7 2
    ♡ K 6                           ♡ A J 7 4
    ◇ J 10 6 2                      ◇ 9 7 4
    ♣ A K J 8 2                     ♣ 9 5 4 3
                    ♠ K Q J 8 6 5 3
                    ♡ Q 3
                    ◇ A K 5 3
                    ♣ —
```

West	North	East	South
			1♠
2♣	Pass	3♣	4♠
Dble	Pass	Pass	Pass

West led the king of clubs. South ruffed, crossed to the queen of diamonds, returned to the ace, and ruffed the five of diamonds in the dummy. However, when next declarer played a spade, West won with the ace and gave his partner a diamond ruff, defeating the contract.

Declarer had two ways to make the contract. He could have cashed the king of diamonds before ruffing his low diamond in the dummy; or, preferably, South should have returned to hand via a club ruff and trumped the king of diamonds with dummy's ten of spades. Then he would have lost only two hearts and the ace of trumps.

There was a chance to make the contract even if West had led the ace and another spade. South should win in the dummy and play a low heart. If the defenders do not switch to diamonds soon enough, a squeeze develops on West.

Suppose West wins the heart with the king and tries to cash the ace of clubs. South ruffs and plays another heart. East can still defeat the contract by switching to a diamond because it destroys declarer's communications, but if he just leads a third heart or a second club, South ruffs and runs his trumps. With one round remaining, this will be the position:

```
                    ♠ —
                    ♡ 10 9
                    ◇ Q 8
                    ♣ Q
    ♠ —                              ♠
    ♡ —                              ♡ Immaterial
    ◇ J 10 6 2                       ◇
    ♣ K                              ♣
                    ♠ 6
                    ♡ —
                    ◇ A K 5 3
                    ♣ —
```

West is squeezed by the final spade.

RESTRICTIONS ON BIDS

The guiding principle in partnership bidding should then be expressed as follows: A player must not make a bid in dependence upon cards his partner may hold, *if his partner, holding those cards, could reasonably be expected to make the bid for himself.*

In the case of high cards and measurable distributional strength, partner can recognize and bid his own values. There should be no gambling on finding aces and kings, or trump length, in partner's hand. A gambling bid is justified only when it seeks to find distinctly unbiddable values in partner's hand.

The partnership factor exerts much restraint on bidding. Each bid must be made in full awareness of the message it will carry to the partner, and in full preparation for any action partner may take on the strength of that message.

The fact that some contract is superior may not be sufficient excuse for bidding it. Holding the following hand, when his partner makes an opening bid of one spade, a player may feel fairly sure that two diamonds would be a better contract than one spade:

♠ —   ♡ 7 5 3   ◇ 10 9 7 6 4 3 2   ♣ 8 7 5

Nevertheless he must pass. He cannot bid two diamonds, for his partner would have no way of knowing that the two-diamond bid is designed only to provide a safer contract. The consequence of the two-diamond bid might be a final contract of two or three spades, or of four diamonds, which would be far more dangerous than one spade. In these circumstances, the best contract, two diamonds, is unattainable. If the opponents so will, the hand must be played at an inferior one-spade contract. If this be a weakness in expert bidding methods, at least it is a proper subordination to the more important partnership factor; and experience in play has not shown the passing of such hands to be ultimately costly.

♠
♡
3 **Obstructive Bidding**
♢
♣

The major object in the building of any bidding system is to permit valuable information to be supplied to the bidder's partner and at the same time be withheld from his opponents. Fortunately for the system maker, the achievement of this apparent paradox is not overwhelmingly difficult.

Undeniably an exchange of information between partners is necessary. There are few cases in which one partner alone can decide the best final contract.

1. ♠ A K 10 9	2. ♠ K Q J 10 9 8 7
♡ A K 8 4	♡ 8 3
♢ A Q J 10	♢ 7 5
♣ 6	♣ 5 3

The player who holds hand number one is willing to insist on reaching game, but he must know his partner's distribution before he can decide the suit in which the contract is to be played.

The player who holds hand two is willing to insist on spades as the trump suit, but he must know his partner's high-card strength before he can decide how high to go.

For these choices precise information is not necessary. The partners need not waste time seeking absolute assurance that they can make game. As seen in the earlier chapter on scoring, in a team event scored using International Match Points, a non-vulnerable game should be bid when the chance of success is around the 50 percent mark; whereas when vulnerable only a probability of some 37 percent is needed (assuming no risk of an opposing penalty double). If it appears that game should not be bid, it is desirable to stop at the lowest safe contract, and the two partners need not know whether they will win seven, eight, or nine tricks. As between two or more prospective trump suits, it is enough merely to know which is best, and there need be no effort to determine the exact length and strength of each.

The information exchanged between partners sometimes is purposely kept vague. This does not prevent their reaching the most desirable contract, and it permits them to devote a part of their bidding energy to the thwarting of their opponents.

The essential requirement of every bid in contract bridge is that it be obstructive. When a partnership has the superior cards, it may choose its bids so as to mislead, or at least so as not to assist, the opponents' defense. When a partnership's cards are inferior to, or no better than, its opponents' cards, it must so bid as to discourage or hamper its opponents' bidding.

DEFINITION OF OBSTRUCTIVE BIDS

An opening bid or response is satisfactorily obstructive when it is dangerous to overcall it.

Overcalling is dangerous in direct proportion to the risk of being doubled; hardly ever is an appreciable loss suffered from playing in an undoubled contract. The degree of danger of being doubled depends, in most cases, upon the number of tricks bid for. It would appear that it is no greater overbid to bid for seven tricks when able to win only five than to bid for ten tricks when able to win only eight. In either case, the result will be a two-trick penalty. In practice, however, the former is no overbid because it will not be doubled; the latter is an overbid because it will be doubled.

Assume that a player, in overcalling, undertakes a contract he cannot make. He will be doubled almost invariably if his overcall is a four-bid; usually, if it is a three-bid; occasionally, if it is a two-bid; and almost never if it is a one-bid.

An opening bid or response at the two-level or higher is inherently obstructive. Often it does not leave the opponents time enough to discover their best trump suit and the extent of their combined strength. Thus they are doubly handicapped: to overcall is dangerous and must be balanced by a chance to find a profitable contract they can make; therefore to overcall is futile even when there is a contract they can make, if they are unable to reach that contract. Faced with such a doubtful choice, they frequently decide not to bid. Consider again these hands (from page 84):

♠ A 9 7 4 2	♠ K 8 6
♡ A K 10 8 6	♡ 7 5
◇ K 6	◇ A Q 4 3 2
♣ 9	♣ 8 6 5

Suppose South, not vulnerable, makes an opening bid of four clubs. West may suspect that his side can make ten tricks in whichever major suit East can better support. For West to show both his suits, however, would require two bids. This would necessitate a contract at the five-level, which might go down. For West to attempt, by guessing, to select the better suit would be equally dangerous. Finally, there is the danger that East can support neither suit, and that North can double and severely penalize any overcall. West may find in these circumstances that it is safer merely to double South's four-club bid. If East passes, East-West will probably collect a penalty of 300 points, perhaps less 100 honors—poor pay for the spade game they could have reached and made if South had passed.

To the two-, three-, four-, and higher-level bids that stand as inherently obstructive must be added one notrump. For one thing, a two-bid is required to overcall it; but even more important is the manner in which it increases the danger of being doubled.

Dlr: East
Vul: Both

	♠ 8 4	
	♡ 8 5 4 2	
	◇ K 9 4 2	
	♣ Q 7 4	
♠ Q 9 7 2		♠ A 10
♡ J 10 3		♡ K Q 6
◇ J 6 5		◇ Q 10 8 7
♣ K 10 9		♣ A J 5 3
	♠ K J 6 5 3	
	♡ A 9 7	
	◇ A 3	
	♣ 8 6 2	

If East should make an opening bid of one club or one diamond, South may overcall with a bid of one spade, and West will hardly double. For all West knows, East may have a worthless singleton in spades, and North-South will have enough spade strength to make the contract with ease.

If East should make an opening bid of one notrump, South cannot overcall it with a bid of two spades; for not only would the contract be one trick higher, but West's double would become automatic. West would know, from the notrump bid, that East holds some spade strength. A two-spade overcall would be doubled and would go down three tricks, 800 points.

For this reason South dare not overcall a notrump bid; yet consider the possible consequences to South of his failure to overcall. If the West and North hands were exchanged, East-West could make one notrump while North-South could make two spades. By his failure to overcall South would lose 40 points plus the value of the partscore, instead of scoring 60 points plus the value of the partscore—an ultimate difference of 200 points in a duplicate team game or of perhaps 300 points in rubber bridge. Such is the value, in this case, of the obstructive function of East's opening bid.

WHY ONE-BIDS ARE GIVEN A WIDE RANGE

The inherently obstructive bids are only occasionally available. In most hands that are strong enough to bid, the trump suit is too uncertain or the hand is too weak to bid more than the allowed minimum. This means a one-bid in a suit, and the one-bid is not high enough to be inherently obstructive. It does not sufficiently discourage an overcall; it does not rob the opponents of the bidding rounds they need to find their best trump suit. Yet the one-bid, to meet the test of a proper systemic bid, must in some way be made obstructive.

What cannot be done by force can often be done by indirection. In the case of the opening one-bid, the purpose is accomplished by creating uncertainty in the opponents' minds. When the opponent must guess, he may guess wrong, and often, rather than risk the consequences of incorrect action, he will take no action at all. To create this uncertainty, to necessitate this guess, the opening one-bid is given as wide a range as possible.

In general expert practice, either of the following hands would be opened with a bid of one heart:

	1.		2.	
♠	6		♠	A 3
♡	A K J 6 5 3		♡	A Q 9 7 2
◇	K J 5		◇	A K 8 3
♣	8 4 2		♣	Q 7

Suppose South has made an opening bid of one heart; West, his opponent, must consider whether or not to overcall.

If South holds hand number one, West can probably overcall without serious risk of having to play his contract doubled. If South holds hand number two, an overcall by West may result in a double and a disastrous penalty.

This uncertainty alone is a serious deterrent upon West, but far more important to West is this: without knowing the nature of the opening hand, he cannot gauge the extent of his possible gain. If hand one prompted South's bid, it is quite possible that East-West can reach and make a game, and this possibility justifies some risk. If hand two prompted South's bid, game is entirely out of the question for East-West, and if West overcalls he will be in the position of having risked without hope of gain. The expert's psychological makeup being what it is, the unwarranted risk would be seriously detrimental to his self-respect if not to his bridge score.

This psychological factor should not be underestimated. The expert abhors a guess. It may be that he would gain in the long run by overcalling even when the overcall entails some risk—though in the early days of contract bridge weak overcalls were so consistently punished that they were soon abandoned—but the occasional large loss is always more impressive than a series of smaller gains. Thus, while the obstructive function of the one-bid is largely illusory, it is nonetheless effective.

The wide range given to opening one-bids is a matter of necessity as well as of strategy. A single bid cannot completely inform the partner—it can tell of high-card strength or of distribution, but not of both. Therefore the introductory bids are purposely kept vague, since they can be nothing else to partner and should be, ideally, nothing else to the opponents.

THE CODE BIDS

The "mathematical" systems disregard this tenet of theory and so lose much of their effectiveness. Consider the following bidding according to one of the systems in which the preliminary bids precisely define the hands on which they are made.

West	North	East	South
			1 ◇
Pass	1 ♠		

Now, according to the system being employed, South is known to have less than sixteen high-card points since he would have opened one club on any hand with sixteen or more; and North does not have enough points to force to game: less than an opening bid himself. East can read with reasonable accuracy his partner's high-card holding, and may frequently decide to enter the bidding in the secure knowledge that he cannot be caught and punished.

Consider the same bidding when one-bids in suits are given a wide instead of a narrow range. South and North have both bid, yet East knows almost nothing of their holdings. Either or both may be strong; either or both may be weak. If both are weak, they may be headed for a contract above their trick-taking potential, and for East to bid would rescue them; if both are strong, for East to bid would be dangerous. If their hands are but of average strength, for East to pass may cost his side a partscore, especially if East has some such borderline holding as

♠ 6   ♡ A Q 8 6 2   ◇ J 8 2   ♣ K 10 4 3

The bidding proceeds and still little light is thrown on the North-South holdings until it is too late:

West	North	East	South
			1 ◇
Pass	1 ♠	Pass	2 ♠
?			

Now South has limited his hand to a certain extent, but there is still no information on North's hand; and West, though he knows South has no powerful holdings, cannot dare to bid for fear North's first bid has concealed a high-card holding of several tricks.

Finally, the uncertainty ends, but still not to the entire satisfaction of East:

West	North	East	South
			1 ◇
Pass	1 ♠	Pass	2 ♠
Pass	Pass	?	

East now realizes that neither North nor South has a very strong hand; but by this time East is discouraged from overcalling simply because the auction has reached so high a level. Granted North-South are not very strong, but does that necessarily mean East-West can win nine or more tricks?

Thus the unlimited one-bids are designed as a stopgap to confuse the opponents until, on the second round of bidding, those bids which are inherently obstructive come into use.

The above argument was written by the original author of this book for the first edition. The following offers a counter-argument by one of the present coauthors.

THE PROBLEM OF UNLIMITED ONE-BIDS

A feature of traditional American bidding (so-called Standard American) is that many sequences have wide ranges.

Take this uncontested sequence:

North	South
1 ♡	1 ♠
2 ◇	

In terms of high-card points, the opening bid showed perhaps 11-20, and 10, 21, and 22 are not out of the question. The responder showed 6-plus points, but an expert occasionally responds with fewer if he has some distributional strength.

The two-diamond rebid does little to dispel the fog. The opener can still have a minimum, but can also have a near-maximum. Since he did not bid three diamonds, committing the partnership to game, he probably does not have more than 18 points.

This failure to limit the hand in clear fashion can set impossible problems. Suppose the responder has:

♠ A 8 7 3 2   ♡ 6   ◇ Q 8 2   ♣ K 9 4 3

He cannot safely continue the auction. Two notrump would be a clear overbid, suggesting about 11 points. So he must pass, hoping that the opener has either of these hands:

1. ♠ 4	2. ♠ 5 4
♡ A K 9 8 3	♡ K Q 9 8 3
◇ A 9 6 5 4	◇ A K 7 3
♣ 7 2	♣ 7 2

In both cases two diamonds is satisfactory and any higher contract will be in jeopardy. But the pass runs the risk that the opener has either of these hands:

3. ♠ 4	4. ♠ K 9 4
♡ A K 9 8 3	♡ A J 9 8 3
◇ A K 6 5 4	◇ A K J 3
♣ Q 2	♣ 7

Opposite hand three, the partnership misses a sound three-notrump contract, and opposite hand four, a sound four-spade contract.

It is not only the responder who is troubled by this problem. The opener has to worry if he has rebid two diamonds with, say, 16-18 points and the responder's next bid is three notrump. If the opener is concerned about missing a slam, he may well move on and land precariously in four notrump. If this fails by a trick, he has been heavily punished.

Another auction that creates problems is this:

North	South
1♠	1NT
2♡	

Here again the opener has done little to limit his hand, and the responder must guess whether he is facing eleven high-card points or seventeen. And if the opener had eighteen, he had to choose between an overbid and an underbid.

The problem is less serious if the partnership bids three suits at the one-level. The opener is still unlimited, but there is plenty of bidding space in which to maneuver.

In these sequences, standard methods breach a useful principle of bidding: *At least one of the first three partnership bids should be limited.*

And the partnership is even better off if a limited bid comes on the first round.

Earlier editions of this book argued, as above, that the unlimited bid has the advantage of keeping the opponents in the dark and making it harder for them to compete. That is sometimes true, but the disadvantage of keeping partner in the dark is far more serious.

This is the main reason that experts around the world have moved firmly in the direction of strong-club systems in the past twenty years. However, there is a tradeoff in adopting such methods. Strong club systems make it harder to bid minor-suit hands with any real accuracy. The one-diamond opening, especially when also using five-card majors, can show anywhere from zero diamonds on up, and having to open two clubs to show a club suit crowds the subsequent auction. As a consequence, the late 1980s saw a trend back toward natural methods.

In the 1979 Bermuda Bowl, when only six teams were competing, this was the breakdown of the systems being used:

Natural: 5 pairs
Strong club: 12 pairs

Variable club (one club is either natural or strong and
artificial): 1 pair

In the 1989 Bermuda Bowl, however, with ten teams
involved, the systems lined up like this:

Natural: 15 pairs
Strong club: 10 pairs
Variable club: 3 pairs
Forcing pass: 2 pairs (one only when non-vulnerable)

Of course, the fact that the system being employed has a
natural base does not mean it is simple. Most pairs playing at
this level have many, many defined sequences that involve
lots of conventional gadgetry.

Only time will tell in which direction the wheel will
turn—if at all—during the next decade.

♠
♡
4 Limited and
Unlimited Bids
◇
♣

Limited and unlimited are relative terms in bridge. No two hands are exactly alike. Furthermore, the same hand may vary in strength between one bidding situation and another. A limited bid, then, does have some range; an unlimited bid does have certain limits. For purposes of definition, a bid is limited when the weakest hand on which it may be made, and the strongest hand on which it may be made, are no more than one trick apart; a bid is unlimited when its weakest and strongest examples may be more than one trick apart.

Thus: South opens the bidding with one heart. North, his partner, can hardly "limit" South's strength. South may have from a four- to an eight-card heart suit; he may have only 12 or 13 points but he may have 20; he may be unable to make his seven-trick contract without considerable assistance, but he may have enough playing strength to guarantee a ten-trick game without support. Actually there is a bottom limit to South's strength, and a top limit; but they are so far apart that practically the bid is unlimited, for it tells too little to give North any notion of the best final contract.

Ideally, any low bid should be unlimited and any high bid should be limited. The limited bid is always desirable, for it better informs the partner, and the information it gives should be foregone only for purposes of obstruction. The low bid cannot be made obstructive unless it is unlimited, but the high bid can.

Any high opening bid (three or more) is strictly limited. It may be a weak bid, like a shut-out four-spade bid; it may be a powerful bid, like a slam-try five-spade bid; it is still a limited bid. It must be noted that a limited bid is not necessarily weak, nor an unlimited bid necessarily strong.

A low bid should be unlimited because many holdings require two or more bids before the partnership can proceed intelligently to a proper contract. The following example was previous cited (page 355):

♠ A 9 7 4 2   ♡ A K 10 8 6   ◇ K 6   ♣ 9

It was found impossible to bid this hand adequately over an opening four-club bid. The hand suggests a series of two bids, one in spades, one in hearts, so that partner may choose between the suits. The first bid should be made at a low level, leaving room to make the second bid without risking a penalty.

It follows that any low bid carries the implication that the hand may have undisclosed strength, and that the bidding is purposely being kept low so that additional information may be given later.

This principle applies, however, only to a low bid in a suit that has not previously been bid. When a player reverts to a suit that has previously been bid, he clearly implies that he has found an acceptable trump suit and that further distributional information is unnecessary. In this circumstance, why not show the full strength of the hand?

1.	West	North	East	South
				1 ♡
	Pass	1 ♠	Pass	2 ♡/♠
2.	West	North	East	South
				1 ♡
	Pass	1 ♠	Pass	2 ◇

In the first sequence, South limits his hand far more strictly than he does in the second. If South in sequence one were extremely strong, why not bid three or four hearts or spades, or make a splinter bid? South can be interested in no other suit, for if he were he could have bid that suit. But South in sequence two may have left much about his hand unspoken. He may have a club suit that he has not yet had time to show, he may be waiting to learn whether or not North can support hearts or diamonds, or rebid spades. It is not a certainty that South in sequence two has a strong hand, any more than it is ever a certainty that an opening bidder has a strong hand; but it is a possibility. South in sequence one cannot have a very strong hand; he has made a limited bid. Consequently, North will make every effort to rebid in sequence two, but will not fear to pass in sequence one.

Therefore any bid in a suit previously bid (by either partner) is limited; any bid in a new suit (not previously bid) is unlimited, as these terms were defined earlier in this section. This means, it must be remembered, only that an unlimited bid has a range of more than one trick.

FORCING AND NON-FORCING DOUBLE RAISES

Theoretically, no natural bid that limits the strength of a hand should be forcing. If the bidder's partner knows what to expect, he should be able and entitled to make his own decision.

A player limits his hand to some extent whenever he fails to make the strongest bid he has available in the circumstances.

West	North	East	South
			1 ♡
Dble	1 ♠		

Traditionally, North's hand is limited by the fact that he did not redouble. However strong North's later bids may sound, South must keep this fact in mind. South may pass the one-spade bid because North has limited his hand. He cannot have more than 9 or 10 points (and probably has less), and South may know that this is too little for game.

In the modern game, the automatic redouble with 10 or more points has gone out of favor. Many pairs play that a new suit at the one-level "ignores the double" and is still forcing, though most still assume a new suit at the two-level is nonforcing. With the use of a convention often incorrectly known as Jordan (a jump to two notrump over the double to show a high-card raise of partner's suit to at least the three-level), a redouble does tend to suggest a definite desire to penalize the opponents if they do not have a good fit. The omnibus redouble keeps the opener more in the dark as to the exact nature of his partner's hand. (In the mid-sixties one leading American expert, Robert Jordan, told another, Tom Sanders, that he had heard about the use of two notrump over an opposing take-out double to show an invitational raise. Jordan did not claim to have originated the idea, or even to use it, but his name became attached to it by many players. This is a misnomer. The idea is much older, and was suggested in a *Bridge World* article entitled "Competitive Gadgets" by Alan Truscott, published in February 1954. Players who refer to the idea as "Truscott" are historically correct.)

Moving on, consider this simple sequence:

West	North	East	South
			1 ♠
Pass	3 ♠		

The systems—Acol, for example—that use a non-forcing double raise are sounder in theory than the former Standard American treatment that made the double raise forcing to game. As a bid in a suit previously bid, the double raise is limited; being limited, it should not be forcing.

American players have come to realize this, and those few remaining experts who treat the double raise as forcing do have limits for the strength of the bid. It shows some 13-15 points in support of the suit: spades, above. A jump shift, however, carries a different message.

West	North	East	South
			1 ♠
Pass	3 ◇		

North's bid is also forcing to game, but it is unlimited. It could conceal a very strong spade raise.

Consider these two hands:

1. ♠ K 8 7 5 2   2. ♠ K Q 7 5 2
   ♡ A Q 6   ♡ A 6 5
   ◇ 8 4   ◇ A K 6
   ♣ K 6 5   ♣ 8 4

Hand number one justifies a double raise of partner's one-spade opening bid; therefore, hand two does not. There is too great a range between the two hands for both to satisfy the requirements of a limited bid. Unless using a forcing raise, an expert would respond with a jump to three diamonds on hand number two, conforming to theory and making an unlimited bid even at the expense of misinforming his partner as to his diamond holding.

LIMITED NOTRUMP BIDS

Any bid in notrump, whether an opening bid of one or more notrump, a raise in notrump, or a rebid or response in notrump, is invariably a limited bid.

There is a basic theoretical justification for this. The only reason some bids must be unlimited is that it is impossible to show strength and distribution with the same bid. The notrump bid describes its distribution and implies that it has no further distributional information to give. Therefore the quantity of the notrump bid can and should show the full strength of the bidder's hand.

There is a further practical reason why any notrump bid must be limited. Notrump is the easiest denomination for the opponents to double, which makes it too dangerous a bid to keep vague.

1.	North	South	2.	North	South
	1 ♠	2 ♠		1NT	2NT

In sequence one, South may gamble a bit to raise the opening spade bid. If North has a very strong hand, the raise may keep the bidding open to game; if North has a very weak hand, he may pass *and the opponents probably cannot double.* Even if they have great power in aces and kings, the opponents must fear that North-South have enough trump length and distributional power to win eight tricks. The risk, of course, in raising with a weak hand is that North may bid to an impossible game contract.

In sequence two, South cannot so gamble. If the raise proves to be an unwise speculation on the strength of North's hand, North-South will be at the mercy of their opponents, for either of the opponents can safely double a notrump contract with strength in any suit or suits (though, to be honest, this does not happen often—the fourth player, West, will be wondering if North is about to bid three; and East has already passed over one notrump, so why should he double two?).

Suppose North makes an opening bid of one notrump; and suppose North's hand might be either of the following, or anything in between:

	1.	2.
♠	A Q 6	A Q 6
♡	A 7 2	A J 7
◇	J 8 5 3	K 10 9 2
♣	K 5 4	K Q 5

South, after the one-notrump bid, would have no notion what to do with the following hand:

♠ K 7 3   ♡ 10 3   ◇ Q 7 6 4   ♣ A 7 6 2

If South raises to two notrump and North has hand number one, the opponents may double and collect a two- or three-trick penalty; but if in view of this danger South passes and North happens to have hand number two, the pass will surrender a sure game. This dilemma is precluded by so limiting the one-notrump opening bid that its strongest and weakest examples are never more than two points apart, so the partner always knows whether or not he can profitably raise.

♠
♡
5 Unconstructive and Constructive Bids
♢
♣

Earlier editions of this book attempted to modify standard bridge terminology by giving new meanings to the words "forced" and "free." Bowing to the wind, we must now use terms that prevail in tournament play.

If your partner has forced you to bid, some actions will show no more strength than you have already promised. But even when you are not forced, it does not follow that you pass with a bad hand.

Suppose you have this hand:

♠ 6 5 4 3 2   ♡ 6 5 4 3 2   ♢ 4 3 2   ♣ —

If your partner opens one notrump, of any variety, it would be a great mistake to pass. That contract will surely be terrible, and it must be better to play in two hearts or two spades.

In a normal game, there is nothing better than bidding two spades or two hearts, hoping to hit the suit in which partner has some length. This might land you in a 5-2 fit in your chosen suit when the other suit provided a 5-4 fit. Most experts have a solution.

They bid two clubs, Stayman, ready to pass if the opener bids a major suit. If the rebid is two diamonds, denying a major, they continue with two hearts. If the opening bidder has three hearts, he passes. If not, he bids two spades, with three cards in that suit.

This is only possible if the partnership has the agreement that this sequence by the responder is *unconstructive.* The responder has made two bids although he has no interest whatever in reaching a game.

With a different hand he might even make a third bid:

West	North	East	South
Pass	1NT	Pass	2♣
Pass	2♢	Pass	2♡
Pass	2♠	Pass	3♣
Pass	Pass	Pass	

What is going on? South's first two bids suggested a weak unbalanced hand with some major-suit length, the hearts at least as long as the spades. (Possible were 5-5, 4-4, 4-5, or 3-4.) He suggested a final contract of two hearts unless North held a doubleton heart and a tripleton spade. But when he received the preference to two spades, showing that his partner held 3-2 in the major suits and therefore eight cards in the minors, he bid three clubs.

South's hand is probably something like this:

♠ 8 7 2   ♡ 9 8 7 5   ♢ 6   ♣ J 8 7 4 3

South could not find a seven-card or eight-card fit in a major suit, so he has settled for a minor-suit contract that must be at worst a 5-3 fit.

This was an extreme example of unconstructive bidding—an attempt to lurch from a bad partscore contract to one that would be less bad. It was only possible because the partnership had another way (probably a transfer sequence, as on page 132) to show an invitational hand with a five-card major suit. Traditionally, Stayman followed by two of a major would invite a game.

The above sequence ended with three unconstructive bids. The following has two:

West	North	East	South
	1♣	Pass	1♠
Pass	1NT	Pass	2♡
Pass	2♠		

New suit bids by the responder are in general forcing, but those following a one-notrump bid by opener are exceptions. South's two-heart bid is unconstructive, and so is North's preference to two spades. South probably has 5-5 or 5-4 in the major suits, and North probably has 3-3-3-4 distribution. (If North has a doubleton somewhere he might have raised directly to two spades. Some modern players would, but others tend to rebid one notrump lacking four-card spade support.)

So here the last two bids are unconstructive, carrying no hint of game.

A preference bid, when partner has offered a choice of suits, is in general unconstructive. It is often an attempt to escape from a possible six-card fit. Suppose you have as South:

♠ 3 2   ♡ 4 3 2   ◊ A Q 4 3 2   ♣ 4 3 2

The bidding begins:

West	North	East	South
	1♣	Pass	1◊
Pass	1♠	Pass	?

South should not consider passing, for it is highly probable that the partnership is outnumbered in spades—almost certain, indeed, for those who habitually open one spade with five cards in each black suit. Nor should he consider two diamonds. That would indeed be unconstructive, but would be another way of landing in a contract with only six trumps. If North has a singleton, or even a void, he will pass in the expectation that South has at least a six-card suit. Bidding and rebidding a suit with only five cards is almost always an error in a situation in which partner is likely to pass. One notrump is possible but not very attractive. North would pass with:

♠ A Q 7 6   ♡ K 8   ◊ 7 5   ♣ A 9 8 7 6

The contract is then slightly inferior.

The best bid is two clubs, hitting the target with the hand shown. It is unlikely that North has a tripleton club, and if he has, no harm is done. If his distribution is 4-3-3-3, he will make a return preference bid of two diamonds. One unconstructive bid often deserves another.

Rarer are *constructive* bids. These are mild invitations, a little better than unconstructive but less than a clear game invitation. This is an example:

West	North	East	South
	Pass	Pass	1♣
Pass	1♠	Pass	2♠

Opposite a passed partner, South was not forced to rebid. His two-spade raise showed slightly better than a minimum opening.

Another example of a constructive action is a *free* bid made following opposing intervention.

West	North	East	South
			1♣
Pass	1♡	1♠	?

If South has a minimum hand, he is not obliged to bid, although he will do so with any clear-cut action. He will not bid one notrump, for example, without a spade stopper, and he will be happy to pass with a hand that would have presented a rebid problem:

♠ 4 3   ♡ 4 3 2   ◇ A Q 5   ♣ A Q 7 6 5

In the absence of an overcall, South would have to choose between two hearts, poor; one notrump, worse; and two clubs, worst. With the overcall, he is happy to pass.

The corollary is that if South makes a free bid it is an action he is happy to make. It may be a minimum in high cards, but it will have some extra value in terms of distribution or spade strength.

Notice that the overcall permits a double. Without any special agreement, this is an attempt to punish the overcaller when the opener has four spades with at least two honors. But many modern experts use this double as artificial, a "support double," showing exactly three cards in partner's suit. If playing this convention, the above hand would double. Note that this is better than raising to two hearts, even if North would be aware that three-card heart length is likely, as it permits North to pass, bid one notrump, or two clubs (or two diamonds), all of which are impossible after the raise to two hearts.

When the opponents interfere, in general it is true that a pass is weak and a bid shows a little extra. But at higher levels it may be exactly the other way round.

THE FORCING PASS

The forcing pass is made by a player who has shown such great strength that his side can surely make game or penalize the opponents.

West	North	East	South
	2♡ (a)	2♠	Pass
3♠	Pass	Pass	?

(a) Forcing

South must either bid or double, in this instance because North's opening bid was forcing to game and game has not been reached. If South bids three notrump, four clubs, four diamonds, or four hearts, he indicates his distribution but promises nothing in high cards.

Here are some possible hands for South and the actions he should take:

1. ♠ 3 2	♡ 4	◇ Q J 9 8 6 5	♣ 8 6 5 4	Four diamonds
2. ♠ 8 6	♡ 8 6 5	◇ 9 8 6 5 3 2	♣ 5 2	Four hearts
3. ♠ K 4 3	♡ 2	◇ 8 6 5 3 2	♣ 10 9 6 5	Three notrump
4. ♠ 8 7 5	♡ 8	◇ 8 7 5 4	♣ J 7 6 5 4	Double

Suppose the bidding continues:

West	North	East	South
	2♡	2♠	Pass
3♠	Pass	Pass	4♡
4♠	Pass	Pass	?

Again South is forced to bid or double because North showed so much strength by his opening bid that he must be able to beat four spades, if he cannot make five hearts. North's pass merely states that he wishes South to make the decision. South may hold:

1. ♠ 8 7	2. ♠ 8	3. ♠ 8
♡ 10 6 3	♡ 10 7 6	♡ 8 5 4 2
◇ 10 8 4 3	◇ Q 8 4 3	◇ 8 6 4 3
♣ J 7 5 4	♣ J 7 5 4 3	♣ 9 6 4 3

With hand one, South doubles. He has too little to relish undertaking a five-heart contract and he expects North to win at least four tricks in top cards. With two or three, South bids five hearts. He has enough support to expect the contract to be made and it should be more profitable than defeating four spades. The important thing is that South may not pass.

The forcing pass may result from strong bidding by the combined hands.

West	North	East	South
	1♡	2♠ (a)	3♠
Dble	Pass	Pass	4♡
4♠	Pass	Pass	?

(a) Weak

South must bid or double. North has not abandoned the contract; he has merely asked South to make the decision.

In either bidding situation, South's bid (or double) is forced, promising no more than South could be expected to have in light of his previous bids or passes.

FREE BIDS AS SLAM-TRIES

Any bid except one that is forced shows additional strength; therefore a bid that is not forced may be read as a slam-try when it is above game. However, the way to do this is debated by experts.

West	North	East	South
			1♡
3◇ (a)	4◇ (b)	5◇	?

(a) Weak   (b) High-card raise to at least four hearts

As North-South have the high-card values for game, it is logical to deduce that East is sacrificing. As a consequence, a pass by South would be forcing, asking North to choose between doubling and bidding on in hearts. But South has two other options short of committing his side to a slam: he may bid five hearts or he may pass and then bid five hearts after partner doubles. What is the difference between these two sequences?

As noted, experts disagree, but the majority feel that passing and then removing the double is the stronger action, inviting a slam. The immediate bid of five hearts, not asking partner's opinion, is competitive, and North should not bid a slam without considerable extra values.

Here are two possible North hands:

1. ♠ A Q 3
♡ K J 7 5
◇ 4 2
♣ K 7 6 4

2. ♠ A K 2
♡ K J 7 5
◇ 4 2
♣ K Q J 4

The auction has proceeded:

West	North	East	South
			1♡
3◇	4◇	5◇	Pass
Pass	Dble	Pass	5♡
Pass	?		

North doubles in both cases primarily because he has a doubleton diamond; five hearts might go down if North-South lose the first two tricks to the ace and king of diamonds. However, when South removes the double to five hearts he announces at most one diamond and interest in a slam. North passes with the first hand, as it is a minimum; but he bids six hearts with hand two.

This subject is complicated, however, and is the subject of whole books. Consider this sequence:

West	North	East	South
			1♠
Pass	2◇	4♡	Pass
Pass	Dble	Pass	5◇

South's pass over four hearts was forcing: South had the values for an opening bid and North sufficient to respond at the two-level. Is South's subsequent removal to five diamonds a slam-try?

No, it is not. South must be permitted to give his partner a chance to bid four spades, which might be the only making game. However, when North does not indicate spade support, South bids diamonds because he has unknown support for that suit. South holds something like

♠ A K 6 5 4   ♡ 2   ◇ K J 6 5   ♣ J 9 8

As is always the case, the more sequences you discuss with your partner, the better your partnership will do.

6 Percentage Tables

TABLE 1

The chances that the opponents' cards in a suit will be divided in a given way:

Your combined holding in the suit	Opponents hold	Opponents' cards will break	Percentage
11 cards	2 cards	1-1	52.0
		2-0	48.0
10 cards	3 cards	2-1	78.0
		3-0	22.0
9 cards	4 cards	3-1	49.7
		2-2	40.7
		4-0	9.6
8 cards	5 cards	3-2	67.8
		4-1	28.3
		5-0	3.9

Your combined holding in the suit	Opponents hold	Opponents' cards will break	Percentage
7 cards	6 cards	4-2	48.4
		3-3	35.5
		5-1	14.5
		6-0	1.5
6 cards	7 cards	4-3	62.2
		5-2	30.5
		6-1	6.8
		7-0	0.5
5 cards	8 cards	5-3	47.1
		4-4	32.7
		6-2	17.1
		7-1	2.9
		8-0	0.2
4 cards	9 cards	5-4	58.9
		6-3	31.4
		7-2	8.6
		8-1	1.1
		9-0	0.05
3 cards	10 cards	6-4	46.2
		5-5	31.2
		7-3	18.5
		8-2	3.8
		9-1	0.4
		10-0	0.01
2 cards	11 cards	6-5	57.2
		7-4	31.8
		8-3	9.5
		9-2	1.4
		10-1	0.1
		11-0	0.002
1 card	12 cards	7-5	45.7
		6-6	30.5
		8-4	19.1
		9-3	4.2
		10-2	0.5
		11-1	0.02
		12-0	0.0002

Your combined holding in the suit	Opponents hold	Opponents' cards will break	Percentage
0 card	13 cards	7-6	56.6
		8-5	31.9
		9-4	9.8
		10-3	1.6
		11-2	0.1
		12-1	0.003
		13-0	0.00002

TABLE 2

Distributions of the cards of a suit among the hands of the four players (or of the four suits in one player's hand):

Distribution (of Hand or Suit)	Percentage	Approximate Odds Against
4-4-3-2	21.55	4 to 1
5-3-3-2	15.52	6 to 1
5-4-3-1	12.93	7 to 1
5-4-2-2	10.58	9 to 1
4-3-3-3	10.54	9 to 1
6-3-2-2	5.64	17 to 1
6-4-2-1	4.70	20 to 1
6-3-3-1	3.45	27 to 1
5-5-2-1	3.17	30 to 1
4-4-4-1	2.99	33 to 1
7-3-2-1	1.88	50 to 1
6-4-3-0	1.33	75 to 1
5-4-4-0	1.24	80 to 1
5-5-3-0	0.90	100 to 1
6-5-1-1	0.71	140 to 1
6-5-2-0	0.65	150 to 1
7-2-2-2	0.51	199 to 1
7-4-1-1	0.39	249 to 1
7-4-2-0	0.36	275 to 1
7-3-3-0	0.27	399 to 1
8-2-2-1	0.19	499 to 1
8-3-1-1	0.12	850 to 1
7-5-1-0	0.11	900 to 1
8-3-2-0	0.11	900 to 1
6-6-1-0	0.07	1,400 to 1
8-4-1-0	0.045	2,499 to 1
9-2-1-1	0.018	4,999 to 1
9-3-1-0	0.010	9,999 to 1
9-2-2-0	0.008	12,500 to 1
7-6-0-0	0.006	16,666 to 1
8-5-0-0	0.003	33,332 to 1
10-2-1-0	0.0011	99,999 to 1
9-4-0-0	0.0010	99,999 to 1
10-1-1-1	0.0004	333,332 to 1
10-3-0-0	0.00015	499,999 to 1
11-1-1-0	0.00002	4,999,999 to 1
11-2-0-0	0.00001	9,999,999 to 1
12-1-0-0	0.0000003	333,333,332 to 1
13-0-0-0	0.0000000006	158,755,357,992 to 1

Glossary

Terms listed in the Contents and defined in the text are not necessarily included in this Glossary.

Anchor Suit A suit shown inferentially through the use of an artificial bid such as a transfer or Astro bid.

Artificial Bid A bid giving or requesting information as to strength and/ or distribution and/or specific cards not necessarily related to the denomination named in the bid.

Auction The period or process of bidding.

Balance Reopen the bidding, often relying on the strength assumed to be in partner's hand because the opponents have stopped at a low level.

Balanced Hand A hand that contains no void or singleton, and has at most one doubleton.

Bath Coup The play of the low card from A-J-x (or longer) when an opponent leads the king.

Bermuda Bowl The trophy now awarded biennially to the winners of the World Team Championship. First held in 1950.

Bid Usually an offer to contract to win at least a stated number of tricks with the named suit as trumps or in notrump.

Biritch A card game considered by most authorities to be one of the forerunners of bridge. It was first described in print in England in 1886 under the title of *Biritch, or Russian Whist.*

Blackwood A convention invented by Easley Blackwood in 1933. It is used to locate the number of partner's aces and kings by means of conventional bids of four and five notrump. It should be used to avoid slams in which there is a paucity of top controls rather than to reach a slam because these top cards are held.

Board The device in which the four players' hands are kept in a duplicate tournament; a deal in duplicate; the dummy (North American colloquial).

Board-a-Match A scoring method whereby a team having a higher score on a deal receives one point, and a tie gives each team half a point.

Business Double A double made for the purpose of collecting an increased penalty. "Penalty Double" is a more popular term.

Bust A very bad hand.

Cash Lead a high-card winner or an established card and win the trick with it.

Chicago Four deal bridge usually played in North America in place of rubber bridge. The game originated in the Standard Club, Chicago.

Contract The obligation to win a minimum number of tricks in a suit or in notrump.

Control Holding the ace, a void, the king, or a singleton in a suit; or, in some conventions, a count in which an ace is worth 2 points and a king 1.

Convention A bid or play whose meaning is known only by prior agreement, and of which the opponents should be made aware.

Conventional Systematic; in accordance with an agreed system.

Cue-Bid Either a bid of an opponent's suit below the level of game, asking for further information in order to try to select the best game (or slam); or a bid to show a control in a suit when moving toward a slam.

Cut The division of the cards into two parts upon completion of the shuffle.

Deal The distribution of the cards after the shuffle and cut; it is the whole board: the bidding and play.

Dealer The person who distributes the cards and who starts the auction.

Deck The fifty-two cards.

Declarer The person who plays the cards for the side that won the auction.

Defender One of the two players who try to stop the declarer from making his stated contract.

Discard Play a card from a non-trump suit when unable to furnish a card from the suit led.

Discouraging Signal The play of a card in a suit by a defender to signify no desire to have partner lead or continue that suit.

Double Jump A bid two levels higher than was necessary to make a legal call. For example, bidding three hearts over one diamond.

Double Raise A raise of partner's suit by two levels, such as three spades over partner's one spade.

Doubleton Exactly two cards in a suit.

Duck To play a low card rather than try to win the trick.

Dummy The declarer's partner, who puts his hand face up on the table after the opening lead has been made.

Dummy Reversal A play technique in which declarer ruffs dummy's losers with his own, longer trumps, and uses dummy's trumps to draw those of the opponents.

Duplicate Bridge The form of bridge in which all contestants play the same hands. In this way, the element of luck is lower than it is in rubber bridge or Chicago.

Duplicate Board A device for keeping separate the four players' hands so that the same deal may be played at more than one table.

Echo A signal in which a high card is played before a lower one in the same suit. It is traditionally used to request the lead or continuation of that suit, or to indicate an even number of cards in the suit (except in trumps; see Trump Echo).

Elimination A process in play whereby declarer removes from the hand of an opponent all cards that can safely be led or played against him. Once the elimination is complete, the opponent is given the lead and is forced to make a play beneficial to the declarer. This same technique can be used by the defenders, but it is very rare.

Encouraging Card A card played (usually an unnecessarily high one) to show a desire to have the suit led or continued by partner.

Endplay Giving the lead to an opponent when it is to declarer's advantage. Also known as a throw-in.

Entry A card with which a hand can win a trick and so gain the lead.

Establish Set up one or more cards as winners by forcing out adverse higher cards.

Exit To lead a losing card that compels another hand to win the trick.

Exposed Card A card shown inadvertently during the bidding or play. The Laws cover the various possibilities.

False-Card To play a card with the intention of misleading an opponent.

False Preference To give a preference between partner's two suits by choosing the one in which one has the fewer number of cards. This is normally done in order to keep the bidding open so that partner has another chance to describe his hand further.

Finesse An attempt to win a trick with a card lower than the highest held by the opponents. To succeed, it requires a favorable location of the outstanding higher card.

Force To lead a suit that an opponent must ruff if he wishes to win the trick. It is usually done to weaken that player's trump holding.

Fourth Highest or Fourth Best The traditional lead of the fourth card from the top in a long suit.

Game   A contract for which the trick score is at least 100 points, but not one that requires twelve or thirteen tricks for success. They are three notrump and all possible contracts between four hearts and five notrump, inclusive.

Game-Forcing   A bid that commits the partnership to reaching at least a game contract.

Grand Coup   The ruffing of one of partner's winners to reduce one's trump length prior to executing a trump coup.

Grand Slam   A seven-level contract requiring all thirteen tricks to be won.

Guard   A holding in a suit that will win a trick (sometimes unless the opposing cards are unfavorably distributed).

Hand   The cards dealt to a player; or the whole deal.

High-Card Point   The initial hand-strength evaluation method used by virtually all players. An ace counts as 4 points, a king as 3, a queen as 2, and a jack as 1.

High-Low   An echo.

Hold Up   To refrain from playing a high card with which a trick could be won, usually in a suit in which an opponent is long and strong.

Honor Card   An ace, king, queen, jack, or ten.

Honors   A bonus of 100 points awarded to a player holding four of the five trump honors; or 150 to a player with all five trump honors or all four aces when the hand is played in notrump. (These bonuses are not applicable in duplicate bridge.)

Hook   A finesse (colloquial).

Intermediate Cards   The middle cards: the eights, nines, and tens. They are particularly useful in notrump contracts.

IMP   International Match Point, the scoring used in most duplicate team games.

Insufficient Bid   Making a bid that is lower than the previous highest bid. The penalties are explained in the Laws.

Inverted Minor-Suit Raises   A method in which a single raise of a minor suit (e.g., 1 ◇ –2 ◇) is forcing, showing at least ten high-card points, while a jump raise to the three-level (e.g., 1♣–3♣) is pre-emptive.

Jump Bid   Any bid that is at least one level higher than was necessary to bid the denomination legally.

Kibitzer   A spectator.

Laws   "Laws of Contract Bridge (1981)" for rubber bridge and Chicago; or "Laws of Duplicate Bridge (1987)" for tournament play.

Laydown   A contract so easy to fulfill that declarer does or might expose his hand and claim.

Lead   To play the first card to a trick; the card so played.

Left-Hand Opponent (LHO)   The opponent sitting on one's left.

Leftie   Left-hand opponent (colloquial).

Lightner Double   A lead-directing double, usually of a slam contract. It asks partner to make an unusual lead. The doubler normally wants a ruff or the lead of dummy's first-bid suit.

Limit Raise   A jump raise to the three-level (e.g., 1♡–3♡) that is invitational but non-forcing. It shows about 11 points (a good 10 to a bad 12) and four-card or longer trump support. The opener may pass with a minimum opening bid, but is being encouraged to bid game with anything more.

Loser-on-Loser   To discard one loser on another losing card. Usually made to cut the communications between the opposing hands, but sometimes to avoid weakening one's trump holding.

Love All   The British expression for neither side vulnerable.

Major Suit   Spades or hearts.

Make   To succeed in bringing home the required number of tricks in one's contract.

Matchpoint   The form of scoring used in duplicate pair events. One point is awarded for each pair sitting in the same direction that scores worse on a deal, and half a point is given for a tie.

Minor Suit   Diamonds or clubs.

Mixed Pairs   A tournament event in which a man plays with a woman.

Negative Double   A double made after partner's opening bid has been overcalled by one's right-hand opponent. It is not for penalties, and usually indicates four cards in an unbid major suit.

Non-vulnerable   Said of a side that has not won a game. In duplicate bridge, a side will be arbitrarily non-vulnerable (or vulnerable) depending upon direction and board number.

Notrump   The highest-scoring denomination; to play without a trump suit.

Offside   A card so situated that a finesse against it will lose.

One-over-One   A response at the one-level in a suit.

Onside   A card so situated that a finesse against it will win.

Opener   The first player to make a positive bid during the auction.

Opening Bid   The first bid made by the opener.

Opening Lead   The card led to the first trick. It is made before the appearance of the dummy.

Overbid   To make a bid that describes a stronger hand than the player actually holds.

Overcall   A bid made after an opponent has made a positive bid.

Overruff   To play a trump higher than one previously played to that trick.

Overtake   To play a sequentially higher card than the one contributed by partner.

Overtrick   A trick won by declarer in excess of his contract.

Pack   The deck.

Partial   A partscore.

Partner   The player with whom one shares a common score.

Partnership   The two players who are partners.

Partscore   A contract for which the trick score is less than 100.

Pass   A call usually indicating that the player has no desire to contest the auction further. However, sometimes the pass will be forcing, leaving the next move to partner. This occurs when the partnership is in a game-forcing situation.

Pass Out   When no player makes an opening bid.

Pattern   The shape of a hand.

Penalty Card   A card that is inadvertently exposed during the play. The penalty is covered in the Laws book.

Penalty Double   A double made with the expectation of defeating the opposing contract.

Peter   Another word for an echo or high-low.

Play   To contribute a card to a trick; or the period following the bidding.

Playing-Trick   A card, not necessarily high or a trump, expected to win a trick during the card-play.

Point-a-Board   The British expression for Board-a-Match.

Post-Mortem   A discussion of the merits (or otherwise) of the bidding and/or play of the previous deal.

Powerhouse   A very strong hand.

Precision Club   A system invented by the late C. C. Wei. A one-club opening bid shows at least 16 high-card points (or compensating distributional values), and other opening bids deny the strength to open one club.

Preemptive Bid   A bid that expresses a weak hand with a long suit good for offense but bad for defense. It is usually either a high-level opening bid or jump overcall.

Preference Bid   A bid by which a player indicates which of his partner's suits he prefers.

Protective Bid   Another name for a balancing bid.

Psych or Psychic Bid   A bid that markedly misdescribes the strength and/or suit length of the hand. It is made to try to mislead the opponents, and is probably the most controversial action in the game.

Push   To bid in an effort to persuade the opponents to go one level higher. In scoring of team play, a push is a tie.

Raise   To support partner's suit.

Rebid   Any bid by a player who has previously bid.

Redouble   A call that has the effect of further increasing the premiums or penalties if it is followed by three passes. However, usually the bid is an expression of strength when an opponent makes a take-out double over partner's bid, or requests a rescue to another suit when an opponent makes a penalty double of partner's bid (see SOS Redouble).

Reentry   A card with which a hand can gain the lead after having lost it.

Renege   Revoke (colloquial).

Responder   The partner of the opener.

Response   A bid made in reply to a bid or take-out double by partner.

Reverse   A strength-showing rebid at the two-level (or sometimes higher), in a suit higher in rank than that bid originally (e.g., 1♣–1♡–2♢ or 1♡–2♣–2♠).

Revoke   To play a card of another suit when able to follow suit.

Right-Hand Opponent (RHO)   The opponent sitting on one's right.

Rightie   Right-hand opponent (colloquial).

Rockcrusher   A powerhouse (colloquial).

Roman Leads   See Rusinow Leads.

Rubber Bridge   A form of the game in which the first partnership to score two games wins.

Ruff   To play a trump on a side-suit lead.

Ruff-and-Discard or Ruff-and-Sluff   The result of the lead of a suit held by neither opposing player. It permits one opponent to discard and the other to ruff.

Rule of Eleven   When a player leads the fourth-highest of a suit, the difference of its rank from eleven is the number of higher cards of the suit in the other three hands.

Rule of Two and Three   The classic guideline for preemptive bidding. The bidder should not risk going more than down two when vulnerable, and down three when non-vulnerable.

Run   To cash all one's winners in a suit.

Rusinow (or Roman) Leads   The lead of the second-highest card from an honor sequence. For example, the queen from K-Q or the ten from K-J-10.

Sacrifice or Save   A bid made without expectation of fulfilling the contract, but in the hope that the penalty will be less than the score for the opponents' contract.

Safety Play   A play that guarantees that a certain number of tricks will be won in the suit regardless of the distribution of the opposing cards; or one that improves that chance.

Scissors Coup   A loser-on-loser play that cuts the communication between the two defenders' hands.

Set   To defeat a contract.

Shape   The distribution of a hand; or a hand with (one or) two long suits.

Shift (or Switch)   To win a trick in one suit and lead a card in another suit.

Side Suit   Any of the three non-trump suits.

Signal   Any convention of play whereby the defenders properly give information to each other.

Sign-Off   A bid that asks partner to pass.

Singleton   An original holding of one card in a suit.

Skip Bid   A jump bid.

Sluff   To discard.

Small Slam   A six-level contract requiring twelve tricks to be won.

Solid Suit   A suit composed only of winners, or probable winners.

SOS Redouble   A redouble made after an opponent has made a penalty double. It requests partner to take out into his longest suit.

Split   To play one of equal honors such as the king-queen or queen-jack even though a lower card is held in the suit. It is usually made by the second hand to play to the trick. Or the division of the opposing cards in a suit.

Spot-Card   A non-honor card.

Squeeze   A play that forces an opponent to discard a guarding card from a suit. Sometimes both opponents can be squeezed on the same trick (a simultaneous squeeze) or on different tricks (a non-simultaneous squeeze). A squeeze establishes a card that was not a winner before the squeeze took place.

Stiff   A singleton (colloquial).

Stopper   A holding with which a hand can eventually win a trick against adverse leads of the suit.

Strip   To remove the cards of a suit in one or more hands, usually in preparation for an endplay.

Suit Preference Signal   A defender's signal in play, devised by Hy Lavinthal, whereby the relative rank of a card played or discarded calls for the higher- or lower-ranking of the available suits other than trumps.

Support   To raise partner.

System   The bidding agreements of a partnership.

Take-out Double   A double that requests partner to select an unbid suit.

Tenace   Two honors not quite in sequence, such as ace-queen or king-jack. (From the Spanish *tenaza,* pincer.)

Threat Card   A card that may become established by a squeeze.

Throw-In   An endplay in which an opponent is forced on lead in a position in which he will be compelled to lead to his disadvantage.

Touching Cards   Two or more cards in sequence, such as the K-Q or the 9-8.

Trick   The four cards, one from each player contributed in a clockwise rotation.

Trump   The master suit during the card-play. To play a card from the trump suit when unable to follow suit.

Trump Echo or Trump Signal   A high-low in trumps to indicate an odd number of cards in the suit, and, often, the desire for a ruff.

Two-Bid   An opening bid of two of a suit.

Two-Suiter   A hand containing two five-card or longer suits (though sometimes used for a hand with one five-card or longer suit and one four-carder).

Unbalanced Hand   One with a void, a singleton, or two or more doubletons.

Unblock   To avoid blocking a suit by cashing, overtaking, or discarding cards.

Underbid   To make a bid that describes a weaker hand than the player actually holds.

Underruff   To play a trump lower than one already contributed to the trick.

Uppercut   To ruff with an unnecessarily high trump to force out an opponent's higher trump and establish a trump trick, usually for partner.

Vienna Coup   The cashing of a high card, usually an ace, that temporarily establishes an opponent's card before that opponent is squeezed.

Void   Holding no cards in a suit.

Vulnerable   Said of a side that has won a game. In tournament bridge it is predetermined for each board number which side(s), if either, will be vulnerable.

Winner   A card that wins a trick.

x   The symbol sometimes used to represent a spot-card.

Yarborough   A hand containing no card higher than a nine.

Index